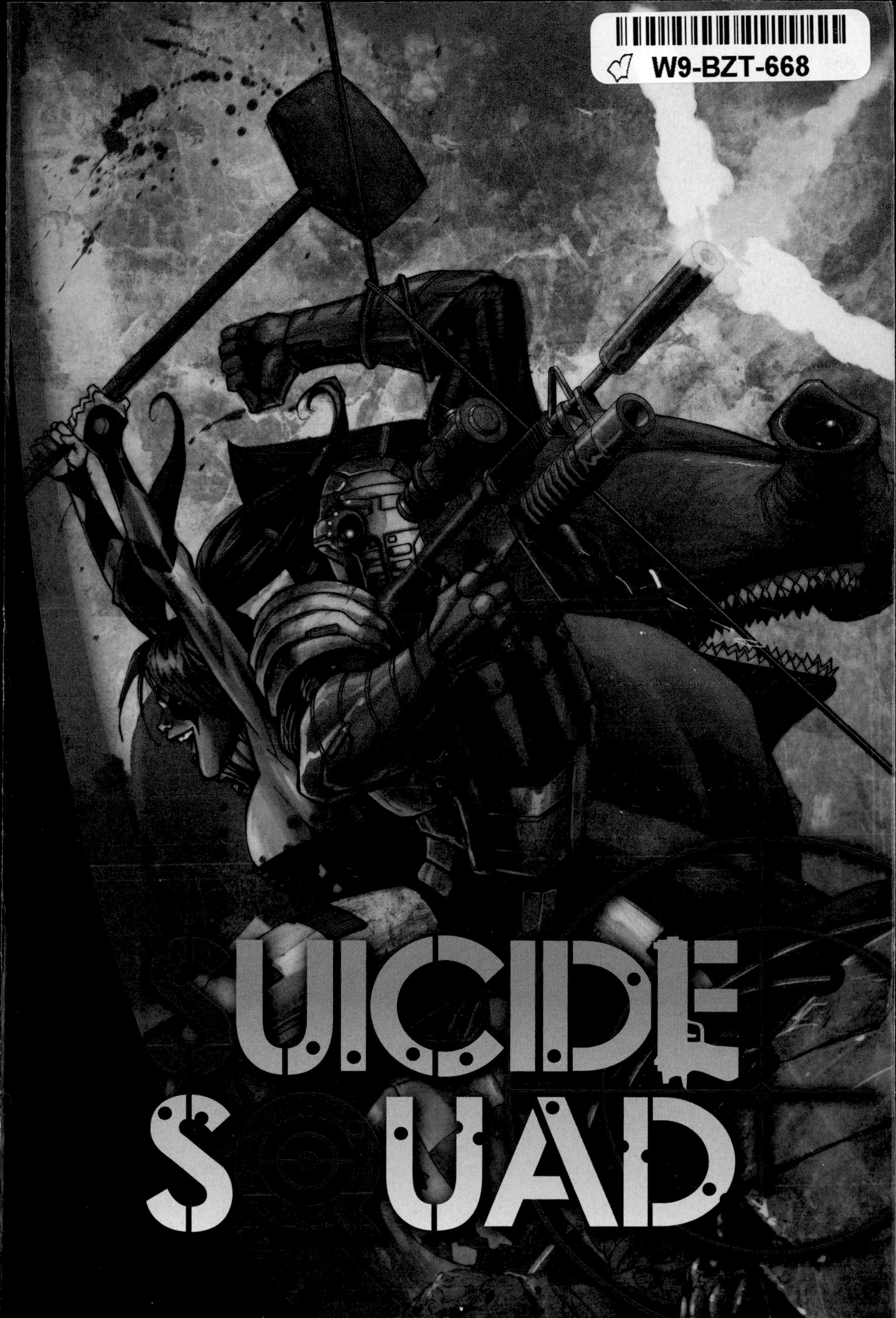

SUICIDE SQUAD

VOLUME 1 **KICKED IN THE TEETH**

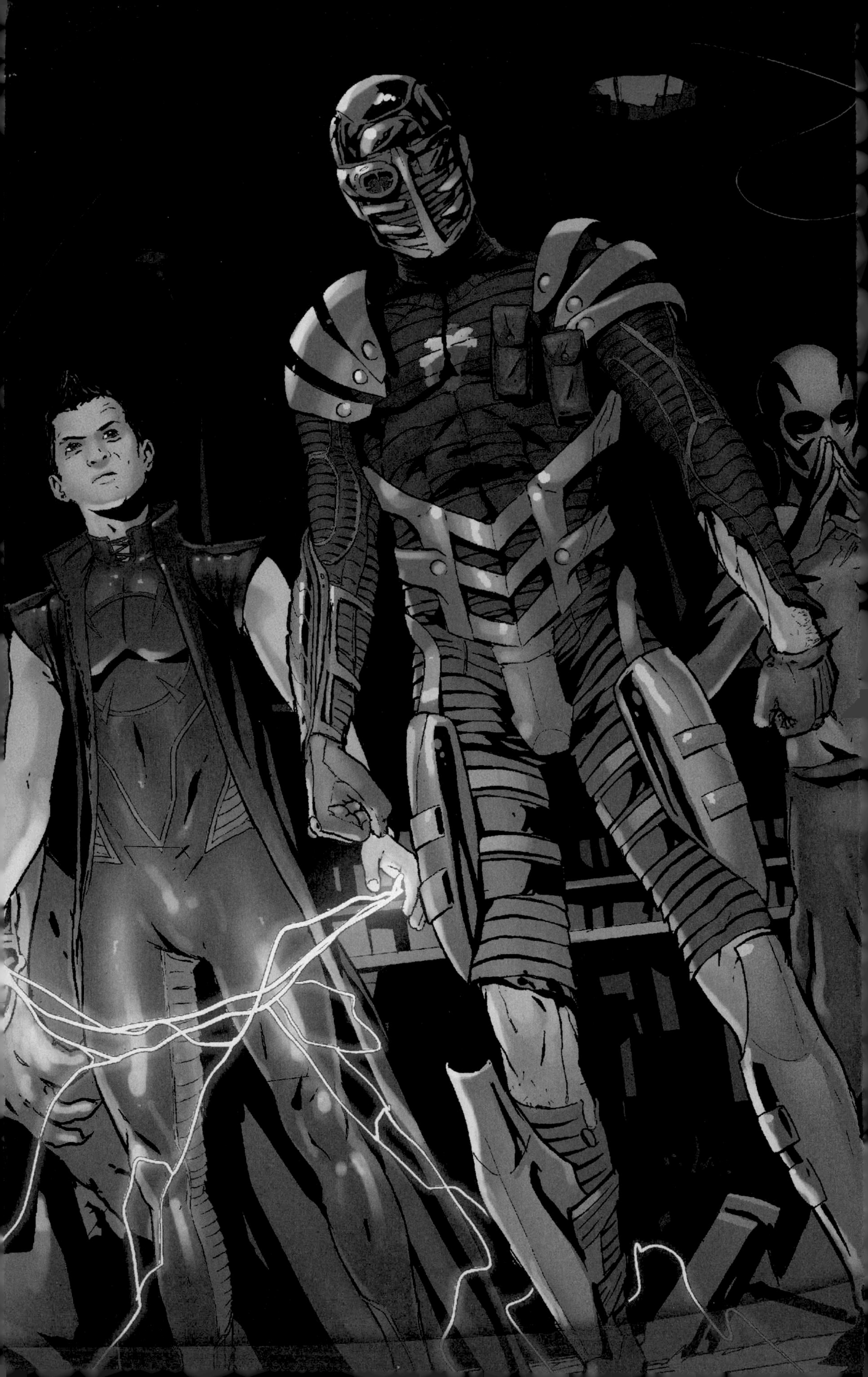

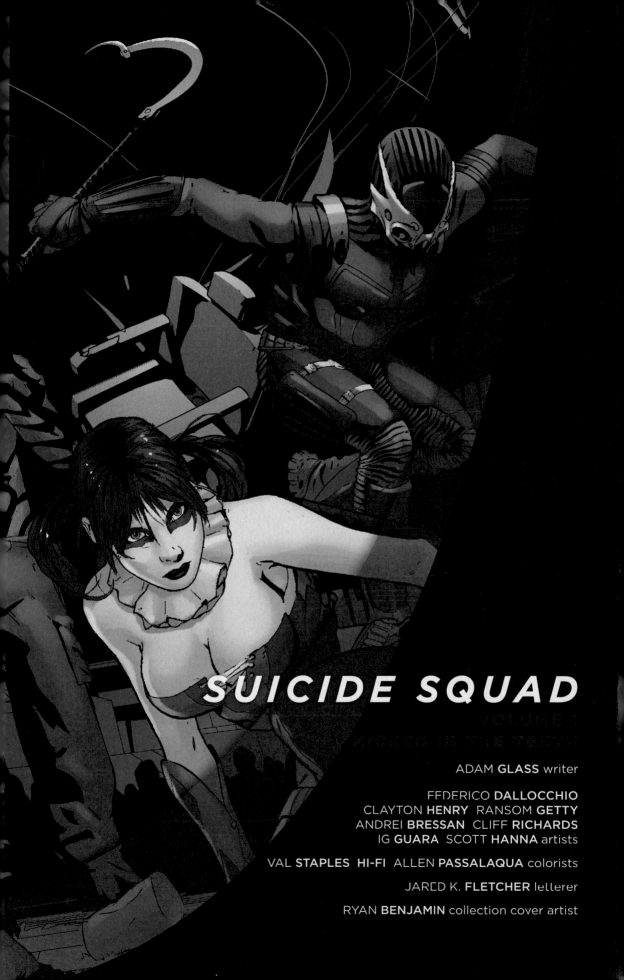

SUICIDE SQUAD

VOLUME 1
KICKED IN THE TEETH

ADAM **GLASS** writer

FEDERICO **DALLOCCHIO**
CLAYTON **HENRY** RANSOM **GETTY**
ANDREI **BRESSAN** CLIFF **RICHARDS**
IG **GUARA** SCOTT **HANNA** artists

VAL **STAPLES** HI-FI ALLEN **PASSALAQUA** colorists

JARED K. **FLETCHER** letterer

RYAN **BENJAMIN** collection cover artist

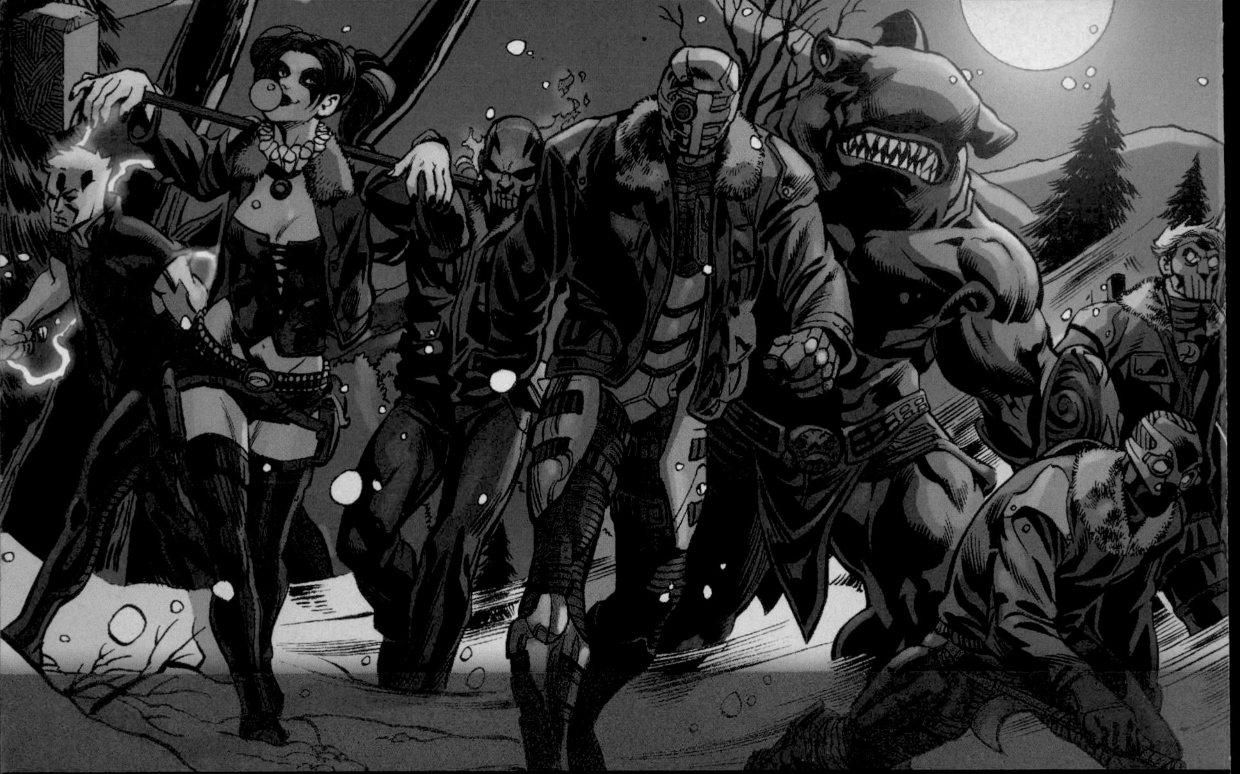

PAT MCCALLUM Editor - Original Series SEAN MACKIEWICZ Assistant Editor - Original Series ROWENA YOW Editor
ROBBIN BROSTERMAN Design Director - Books ROBBIE BIEDERMAN Publication Design

BOB HARRAS Senior VP - Editor-in-Chief, DC Comics

DIANE NELSON President DAN DIDIO and JIM LEE Co-Publishers
GEOFF JOHNS Chief Creative Officer
AMIT DESAI Senior VP - Marketing and Franchise Management
AMY GENKINS Senior VP - Business and Legal Affairs NAIRI GARDINER Senior VP - Finance
JEFF BOISON VP - Publishing Planning MARK CHIARELLO VP - Art Direction and Design
JOHN CUNNINGHAM VP - Marketing TERRI CUNNINGHAM VP - Editorial Administration
LARRY GANEM VP - Talent Relations and Services
ALISON GILL Senior VP - Manufacturing and Operations HANK KANALZ Senior VP - Vertigo and Integrated Publishing
JAY KOGAN VP - Business and Legal Affairs, Publishing JACK MAHAN VP - Business Affairs, Talent
NICK NAPOLITANO VP - Manufacturing Administration SUE POHJA VP - Book Sales
FRED RUIZ VP - Manufacturing Operations
COURTNEY SIMMONS Senior VP - Publicity BOB WAYNE Senior VP - Sales

SUICIDE SQUAD VOLUME 1: KICKED IN THE TEETH

DC Comics, 4000, Warner Blvd., Burbank, CA 91522
A Warner Bros. Entertainment Company.
Printed by Solisco Printers, Scott, QC, Canada. 04/10/15. Seventh Printing.
ISBN: 978-1-4012-3544-4

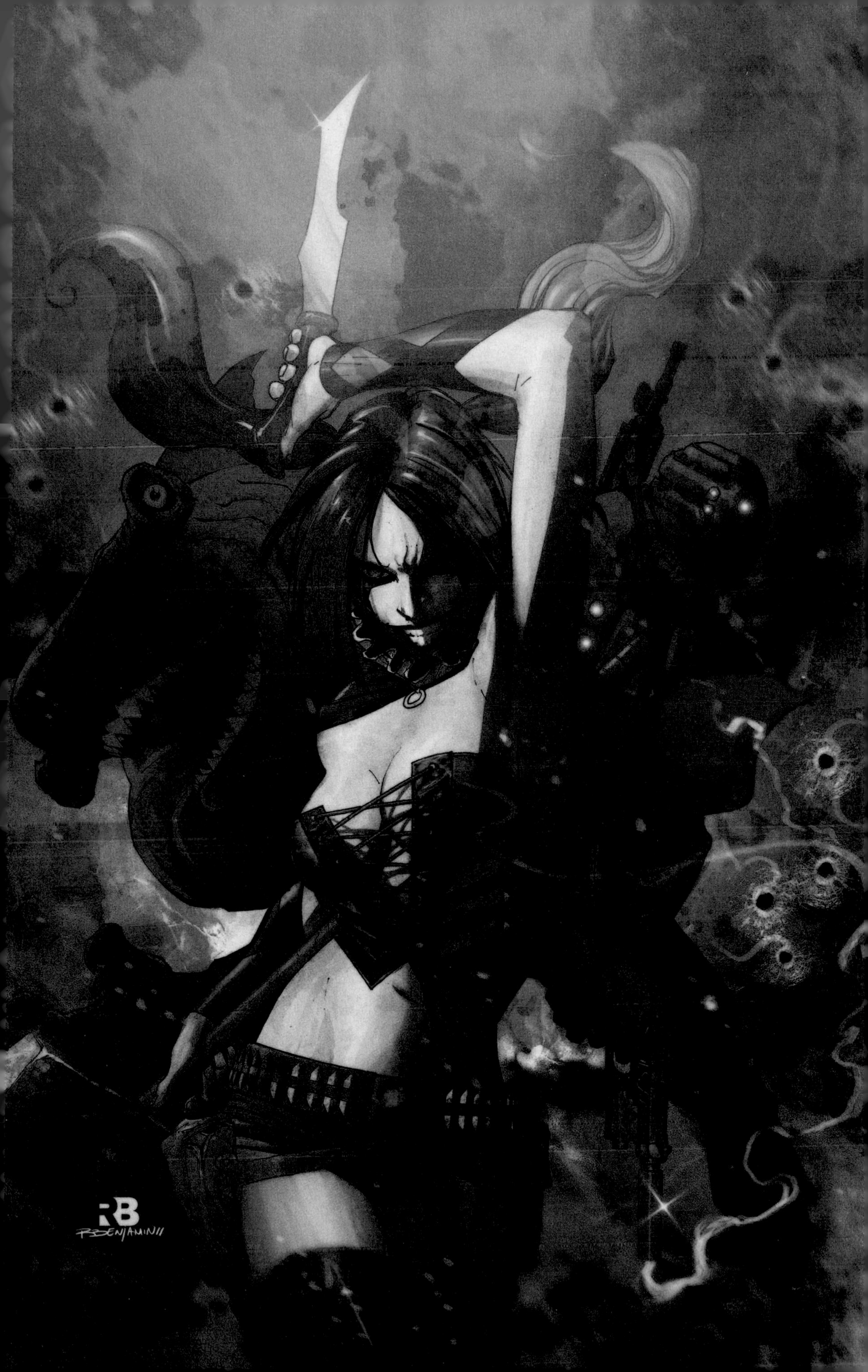
RB

KICKED IN THE TEETH

ADAM GLASS
writer

FEDERICO DALLOCCHIO, RANSOM GETTY & SCOTT HANNA
artists

cover art by RYAN BENJAMIN

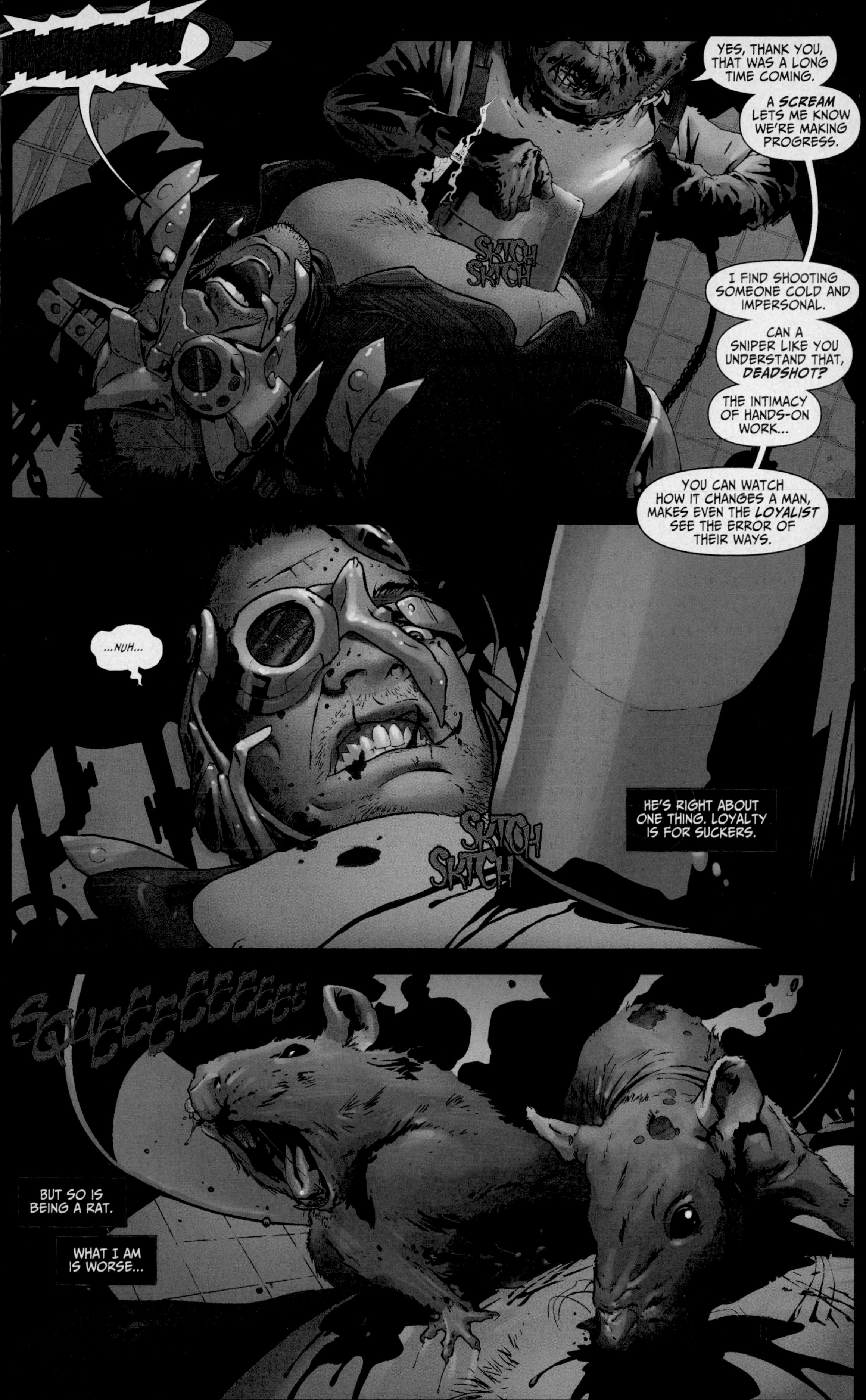
YES, THANK YOU, THAT WAS A LONG TIME COMING.
A SCREAM LETS ME KNOW WE'RE MAKING PROGRESS.
SKTCH SKTCH
I FIND SHOOTING SOMEONE COLD AND IMPERSONAL.
CAN A SNIPER LIKE YOU UNDERSTAND THAT, DEADSHOT?
THE INTIMACY OF HANDS-ON WORK...
YOU CAN WATCH HOW IT CHANGES A MAN, MAKES EVEN THE LOYALIST SEE THE ERROR OF THEIR WAYS.
...NUH...
HE'S RIGHT ABOUT ONE THING. LOYALTY IS FOR SUCKERS.
SKTCH SKTCH
BUT SO IS BEING A RAT.
WHAT I AM IS WORSE...

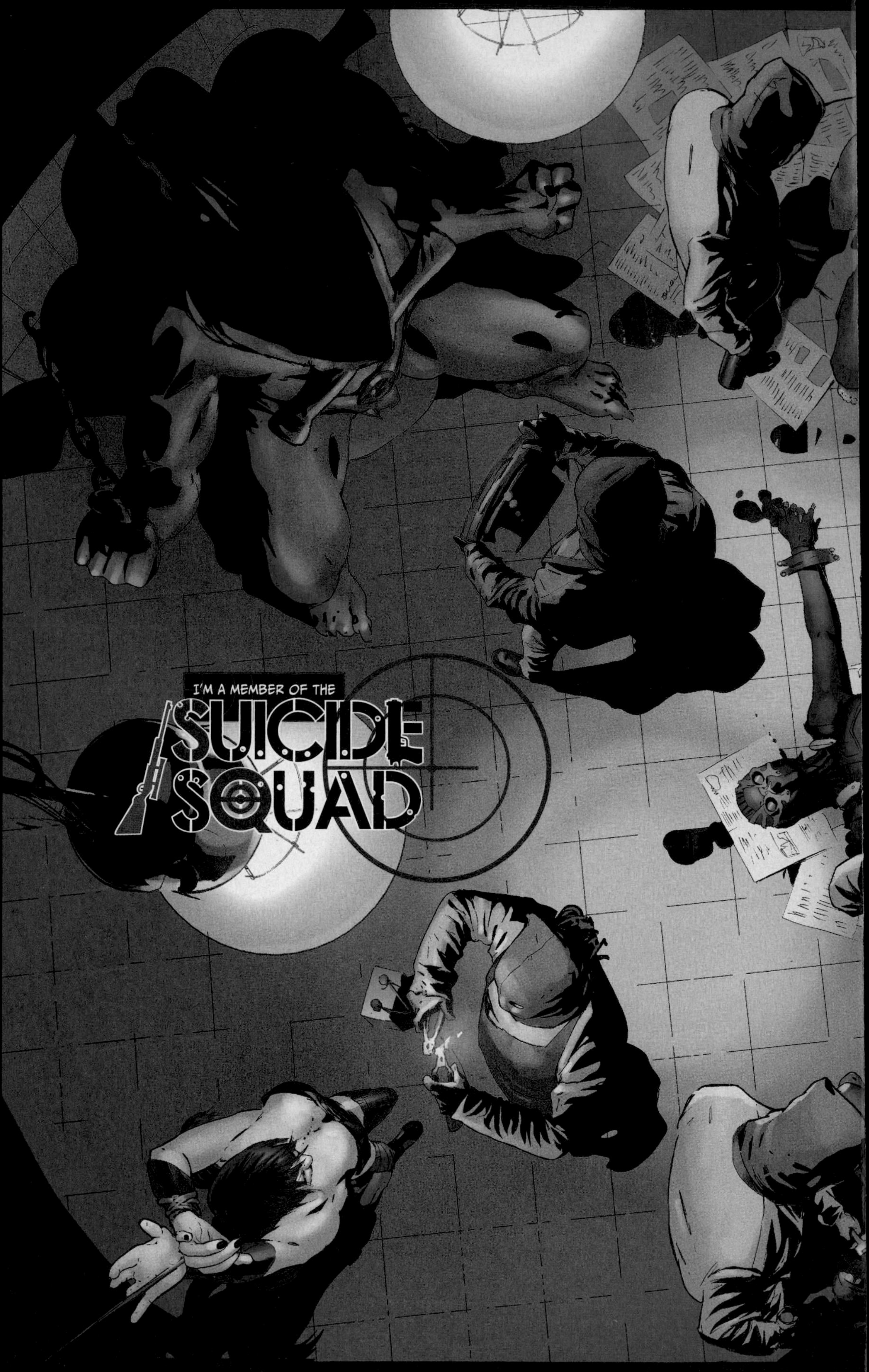
I'M A MEMBER OF THE
SUICIDE SQUAD

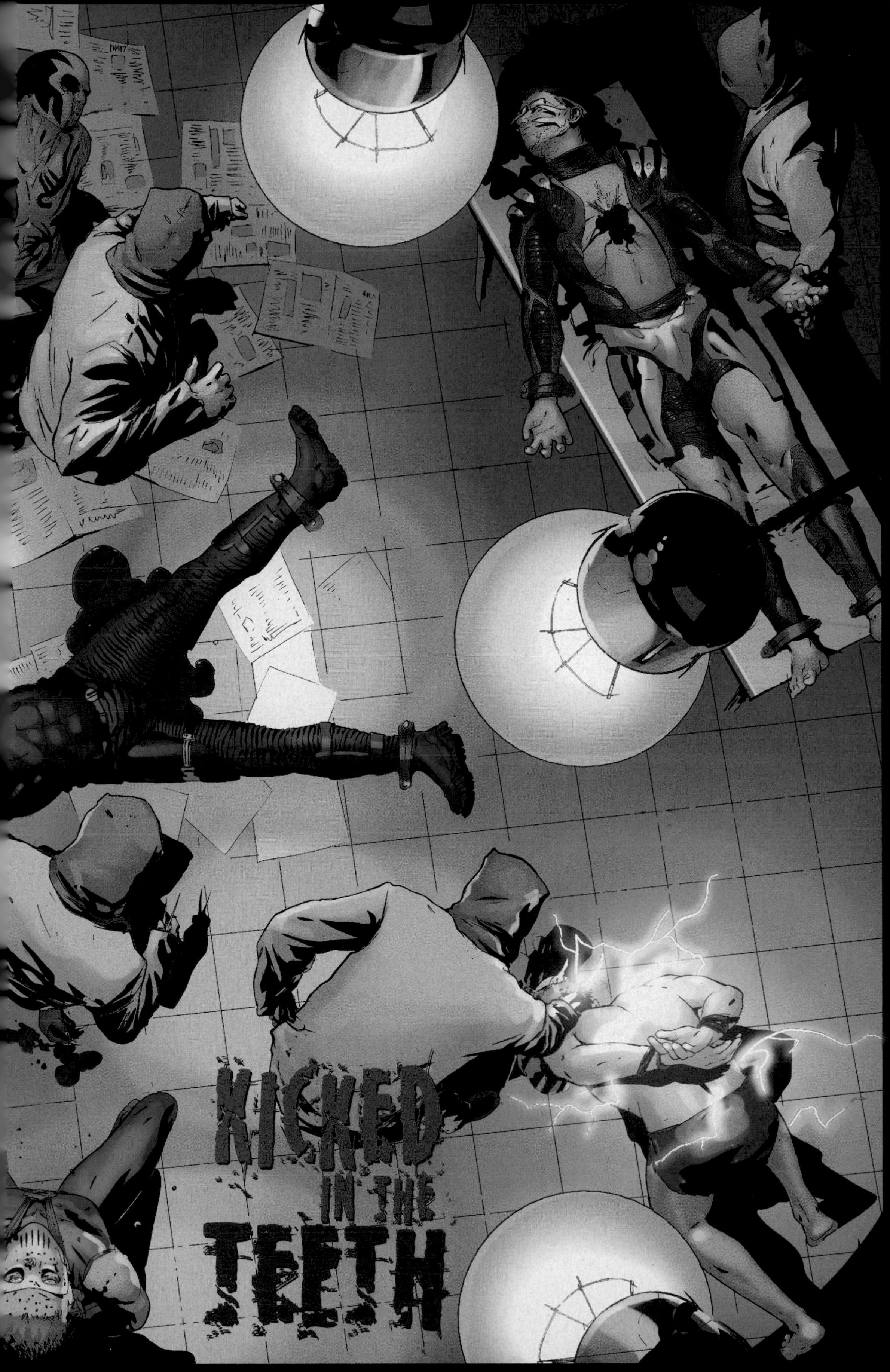
KICKED
IN THE
TEETH

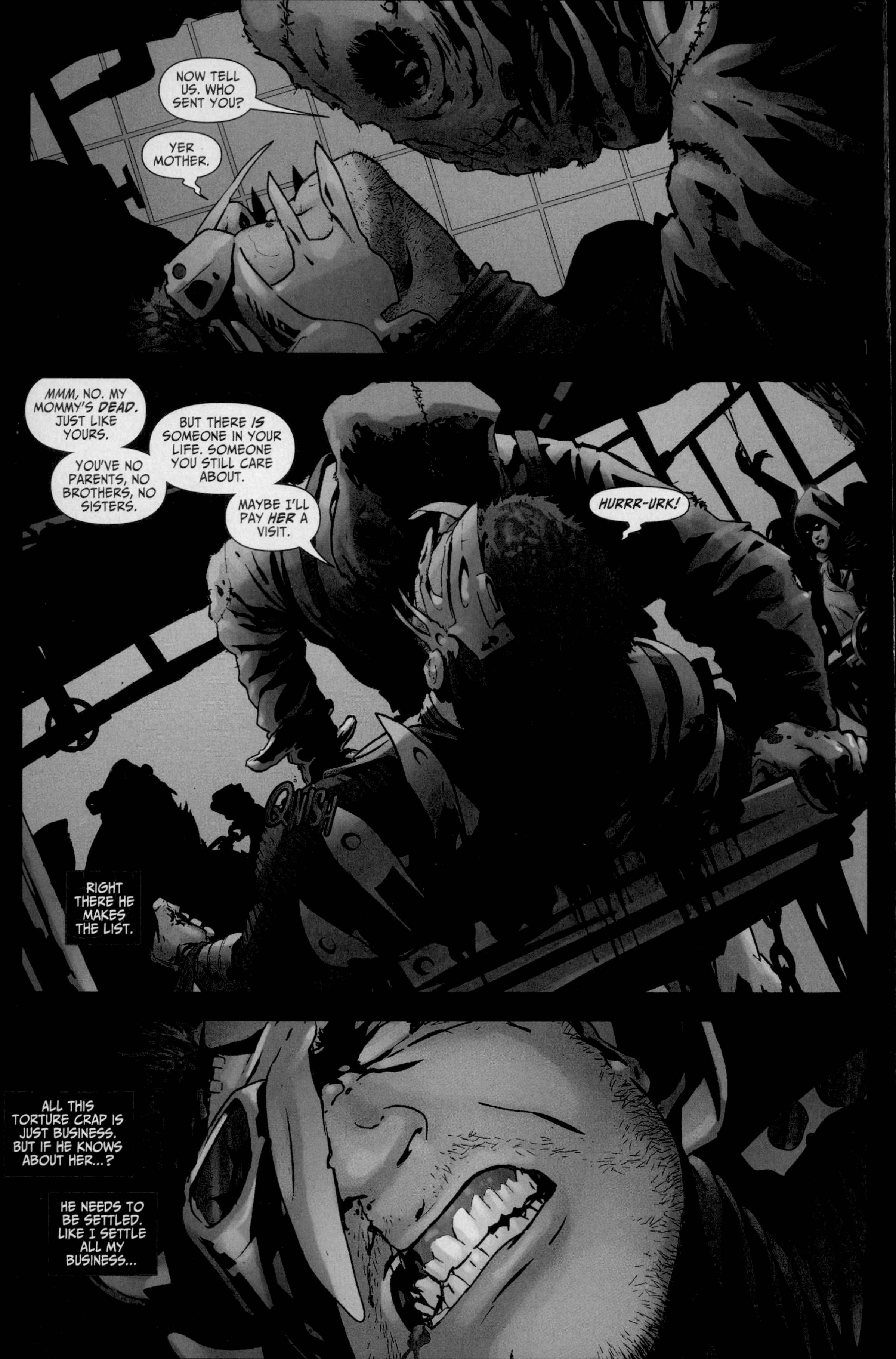
NOW TELL US. WHO SENT YOU?
YER MOTHER.
MMM, NO. MY MOMMY'S *DEAD.* JUST LIKE YOURS.
YOU'VE NO PARENTS, NO BROTHERS, NO SISTERS.
BUT THERE *IS* SOMEONE IN YOUR LIFE. SOMEONE YOU STILL CARE ABOUT.
MAYBE I'LL PAY *HER* A VISIT.
HURRR-URK!
RIGHT THERE HE MAKES THE LIST.
ALL THIS TORTURE CRAP IS JUST BUSINESS. BUT IF HE KNOWS ABOUT HER...?
HE NEEDS TO BE SETTLED. LIKE I SETTLE ALL MY BUSINESS...

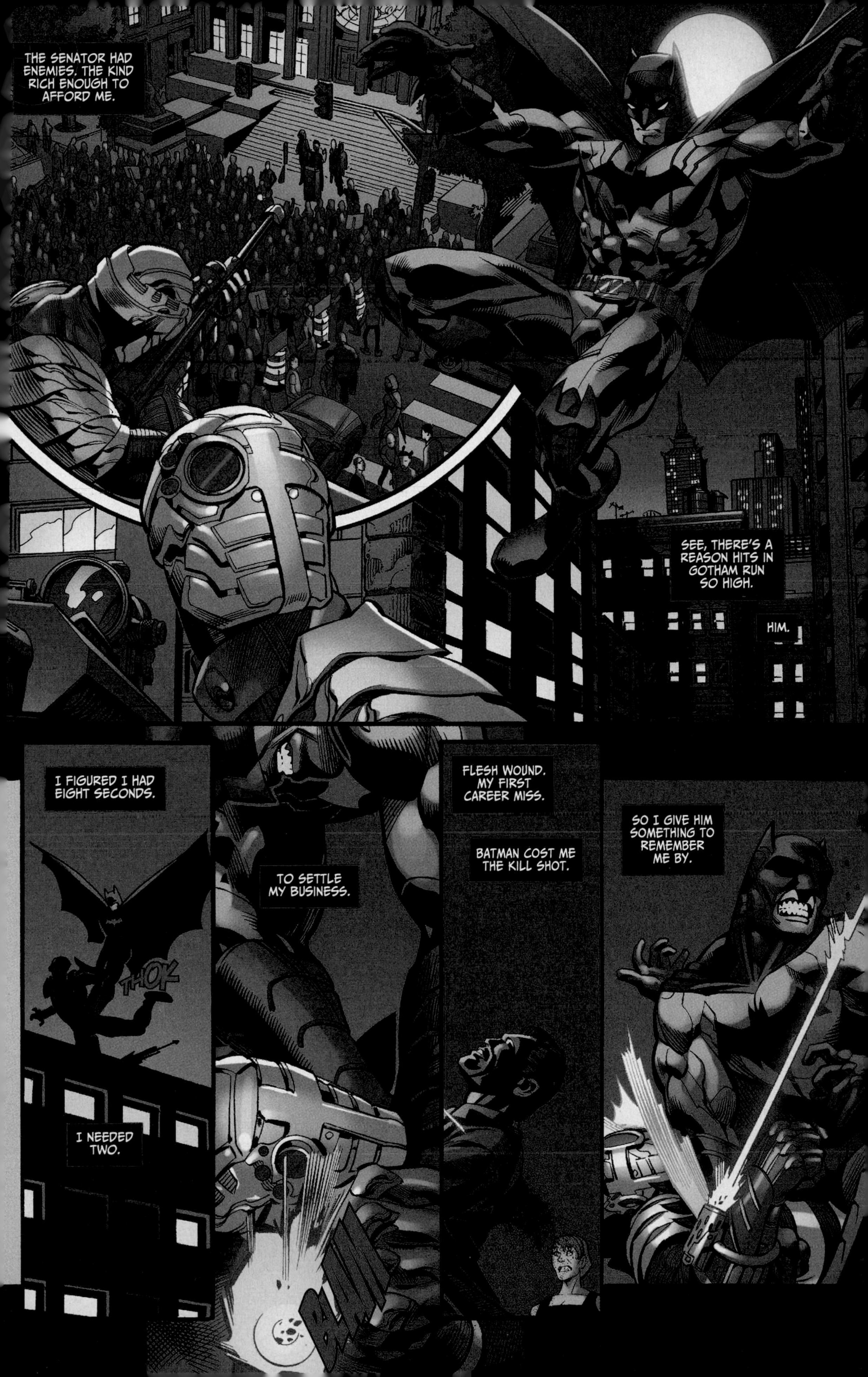
THE SENATOR HAD ENEMIES. THE KIND RICH ENOUGH TO AFFORD ME.
SEE, THERE'S A REASON HITS IN GOTHAM RUN SO HIGH.
HIM.
I FIGURED I HAD EIGHT SECONDS.
THOK
I NEEDED TWO.
TO SETTLE MY BUSINESS.
FLESH WOUND. MY FIRST CAREER MISS.
BATMAN COST ME THE KILL SHOT.
SO I GIVE HIM SOMETHING TO REMEMBER ME BY.

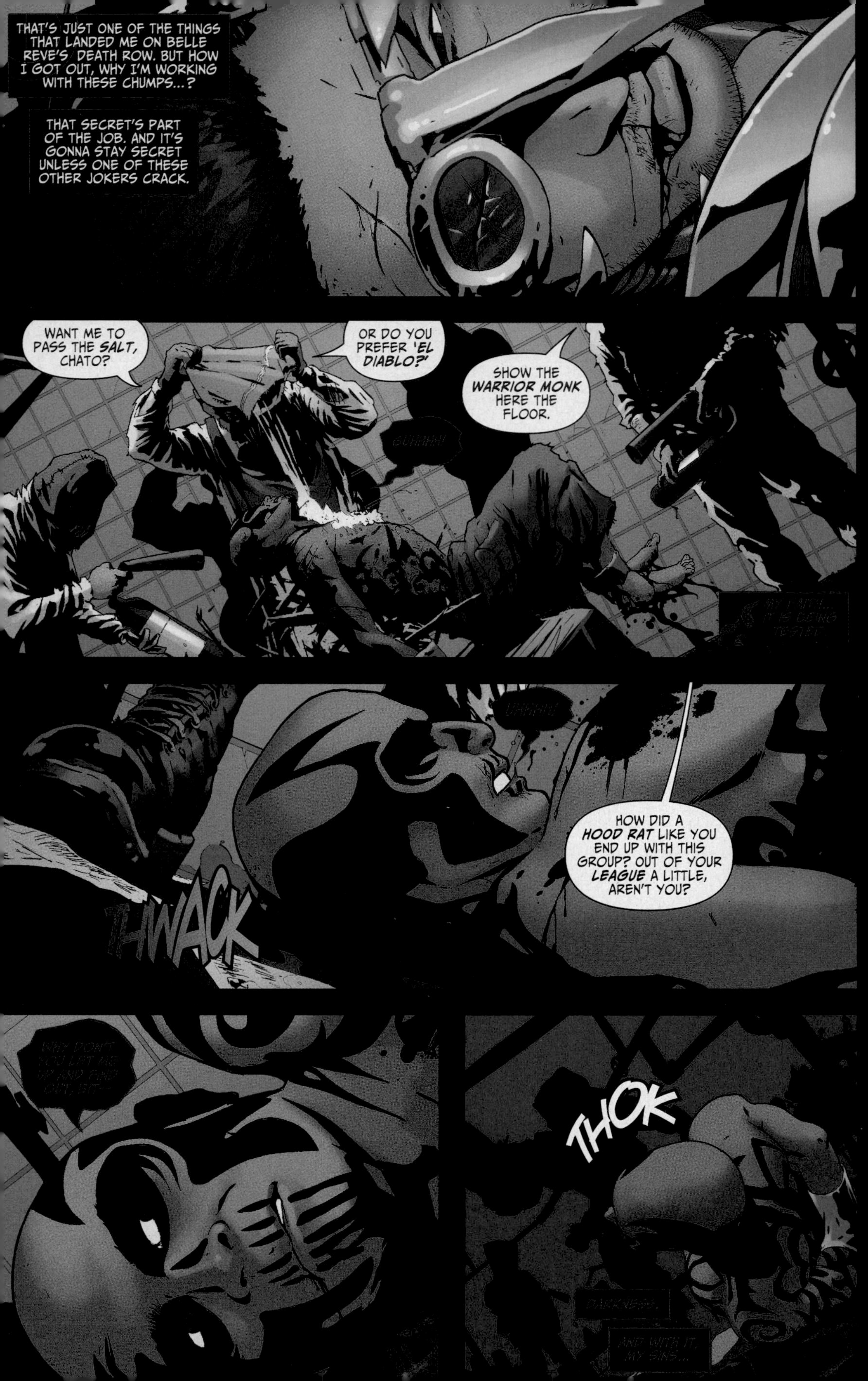
THAT'S JUST ONE OF THE THINGS THAT LANDED ME ON BELLE REVE'S DEATH ROW. BUT HOW I GOT OUT, WHY I'M WORKING WITH THESE CHUMPS...?
THAT SECRET'S PART OF THE JOB. AND IT'S GONNA STAY SECRET UNLESS ONE OF THESE OTHER JOKERS CRACK.
WANT ME TO PASS THE SALT, CHATO?
OR DO YOU PREFER 'EL DIABLO?'
SHOW THE WARRIOR MONK HERE THE FLOOR.
MY FAITH... IT IS BEING TESTED.
HOW DID A HOOD RAT LIKE YOU END UP WITH THIS GROUP? OUT OF YOUR LEAGUE A LITTLE, AREN'T YOU?
THWACK
WHY DON'T YOU LET ME UP AND FIND OUT, ESE--
THOK
DARKNESS.
AND WITH IT, MY SINS...

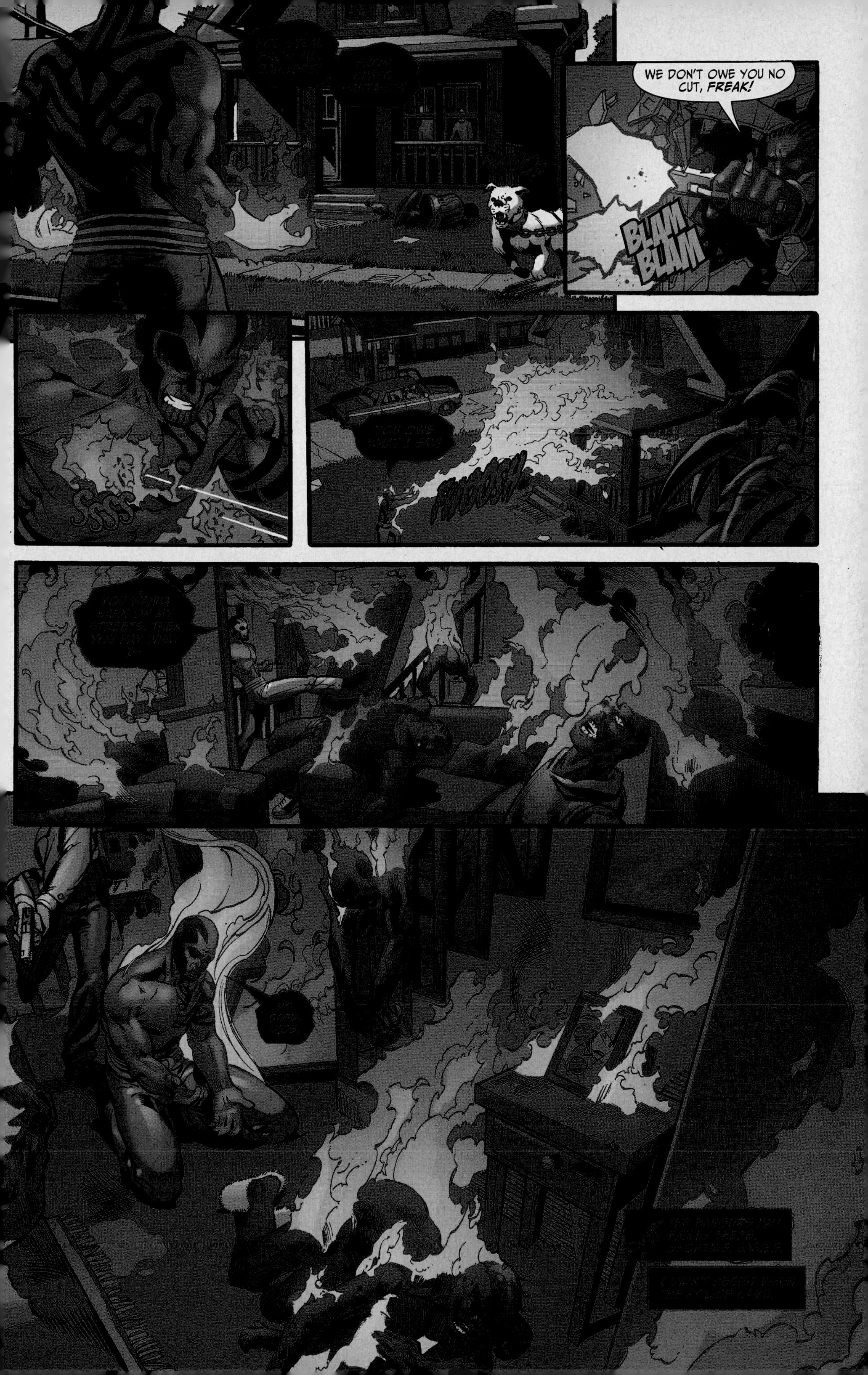
WE DON'T OWE YOU NO CUT, *FREAK!*
BLAM BLAM
SSSS

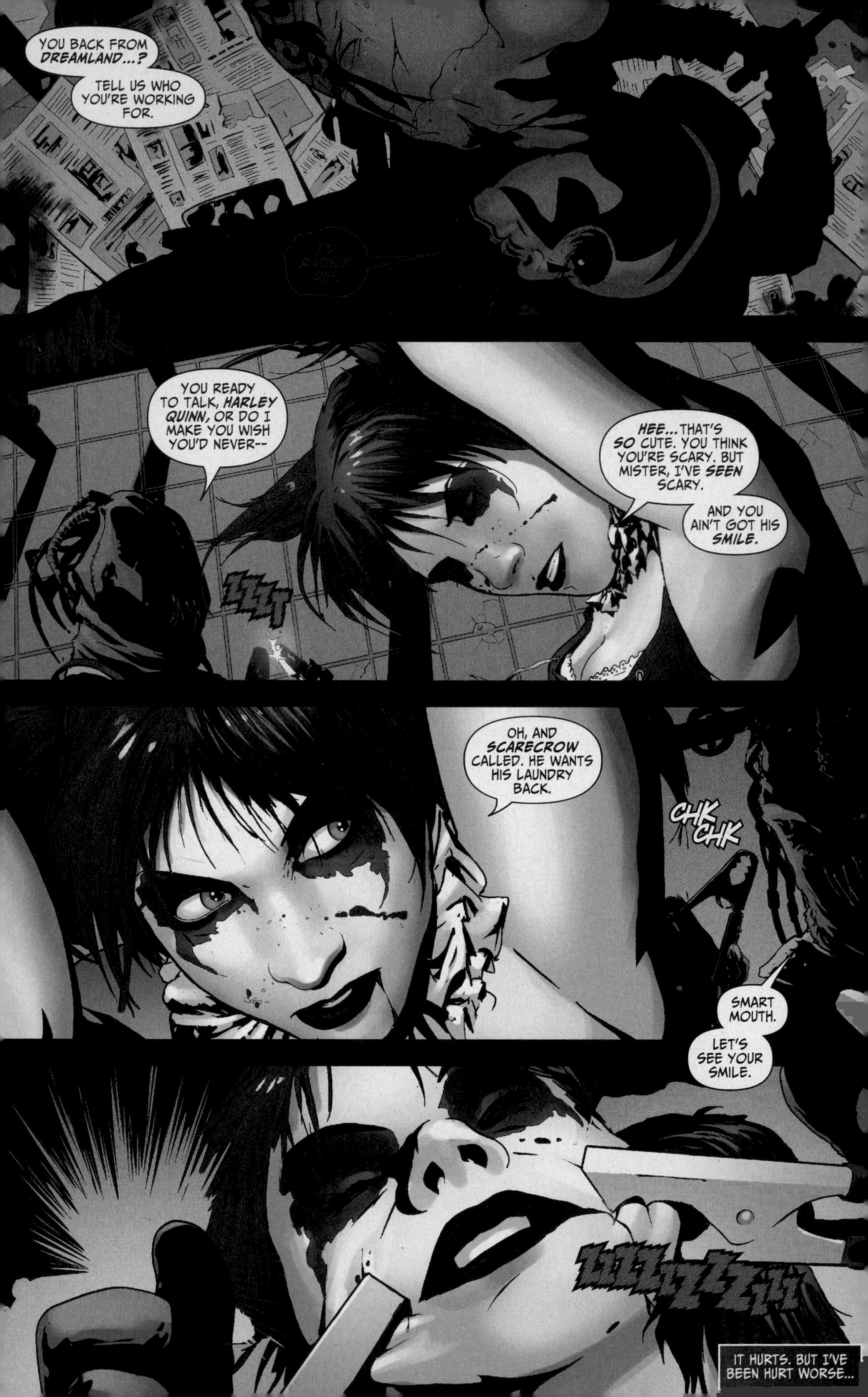

YOU BACK FROM DREAMLAND...?
TELL US WHO YOU'RE WORKING FOR.
I'D RATHER DIE.
THWACK
YOU READY TO TALK, HARLEY QUINN, OR DO I MAKE YOU WISH YOU'D NEVER--
HEE... THAT'S SO CUTE. YOU THINK YOU'RE SCARY. BUT MISTER, I'VE SEEN SCARY.
AND YOU AIN'T GOT HIS SMILE.
ZZZT
OH, AND SCARECROW CALLED. HE WANTS HIS LAUNDRY BACK.
CHK CHK
SMART MOUTH.
LET'S SEE YOUR SMILE.
ZZZZZZZZZZZ
IT HURTS. BUT I'VE BEEN HURT WORSE...

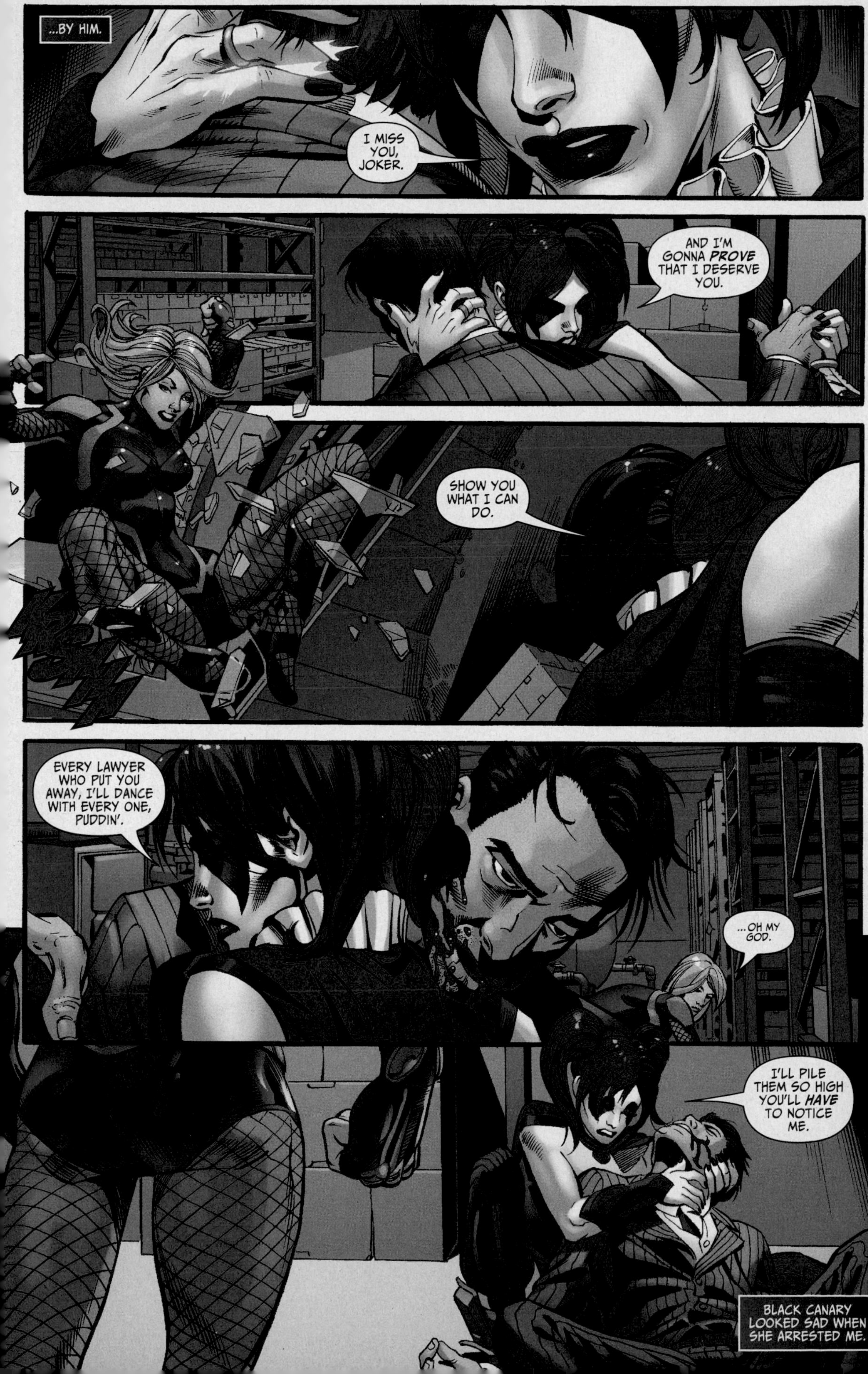
...BY HIM.
I MISS YOU, JOKER.
AND I'M GONNA PROVE THAT I DESERVE YOU.
SHOW YOU WHAT I CAN DO.
EVERY LAWYER WHO PUT YOU AWAY, I'LL DANCE WITH EVERY ONE, PUDDIN'.
...OH MY GOD.
I'LL PILE THEM SO HIGH YOU'LL HAVE TO NOTICE ME.
BLACK CANARY LOOKED SAD WHEN SHE ARRESTED ME.

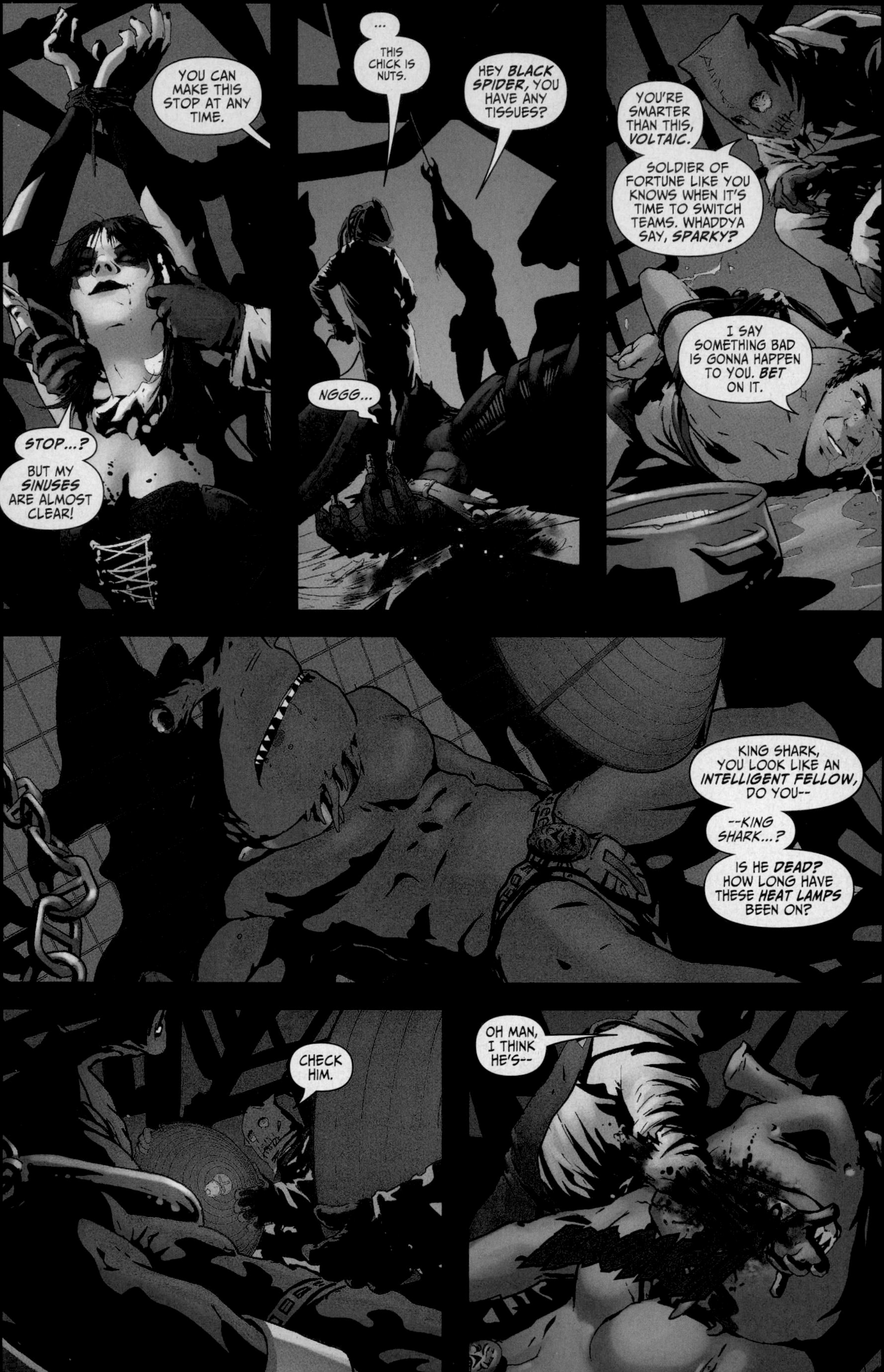
YOU CAN MAKE THIS STOP AT ANY TIME.
STOP...? BUT MY SINUSES ARE ALMOST CLEAR!
...
THIS CHICK IS NUTS.
HEY BLACK SPIDER, YOU HAVE ANY TISSUES?
NGGG...
YOU'RE SMARTER THAN THIS, VOLTAIC.
SOLDIER OF FORTUNE LIKE YOU KNOWS WHEN IT'S TIME TO SWITCH TEAMS. WHADDYA SAY, SPARKY?
I SAY SOMETHING BAD IS GONNA HAPPEN TO YOU. BET ON IT.
KING SHARK, YOU LOOK LIKE AN INTELLIGENT FELLOW, DO YOU--
--KING SHARK...?
IS HE DEAD? HOW LONG HAVE THESE HEAT LAMPS BEEN ON?
CHECK HIM.
OH MAN, I THINK HE'S--

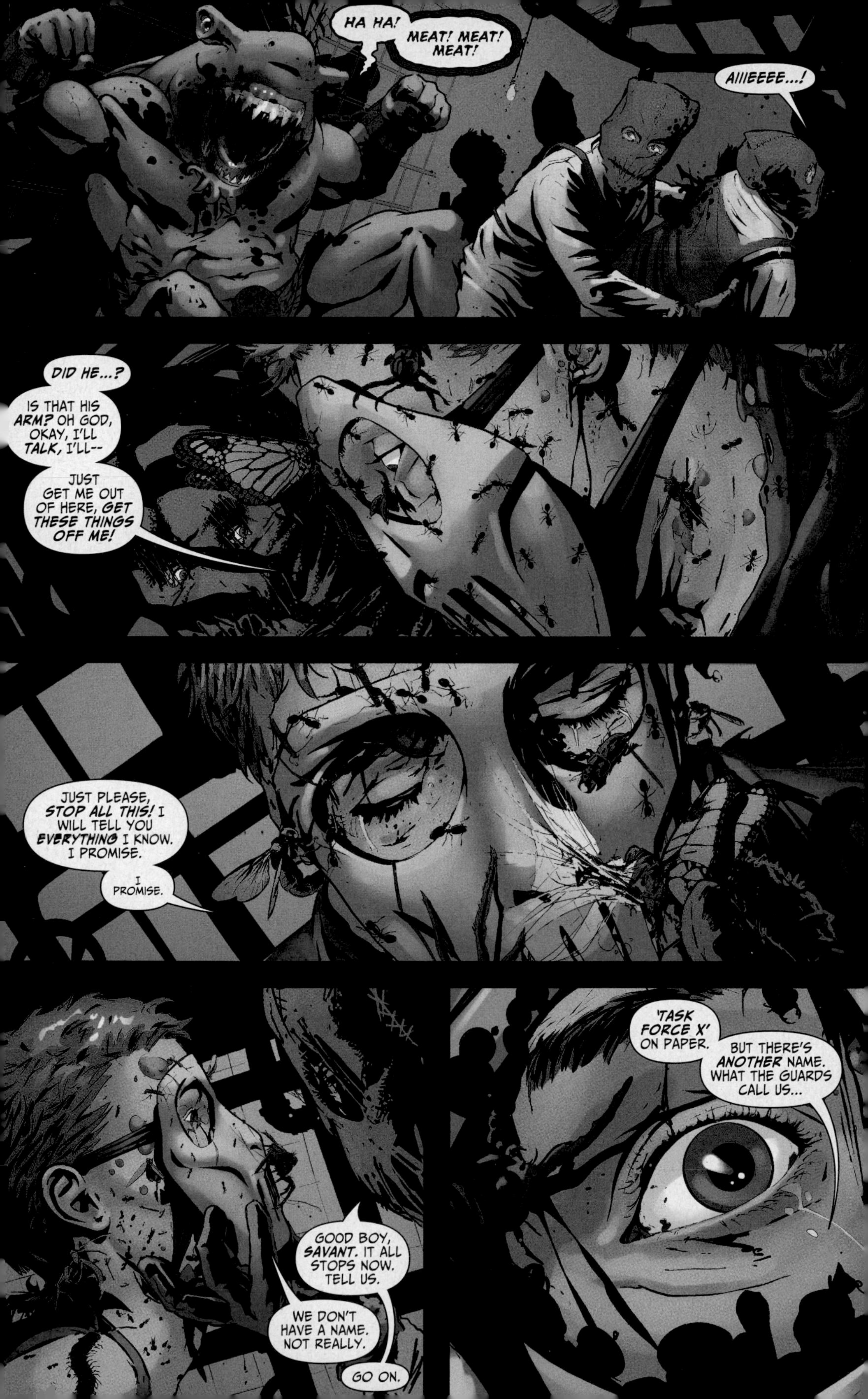
HA HA!
MEAT! MEAT! MEAT!
AIIIEEEE...!
DID HE...?
IS THAT HIS ARM? OH GOD, OKAY, I'LL TALK, I'LL--
JUST GET ME OUT OF HERE, GET THESE THINGS OFF ME!
JUST PLEASE, STOP ALL THIS! I WILL TELL YOU EVERYTHING I KNOW. I PROMISE.
I PROMISE.
GOOD BOY, SAVANT. IT ALL STOPS NOW. TELL US.
WE DON'T HAVE A NAME. NOT REALLY.
GO ON.
'TASK FORCE X' ON PAPER.
BUT THERE'S ANOTHER NAME. WHAT THE GUARDS CALL US...

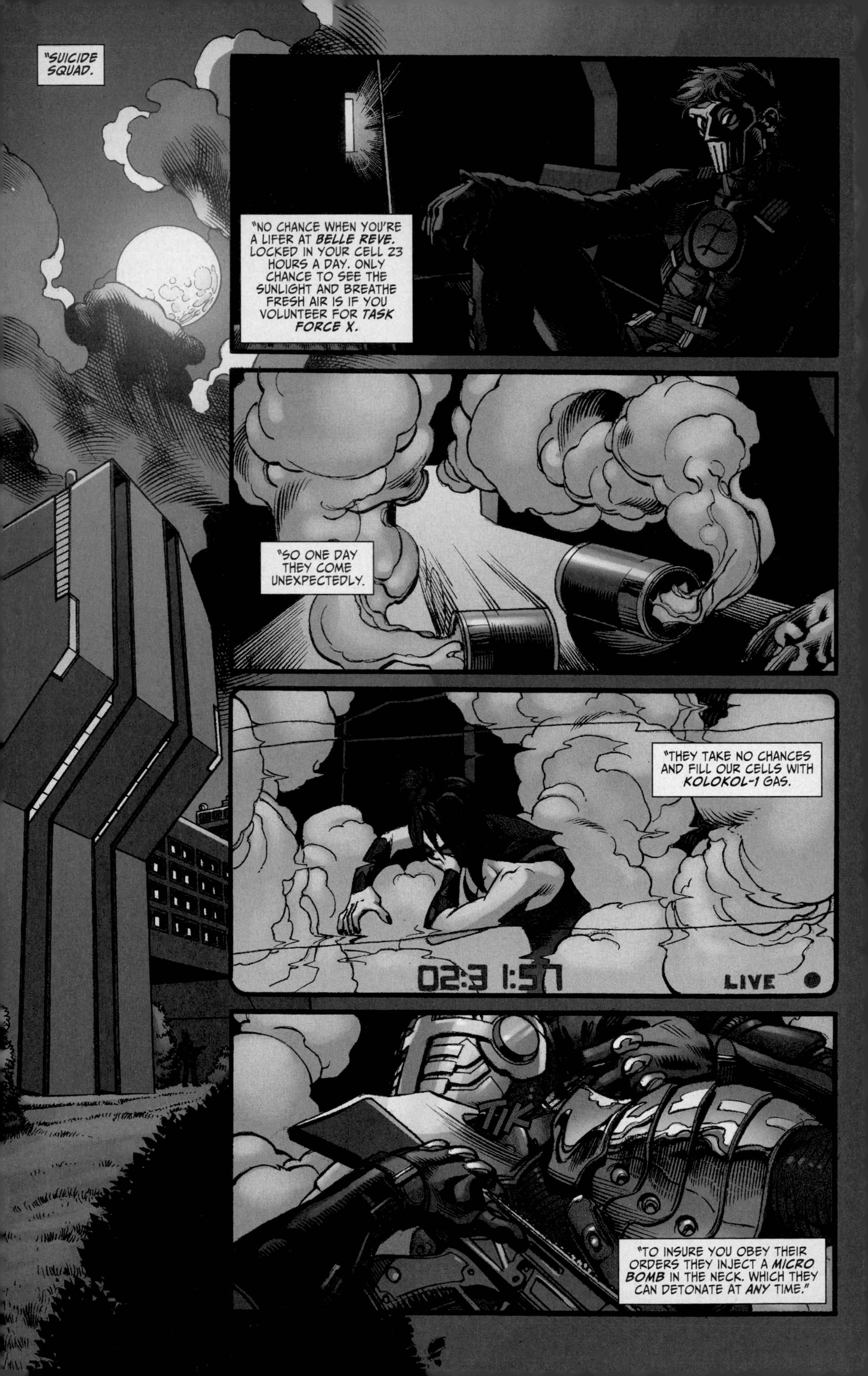
"SUICIDE SQUAD.
"NO CHANCE WHEN YOU'RE A LIFER AT BELLE REVE. LOCKED IN YOUR CELL 23 HOURS A DAY. ONLY CHANCE TO SEE THE SUNLIGHT AND BREATHE FRESH AIR IS IF YOU VOLUNTEER FOR TASK FORCE X.
"SO ONE DAY THEY COME UNEXPECTEDLY.
"THEY TAKE NO CHANCES AND FILL OUR CELLS WITH KOLOKOL-1 GAS.
02:31:57
LIVE
TIK
"TO INSURE YOU OBEY THEIR ORDERS THEY INJECT A MICRO BOMB IN THE NECK. WHICH THEY CAN DETONATE AT ANY TIME."

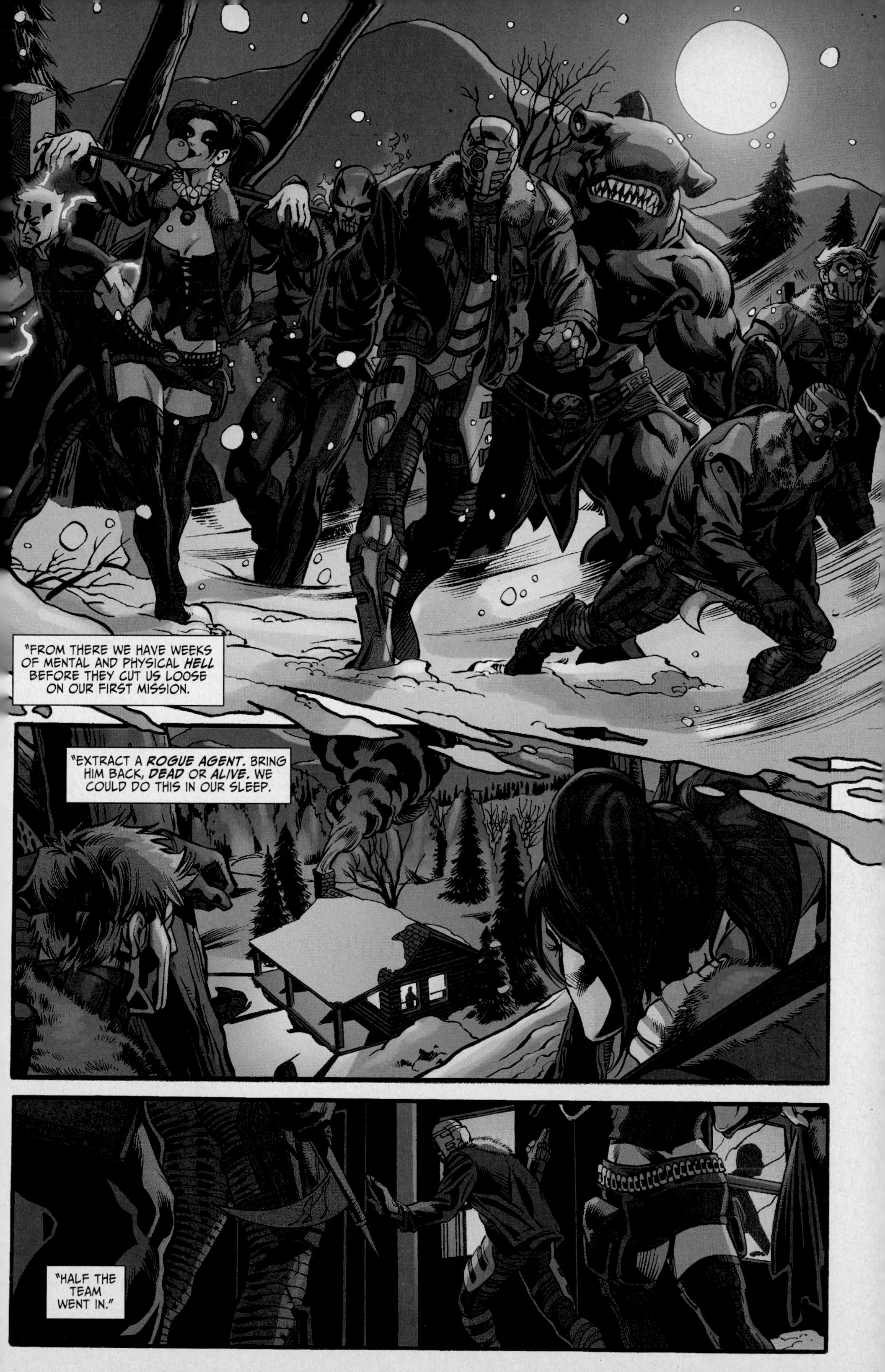
"FROM THERE WE HAVE WEEKS OF MENTAL AND PHYSICAL HELL BEFORE THEY CUT US LOOSE ON OUR FIRST MISSION.
"EXTRACT A ROGUE AGENT. BRING HIM BACK, DEAD OR ALIVE. WE COULD DO THIS IN OUR SLEEP.
"HALF THE TEAM WENT IN."

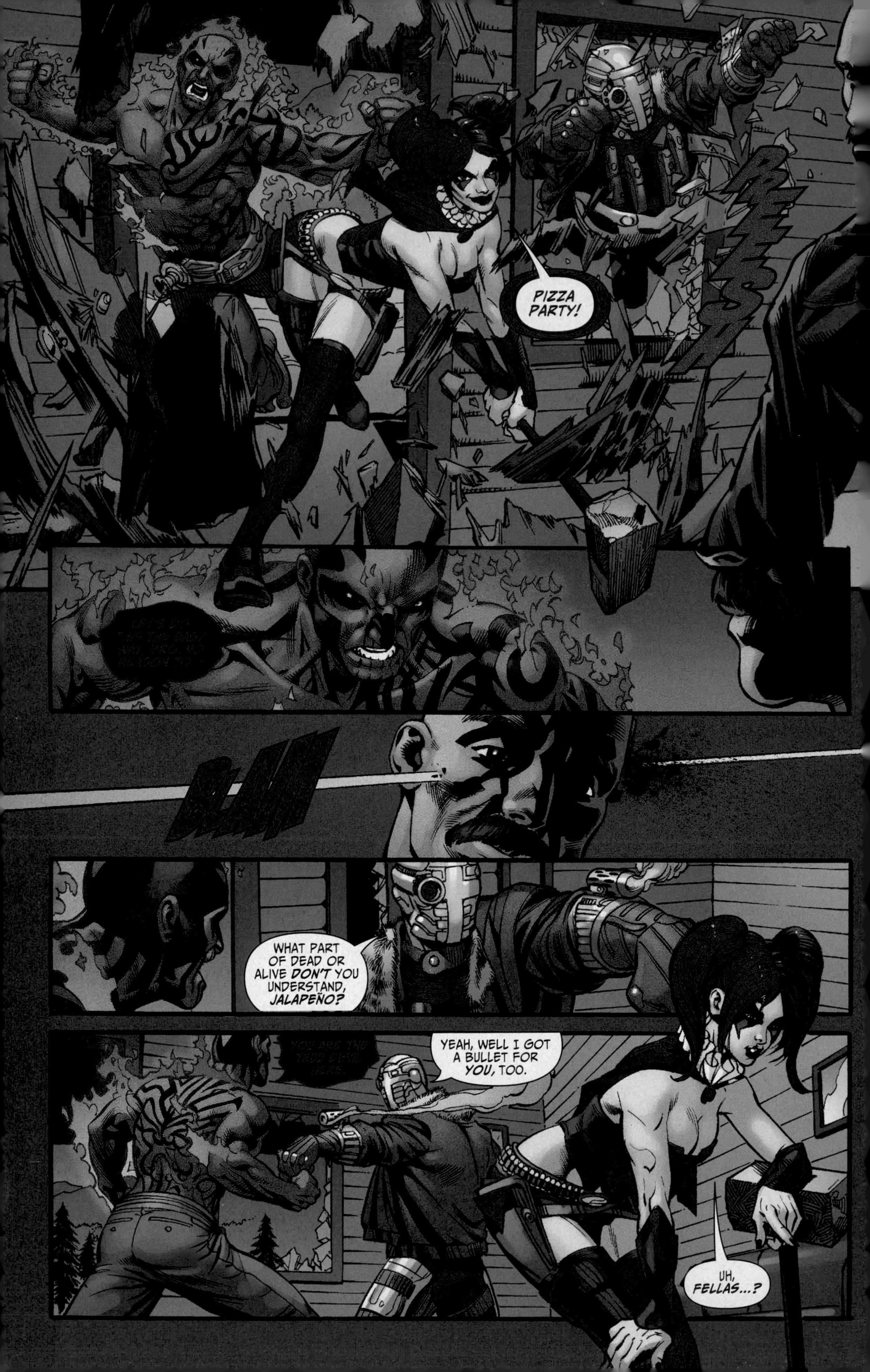
PIZZA PARTY!
WHAT PART OF DEAD OR ALIVE DON'T YOU UNDERSTAND, JALAPEÑO?
YEAH, WELL I GOT A BULLET FOR YOU, TOO.
UH, FELLAS...?

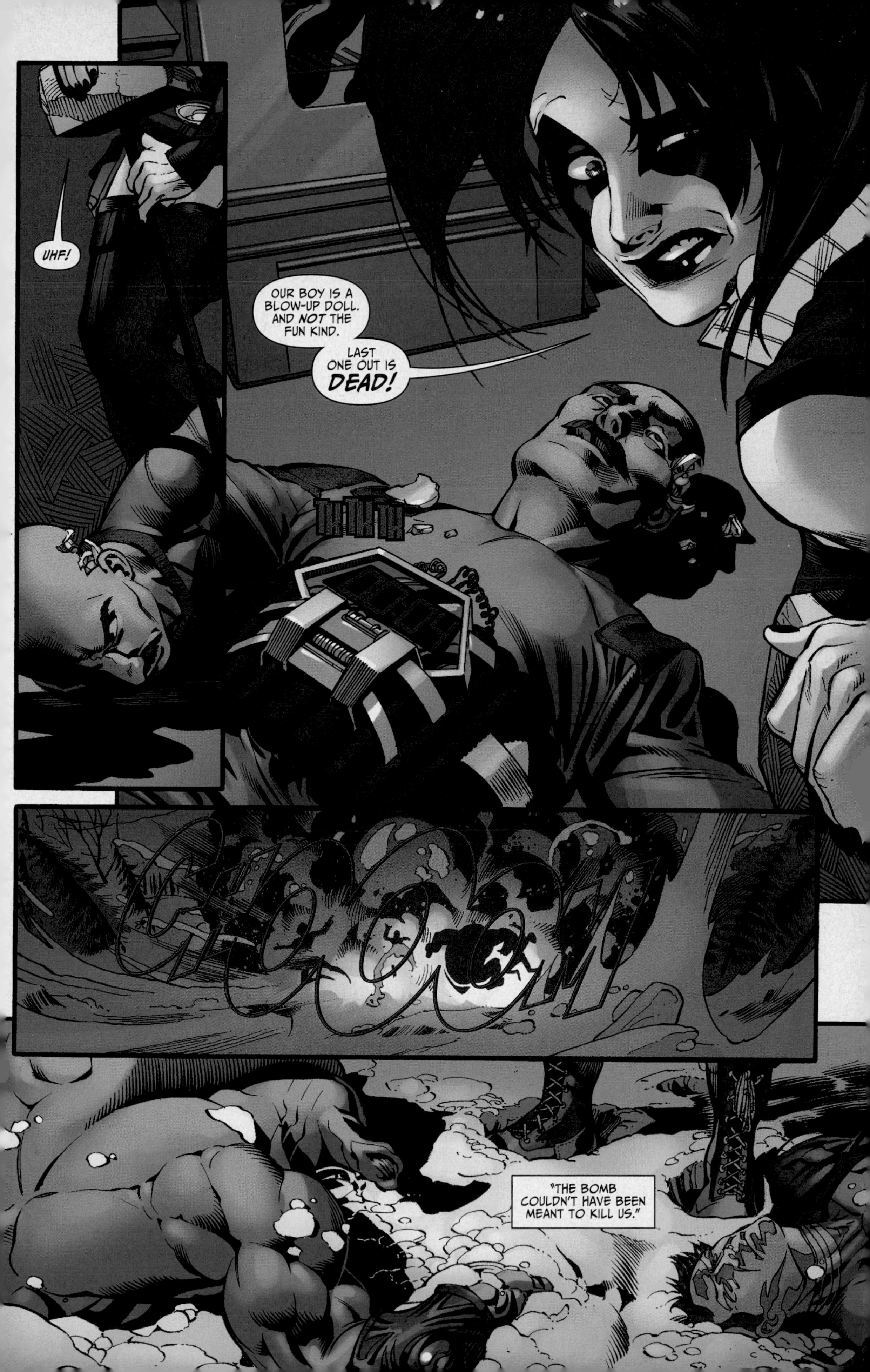
UHF!
OUR BOY IS A BLOW-UP DOLL. AND NOT THE FUN KIND.
LAST ONE OUT IS DEAD!
TIK TIK TIK
"THE BOMB COULDN'T HAVE BEEN MEANT TO KILL US."

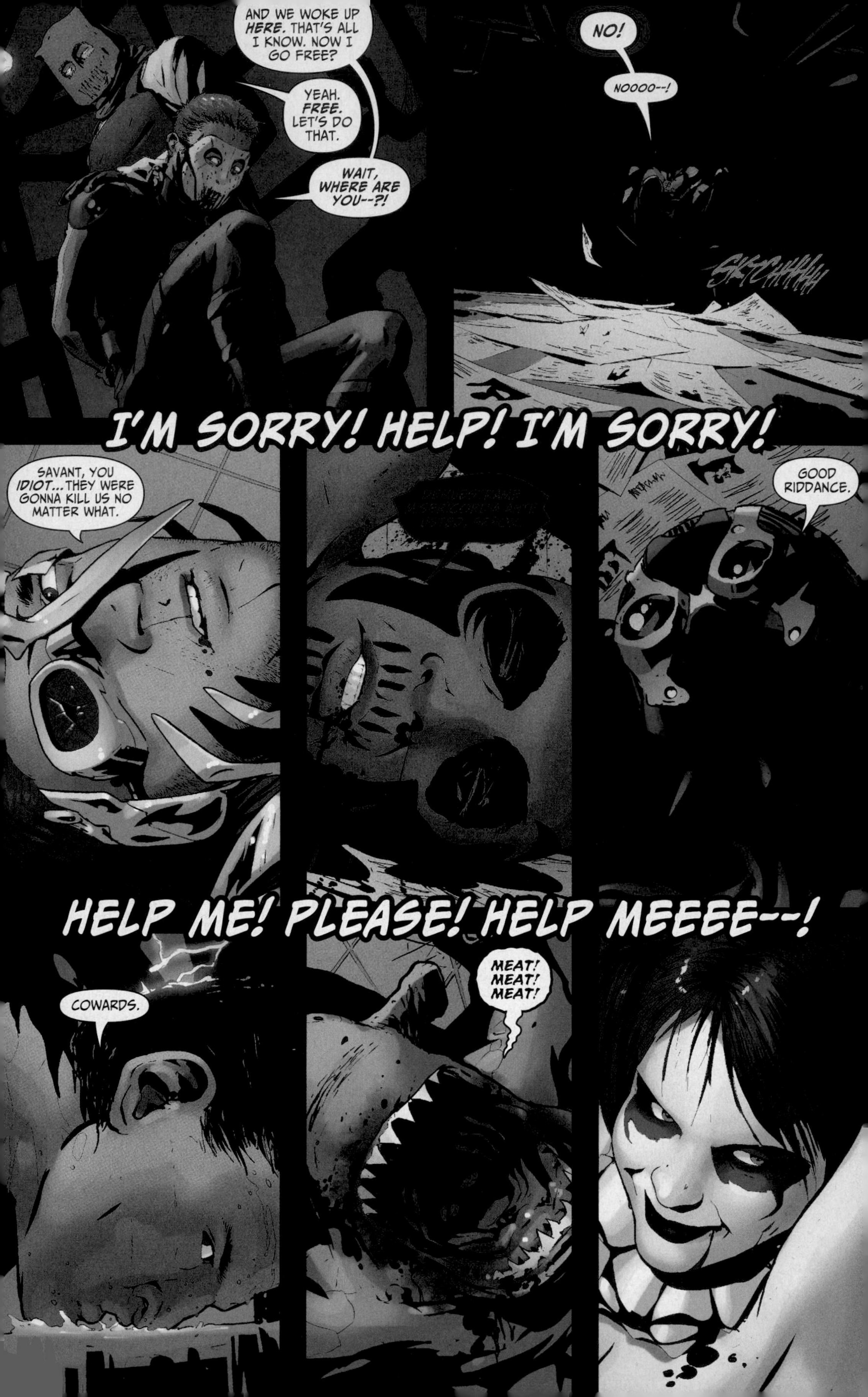
AND WE WOKE UP HERE. THAT'S ALL I KNOW. NOW I GO FREE?
YEAH. FREE. LET'S DO THAT.
WAIT, WHERE ARE YOU--?!
NO!
NOOOO--!
SKTCHHHHH
I'M SORRY! HELP! I'M SORRY!
SAVANT, YOU IDIOT... THEY WERE GONNA KILL US NO MATTER WHAT.
GOOD RIDDANCE.
HELP ME! PLEASE! HELP MEEEE--!
COWARDS.
MEAT! MEAT! MEAT!

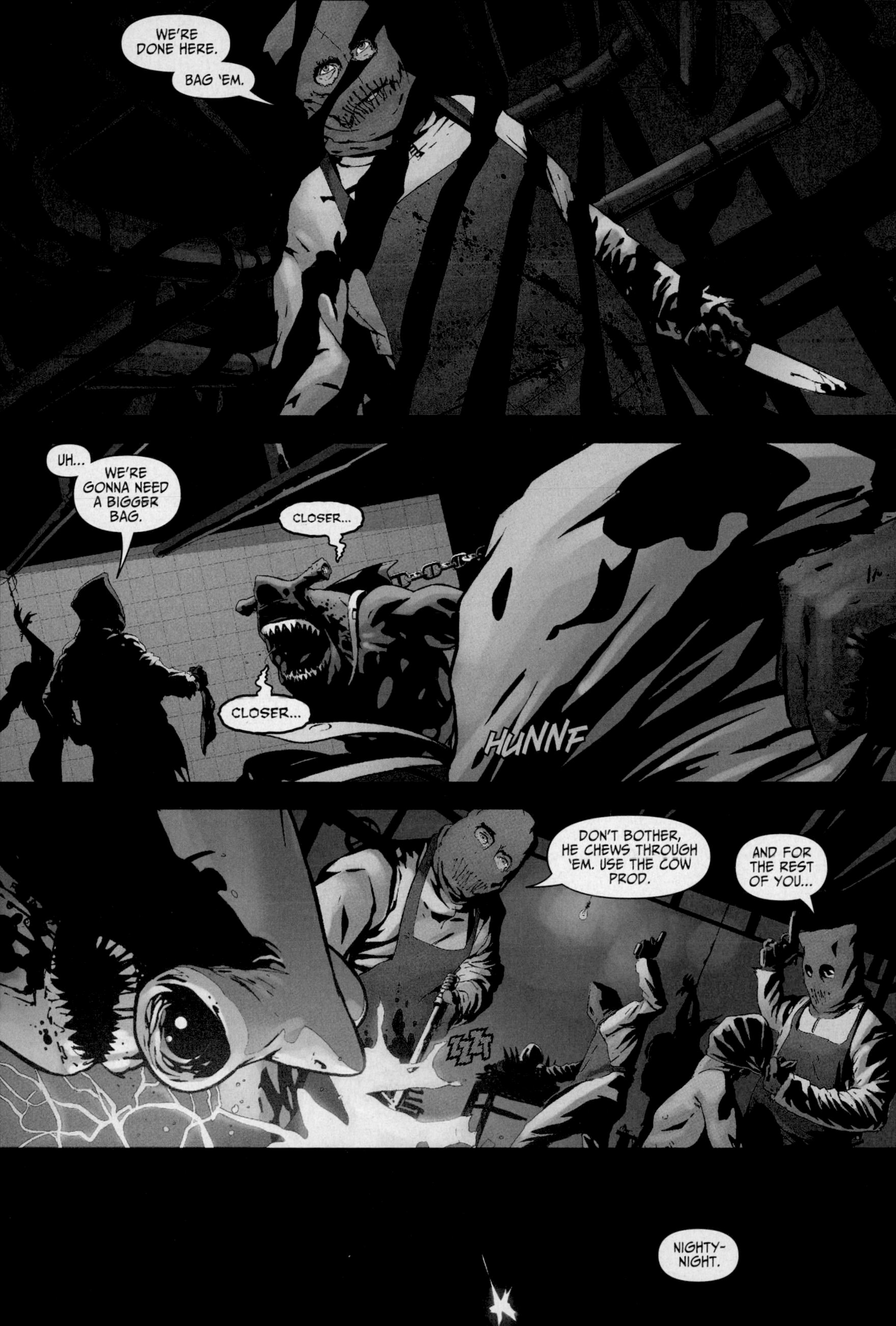
WE'RE DONE HERE.
BAG 'EM.
UH...
WE'RE GONNA NEED A BIGGER BAG.
CLOSER...
CLOSER...
HUNNF
DON'T BOTHER, HE CHEWS THROUGH 'EM. USE THE COW PROD.
AND FOR THE REST OF YOU...
NIGHTY-NIGHT.

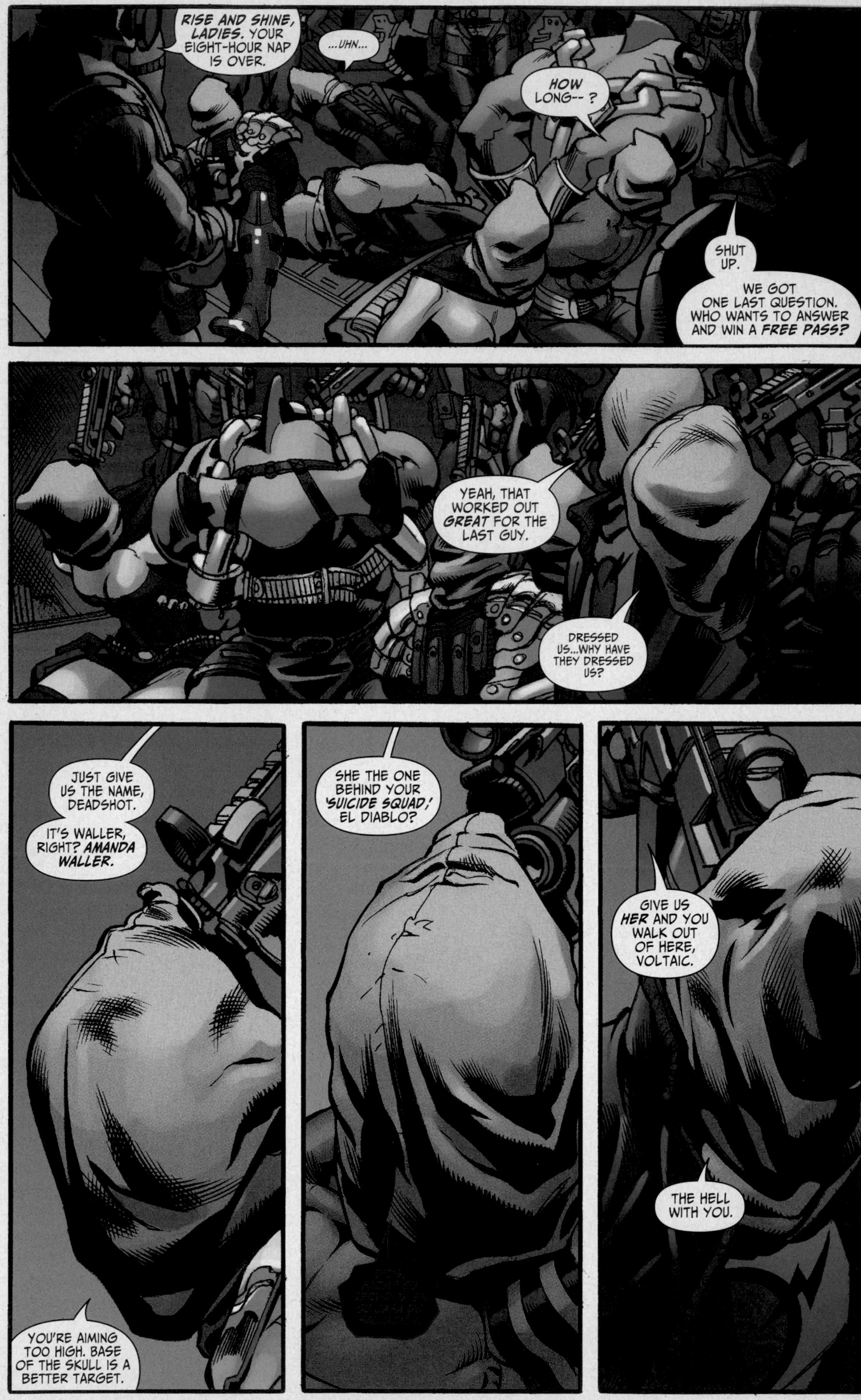
RISE AND SHINE, LADIES. YOUR EIGHT-HOUR NAP IS OVER.
...UHN...
HOW LONG-- ?
SHUT UP.
WE GOT ONE LAST QUESTION. WHO WANTS TO ANSWER AND WIN A FREE PASS?
YEAH, THAT WORKED OUT GREAT FOR THE LAST GUY.
DRESSED US...WHY HAVE THEY DRESSED US?
JUST GIVE US THE NAME, DEADSHOT.
IT'S WALLER, RIGHT? AMANDA WALLER.
YOU'RE AIMING TOO HIGH. BASE OF THE SKULL IS A BETTER TARGET.
SHE THE ONE BEHIND YOUR 'SUICIDE SQUAD,' EL DIABLO?
GIVE US HER AND YOU WALK OUT OF HERE, VOLTAIC.
THE HELL WITH YOU.

YOU HAVE PASSED THE FINAL TEST. YOU ARE ALL OFFICIALLY AGENTS OF TASK FORCE X.

WAIT... WHAT?

YOU WERE PUSHED TO THE BRINK. OUT OF THE THIRTY-SEVEN CANDIDATES, ONLY YOU SIX DIDN'T BREAK.

A *TEST?* THIS HAS ALL BEEN A *FREAKIN'* TEST?!

SOME OF US NEED A DOCTOR.

REQUEST DENIED, BLACK SPIDER.

CHUKUNCH

YOU ARE BEING DEPLOYED TO THE FIELD IMMEDIATELY.

...WALLER. THAT'S WALLER'S VOICE.

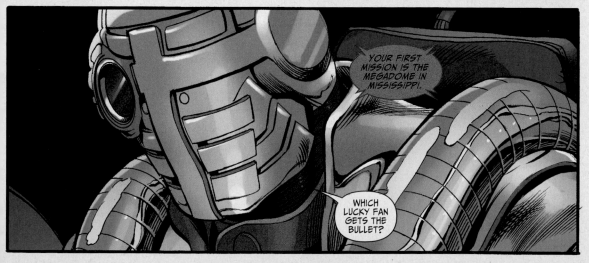

YOUR FIRST MISSION IS THE MEGADOME IN MISSISSIPPI.

WHICH LUCKY FAN GETS THE BULLET?

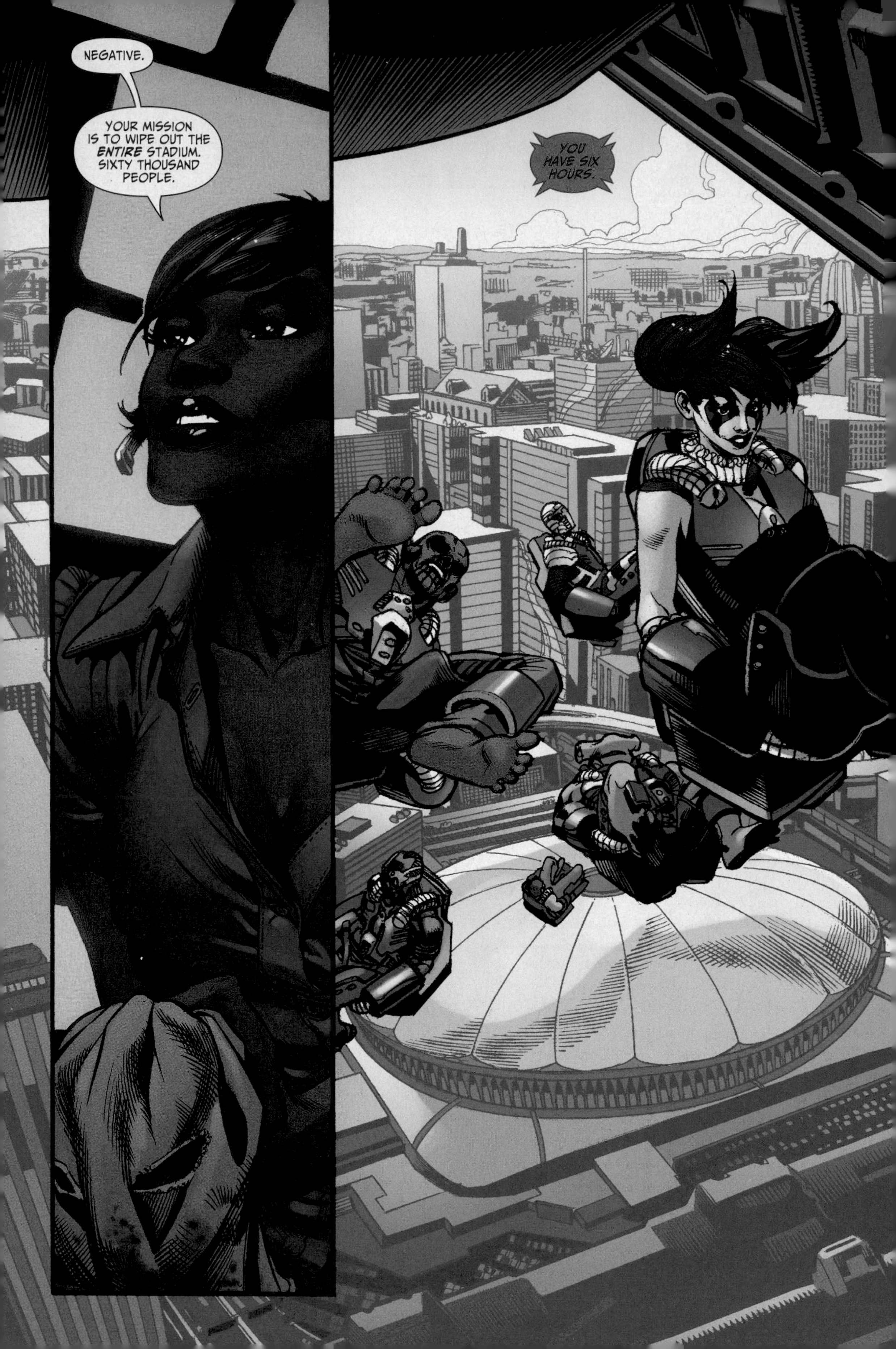
NEGATIVE.
YOUR MISSION IS TO WIPE OUT THE ENTIRE STADIUM. SIXTY THOUSAND PEOPLE.
YOU HAVE SIX HOURS.

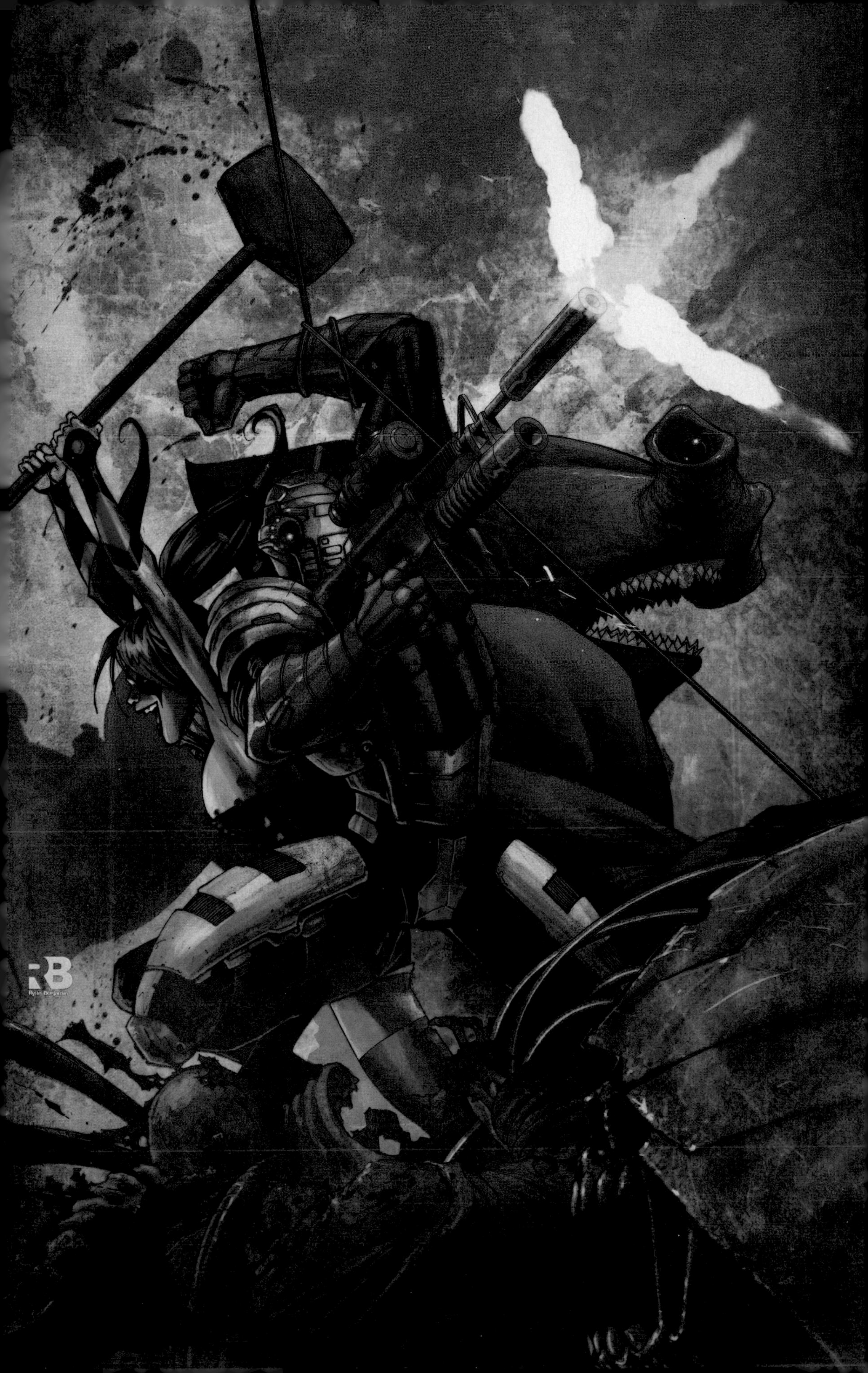
RB

WHEN THE LEVEE BREAKS

ADAM GLASS
writer

FEDERICO DALLOCCHIO & ANDREI BRESSAN
artists

cover art by RYAN BENJAMIN

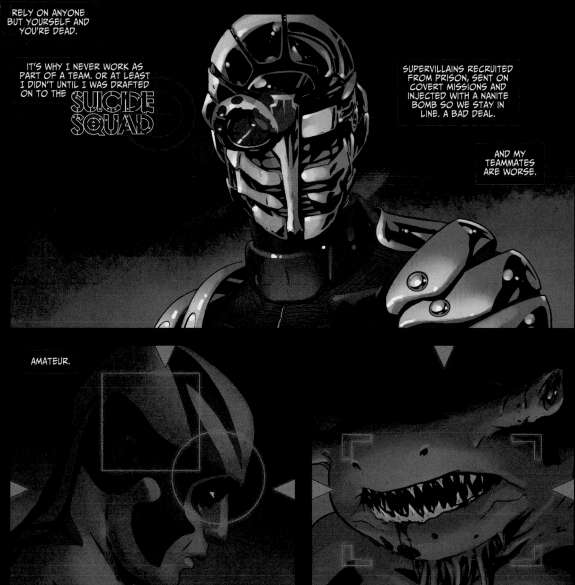

RELY ON ANYONE
BUT YOURSELF AND
YOU'RE DEAD.

IT'S WHY I NEVER WORK AS
PART OF A TEAM. OR AT LEAST
I DIDN'T UNTIL I WAS DRAFTED
ON TO THE SUICIDE SQUAD

SUPERVILLAINS RECRUITED
FROM PRISON, SENT ON
COVERT MISSIONS AND
INJECTED WITH A NANITE
BOMB SO WE STAY IN
LINE. A BAD DEAL.

AND MY
TEAMMATES
ARE WORSE.

AMATEUR.

WILD CARD.

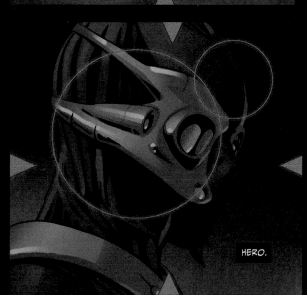

HERO.

AND *CUCKOO FOR
COCOA PUFFS.*

WHEN THE LEVEE **BREAKS**

...OH THANK GOD, THE JUSTICE LEAGUE...

HELP!

KEEP AN EYE ON FATTY. I GOT A CALL COMING IN FROM THE BOSS.

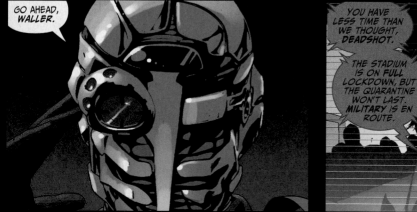

GO AHEAD, WALLER.

YOU HAVE LESS TIME THAN WE THOUGHT, DEADSHOT.

THE STADIUM IS ON FULL LOCKDOWN, BUT THE QUARANTINE WON'T LAST. MILITARY IS EN ROUTE.

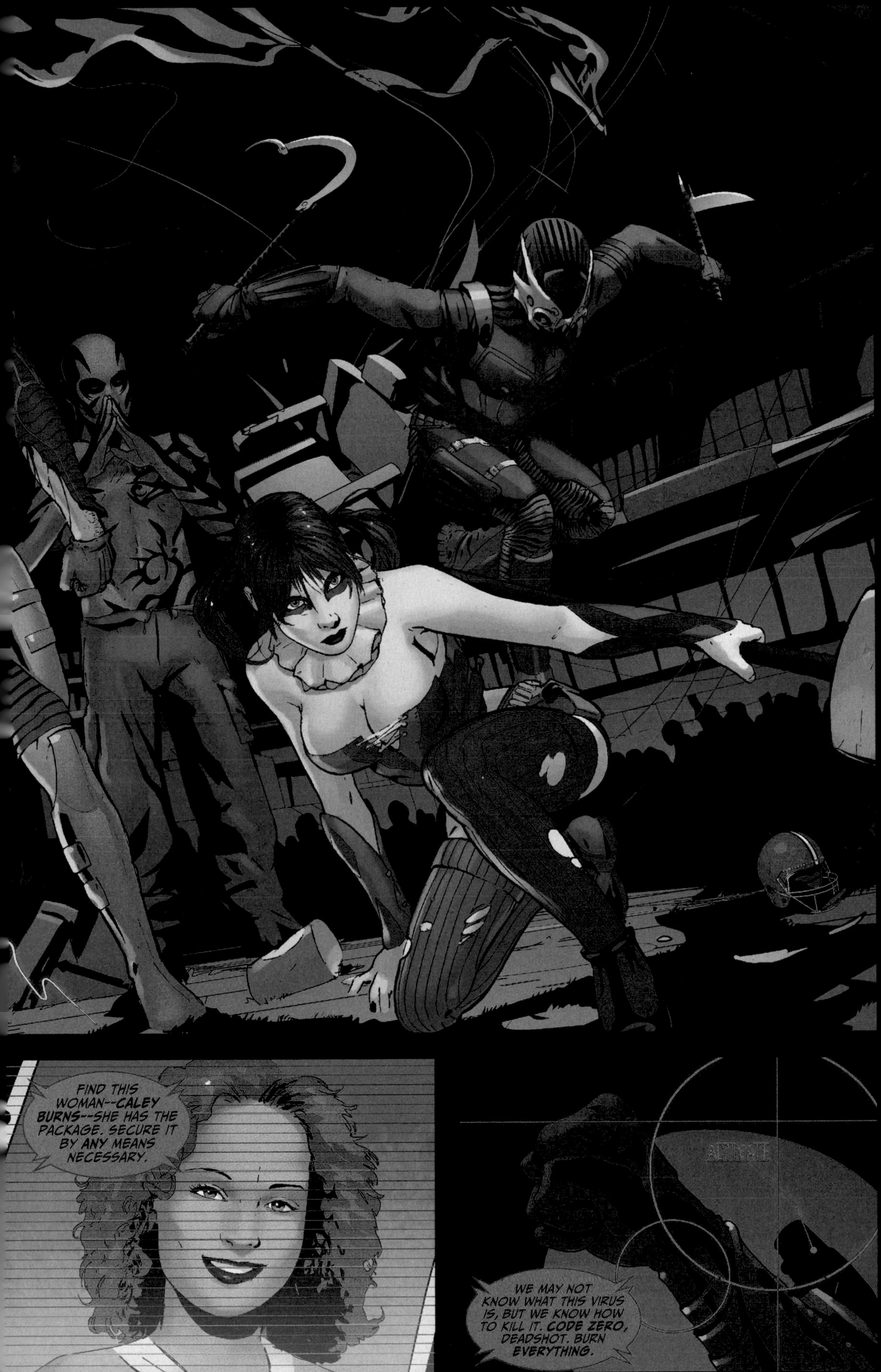
FIND THIS WOMAN--CALEY BURNS--SHE HAS THE PACKAGE. SECURE IT BY ANY MEANS NECESSARY.
WE MAY NOT KNOW WHAT THIS VIRUS IS, BUT WE KNOW HOW TO KILL IT. CODE ZERO, DEADSHOT. BURN EVERYTHING.

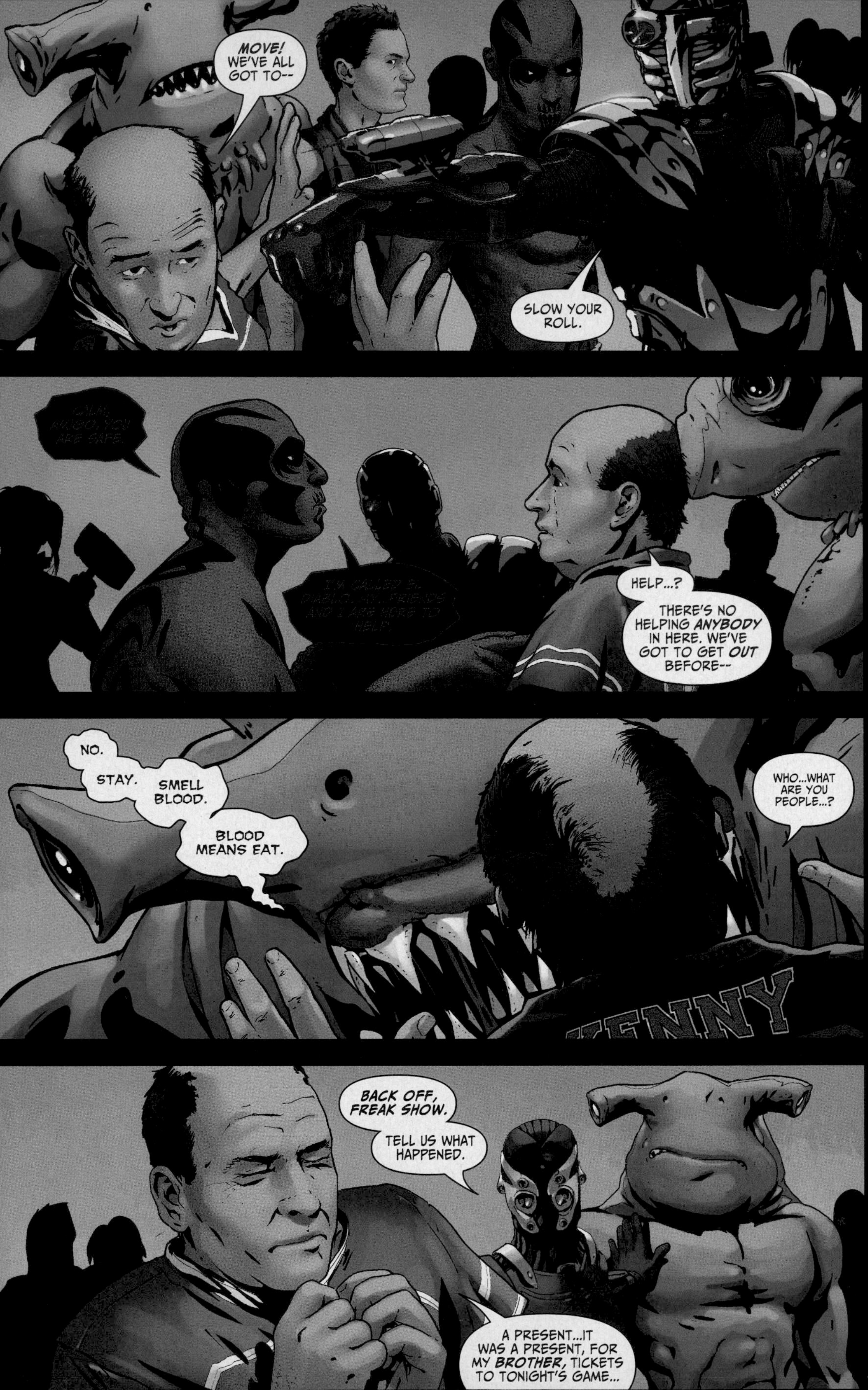

MOVE! WE'VE ALL GOT TO--
SLOW YOUR ROLL.
CALM, AMIGO, YOU ARE SAFE.
I'M CALLED EL DIABLO. MY FRIENDS AND I ARE HERE TO HELP.
HELP...?
THERE'S NO HELPING *ANYBODY* IN HERE. WE'VE GOT TO GET *OUT* BEFORE--
NO.
STAY.
SMELL BLOOD.
BLOOD MEANS EAT.
WHO...WHAT ARE YOU PEOPLE...?
KENNY
BACK OFF, FREAK SHOW.
TELL US WHAT HAPPENED.
A PRESENT...IT WAS A PRESENT, FOR MY *BROTHER,* TICKETS TO TONIGHT'S GAME...

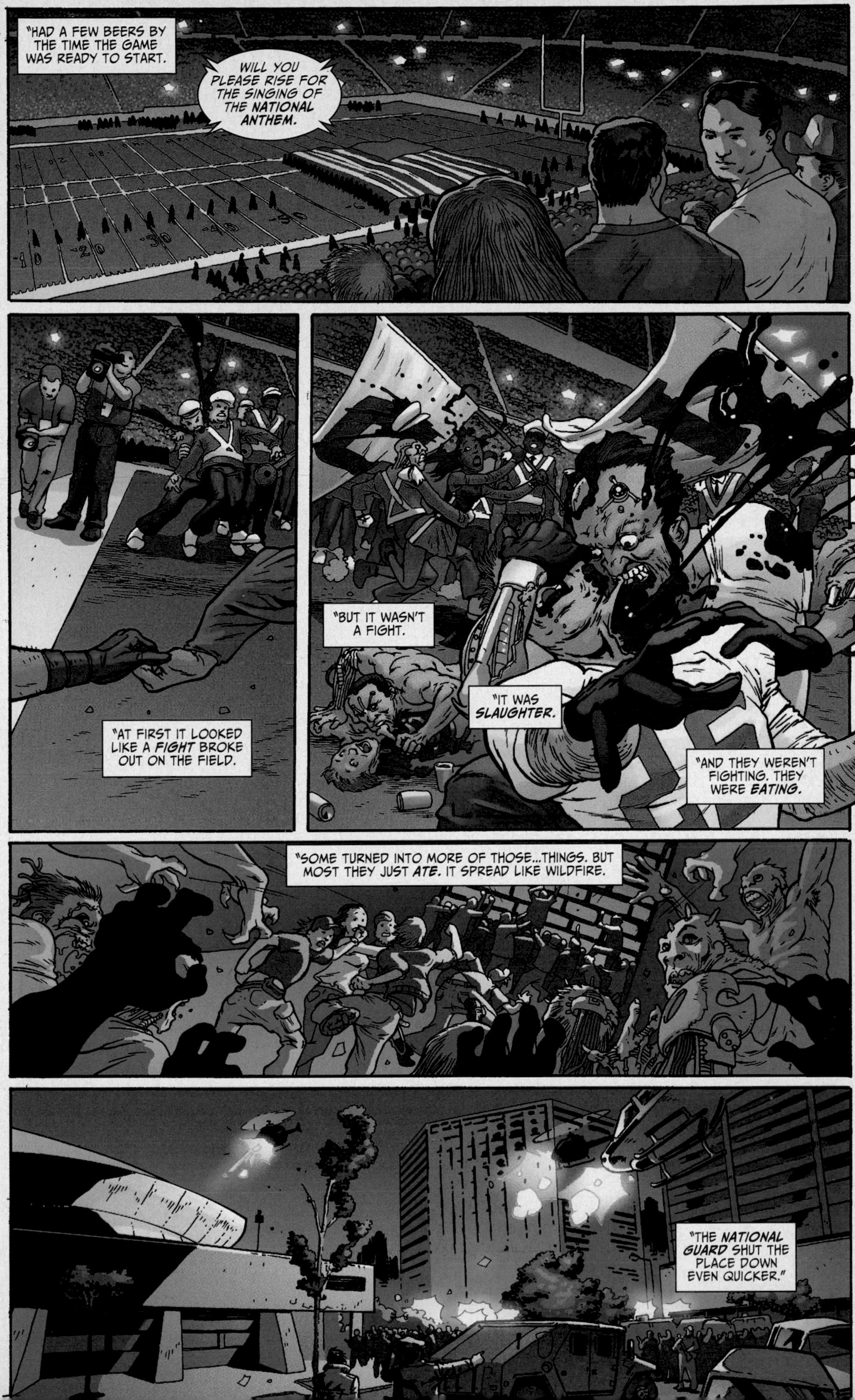
"HAD A FEW BEERS BY THE TIME THE GAME WAS READY TO START.
WILL YOU PLEASE RISE FOR THE SINGING OF THE NATIONAL ANTHEM.
"AT FIRST IT LOOKED LIKE A FIGHT BROKE OUT ON THE FIELD.
"BUT IT WASN'T A FIGHT.
"IT WAS SLAUGHTER.
"AND THEY WEREN'T FIGHTING. THEY WERE EATING.
"SOME TURNED INTO MORE OF THOSE...THINGS. BUT MOST THEY JUST ATE. IT SPREAD LIKE WILDFIRE.
"THE NATIONAL GUARD SHUT THE PLACE DOWN EVEN QUICKER."

THANKS.

BUTCHER! WE COULD HAVE SAVED HIM, BROUGHT HIM WITH US AND--

EASY, *CHILE POWDER*. TAKE A LOOK AT HIS HAND.

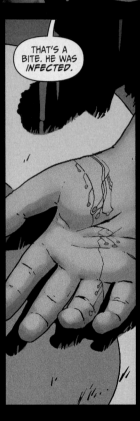

THAT'S A BITE. HE WAS *INFECTED*.

ZOMBIES?!? I'M GOING TO SQUEAL! I *LOVE* ZOMBIES!

IF THEY WANT BRAINS, YOU'RE SAFE, HARLEY QUINN.

LOOK AT HIS SKIN--THERE'S *METAL* IN THERE. THEY'RE TECHNO-ORGANIC, MAYBE A NANOVIRUS. IF IT'S GONE *AIRBORNE*, WE'RE ALREADY DEAD.

HOW DOES THE WORLD NOT KNOW ABOUT THIS?

YOU SAW THE BLOCKADES WHEN THEY *PARACHUTED* US IN. THEY LOCK IT DOWN, FEED THE MEDIA A STORY AND--

NURRR

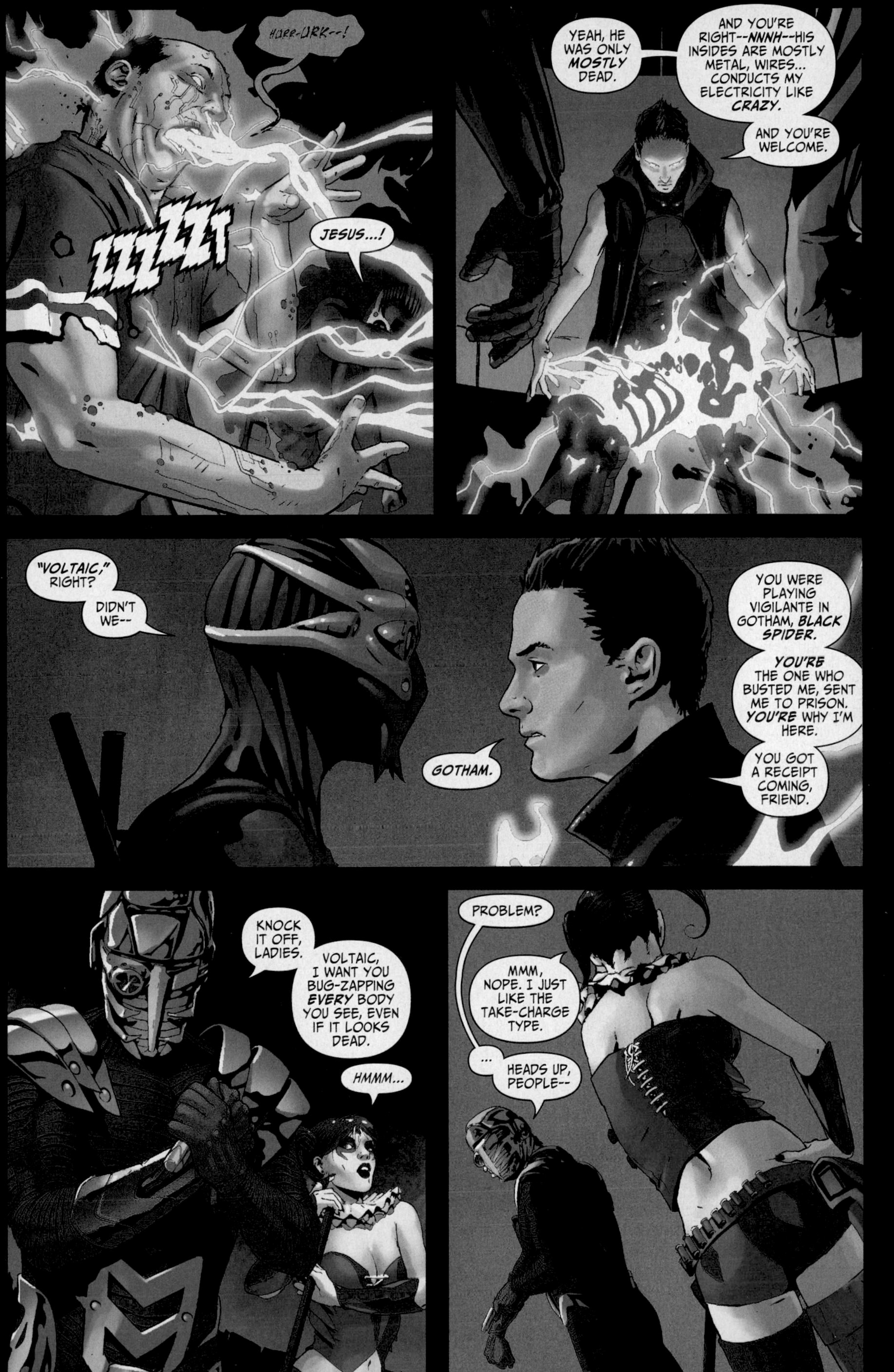
HURR-URK--!
ZZZZZZT
JESUS...!
YEAH, HE WAS ONLY MOSTLY DEAD.
AND YOU'RE RIGHT--NNNH--HIS INSIDES ARE MOSTLY METAL, WIRES... CONDUCTS MY ELECTRICITY LIKE CRAZY.
AND YOU'RE WELCOME.
"VOLTAIC," RIGHT?
DIDN'T WE--
GOTHAM.
YOU WERE PLAYING VIGILANTE IN GOTHAM, BLACK SPIDER.
YOU'RE THE ONE WHO BUSTED ME, SENT ME TO PRISON. YOU'RE WHY I'M HERE.
YOU GOT A RECEIPT COMING, FRIEND.
KNOCK IT OFF, LADIES.
VOLTAIC, I WANT YOU BUG-ZAPPING EVERY BODY YOU SEE, EVEN IF IT LOOKS DEAD.
HMMM...
PROBLEM?
MMM, NOPE. I JUST LIKE THE TAKE-CHARGE TYPE.
...
HEADS UP, PEOPLE--

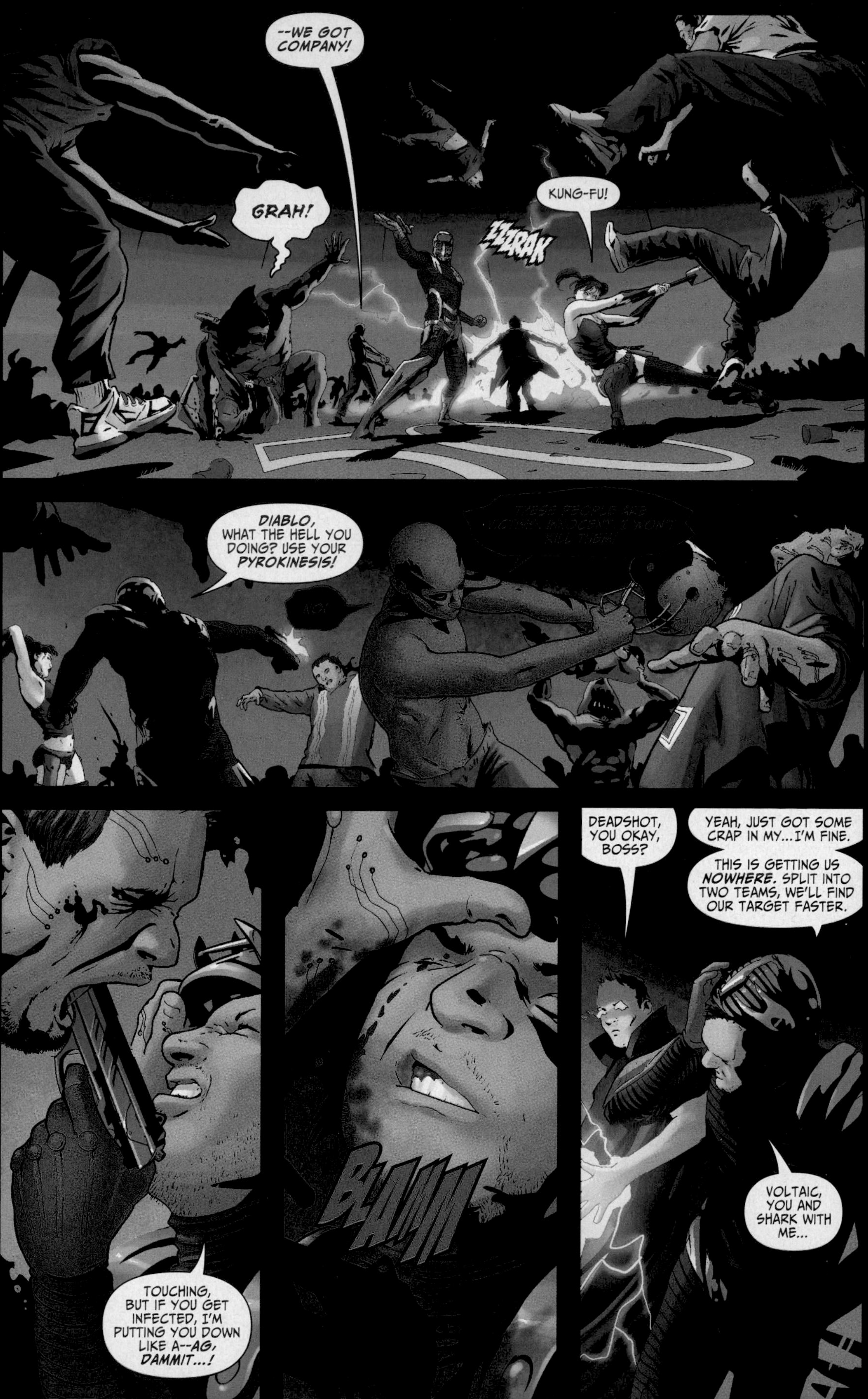
--WE GOT COMPANY!
GRAH!
ZZZRAK
KUNG-FU!
DIABLO, WHAT THE HELL YOU DOING? USE YOUR PYROKINESIS!
THESE PEOPLE ARE VICTIMS. INNOCENT. I WON'T KILL THEM.
TOUCHING, BUT IF YOU GET INFECTED, I'M PUTTING YOU DOWN LIKE A--AG, DAMMIT...!
BLAMM
DEADSHOT, YOU OKAY, BOSS?
YEAH, JUST GOT SOME CRAP IN MY...I'M FINE.
THIS IS GETTING US NOWHERE. SPLIT INTO TWO TEAMS, WE'LL FIND OUR TARGET FASTER.
VOLTAIC, YOU AND SHARK WITH ME...

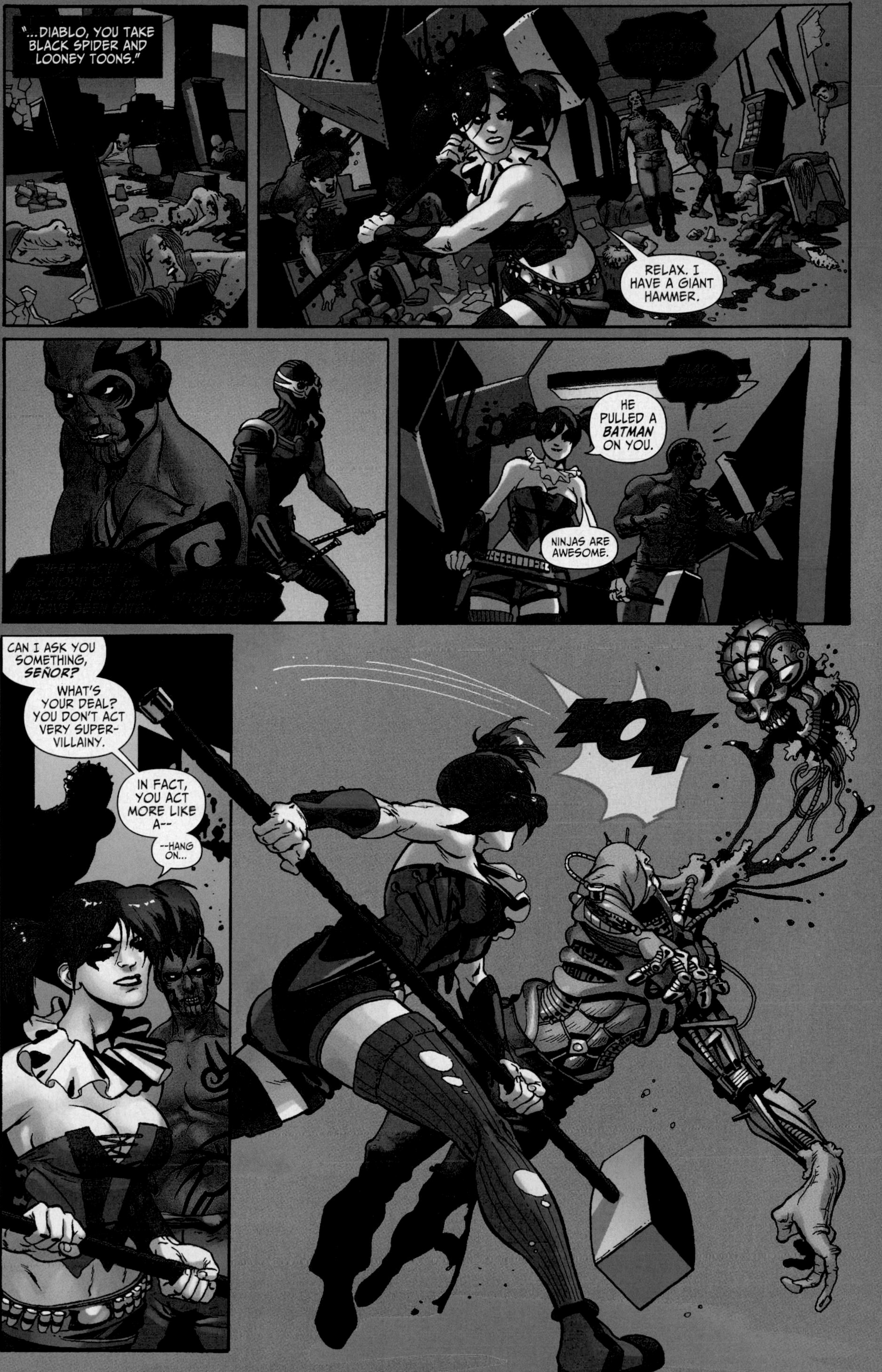
"...DIABLO, YOU TAKE BLACK SPIDER AND LOONEY TOONS."
RELAX. I HAVE A GIANT HAMMER.
HE PULLED A BATMAN ON YOU.
NINJAS ARE AWESOME.
CAN I ASK YOU SOMETHING, SEÑOR?
WHAT'S YOUR DEAL? YOU DON'T ACT VERY SUPER-VILLAINY.
IN FACT, YOU ACT MORE LIKE A--
--HANG ON...

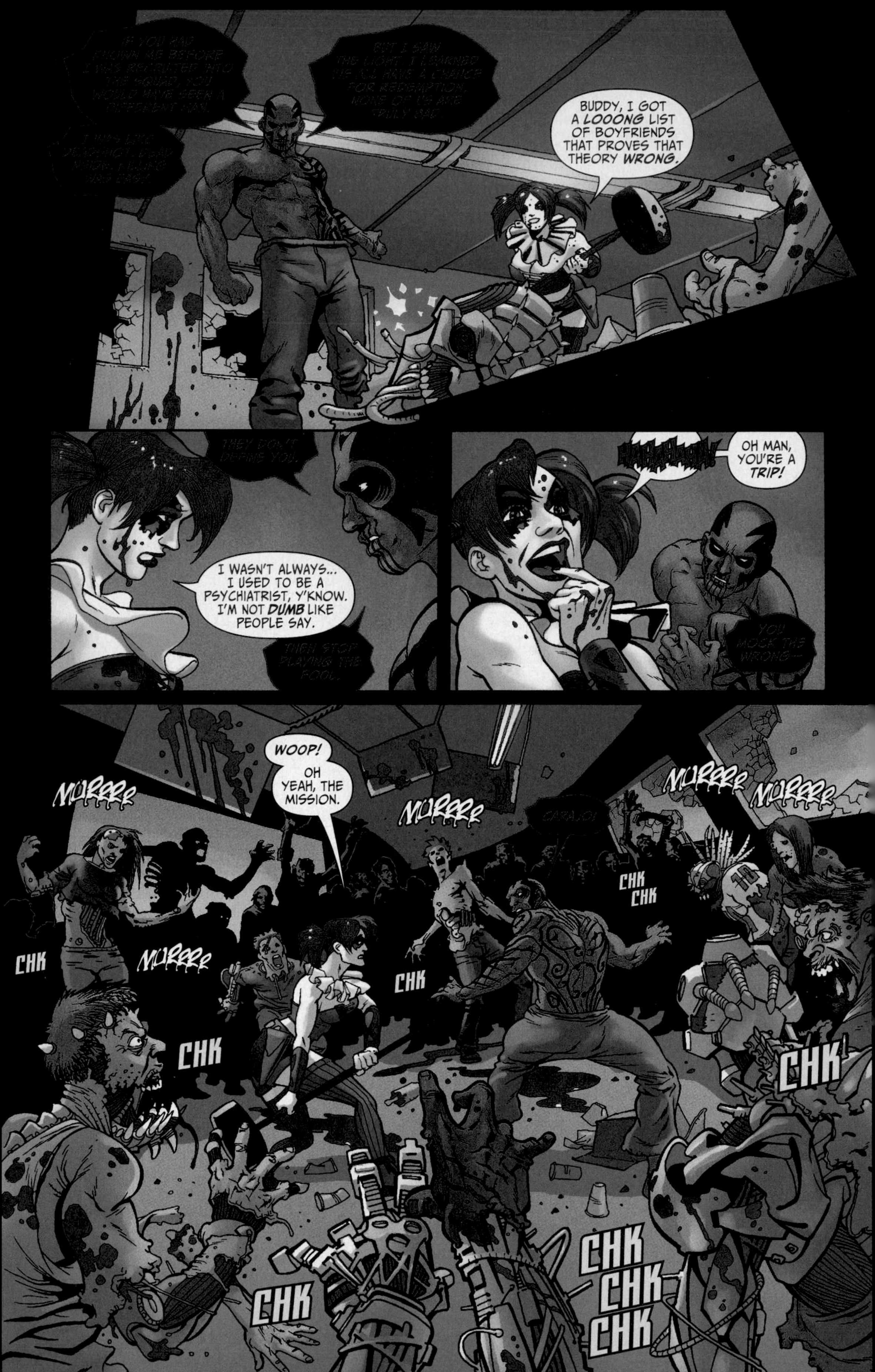
IF YOU HAD KNOWN ME BEFORE I WAS RECRUITED INTO THE SQUAD, YOU WOULD HAVE SEEN A DIFFERENT MAN.
I WAS LIKE PRACTICALLY DEAD
BUT I SAW THE LIGHT. I LEARNED WE ALL HAVE A CHANCE FOR REDEMPTION. NONE OF US ARE TRULY BAD.
BUDDY, I GOT A LOOONG LIST OF BOYFRIENDS THAT PROVES THAT THEORY WRONG.
THEY DON'T DEFINE YOU.
I WASN'T ALWAYS... I USED TO BE A PSYCHIATRIST, Y'KNOW. I'M NOT DUMB LIKE PEOPLE SAY.
THEN STOP PLAYING THE FOOL.
HAHAHAHA!
OH MAN, YOU'RE A TRIP!
YOU MOCK THE WRONG--
WOOP!
OH YEAH, THE MISSION.
MURRRR
MURRRR
CARAJO!
MURRRR
MURRRR
CHK CHK
CHK
MURRRR
CHK
CHK
CHK
CHK
CHK CHK CHK

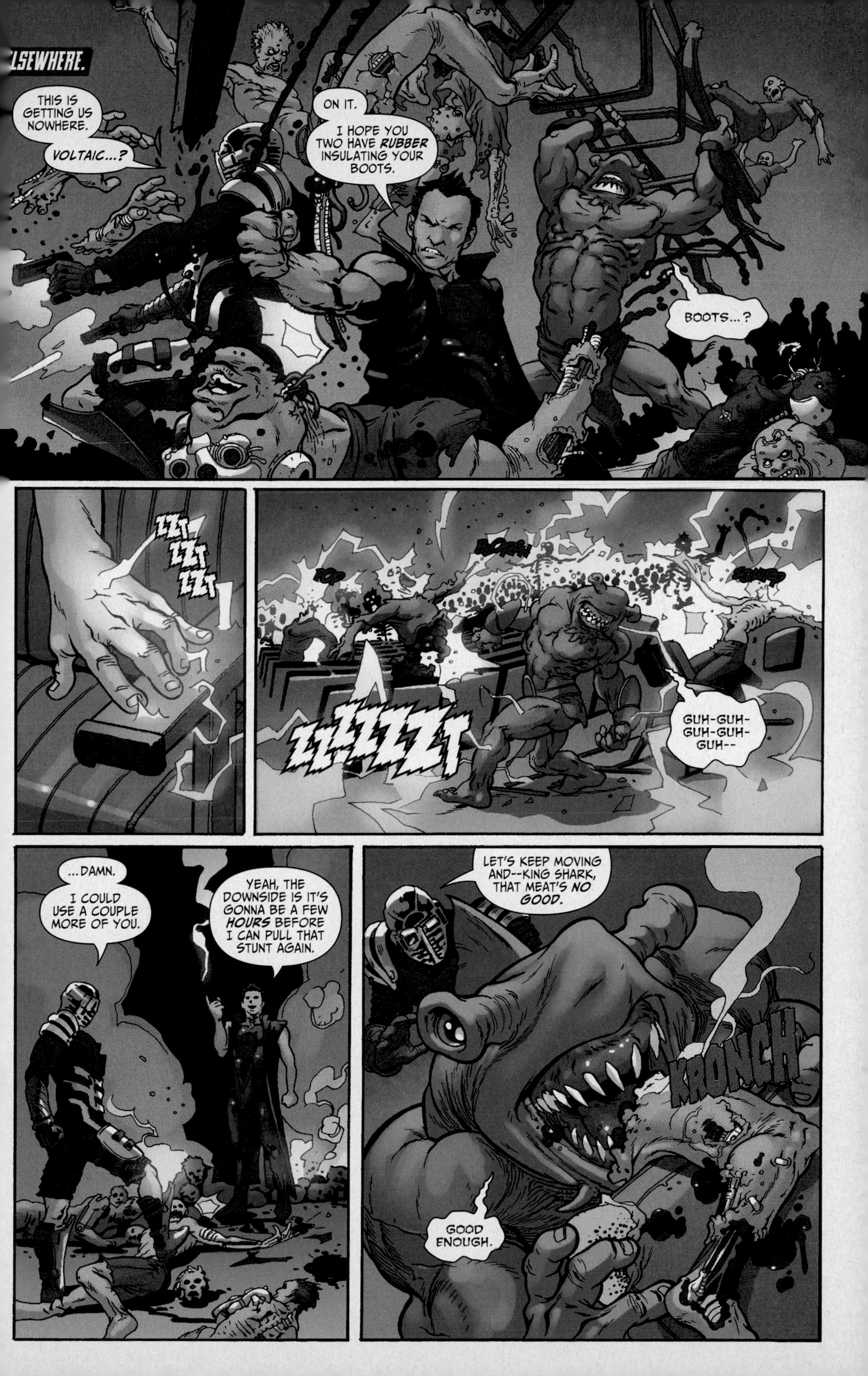

LSEWHERE.
THIS IS GETTING US NOWHERE.
VOLTAIC...?
ON IT.
I HOPE YOU TWO HAVE RUBBER INSULATING YOUR BOOTS.
BOOTS...?
ZZT ZZT ZZT
ZZZZZZZT
GUH-GUH-GUH-GUH-GUH--
...DAMN.
I COULD USE A COUPLE MORE OF YOU.
YEAH, THE DOWNSIDE IS IT'S GONNA BE A FEW HOURS BEFORE I CAN PULL THAT STUNT AGAIN.
LET'S KEEP MOVING AND--KING SHARK, THAT MEAT'S NO GOOD.
KRONCH
GOOD ENOUGH.

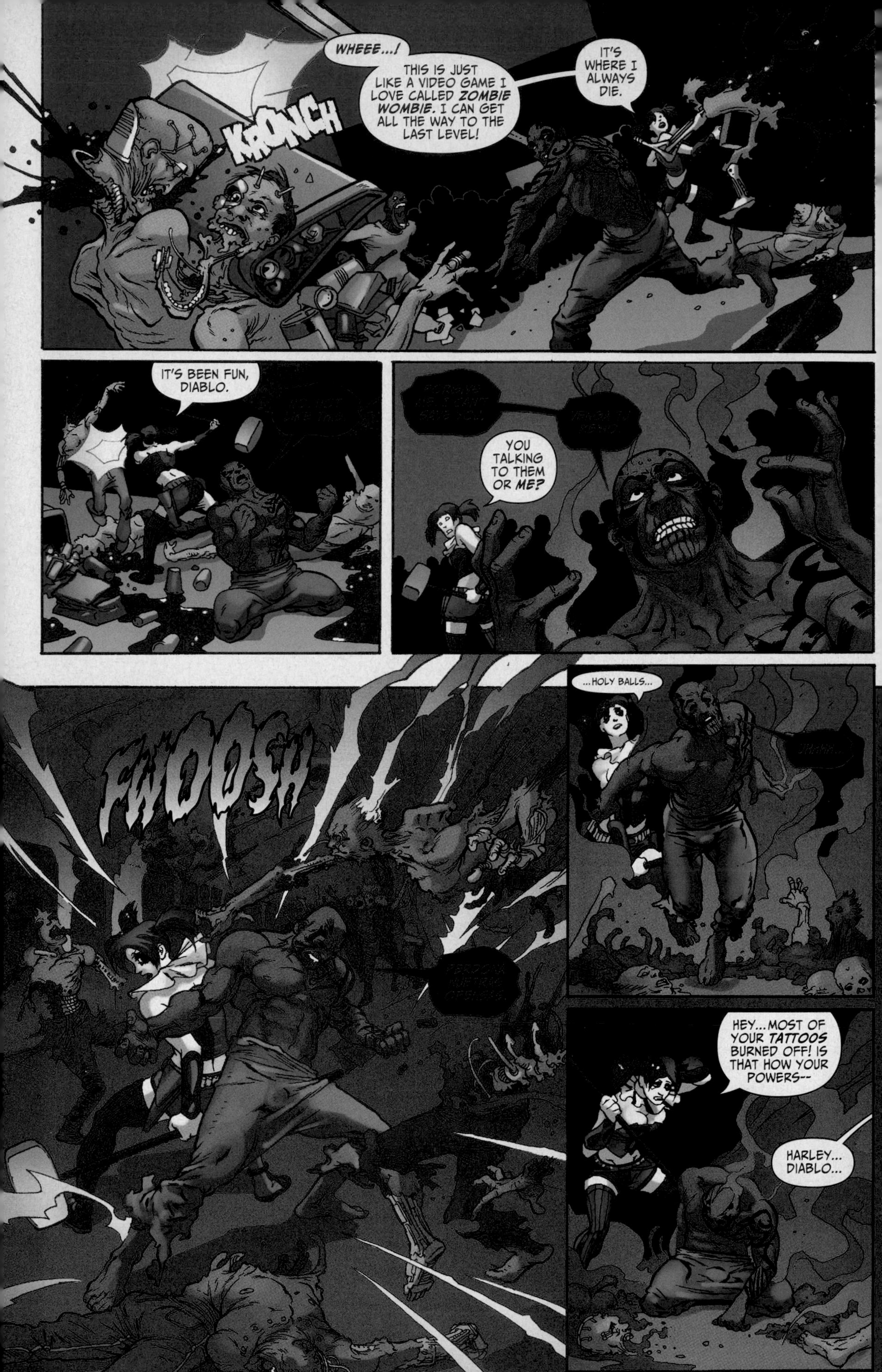
WHEEE...!
THIS IS JUST LIKE A VIDEO GAME I LOVE CALLED *ZOMBIE WOMBIE*. I CAN GET ALL THE WAY TO THE LAST LEVEL!
IT'S WHERE I ALWAYS DIE.
KRONCH
IT'S BEEN FUN, DIABLO.
YOU TALKING TO THEM OR *ME?*
FWOOSH
...HOLY BALLS...
HEY...MOST OF YOUR *TATTOOS* BURNED OFF! IS THAT HOW YOUR POWERS--
HARLEY... DIABLO...

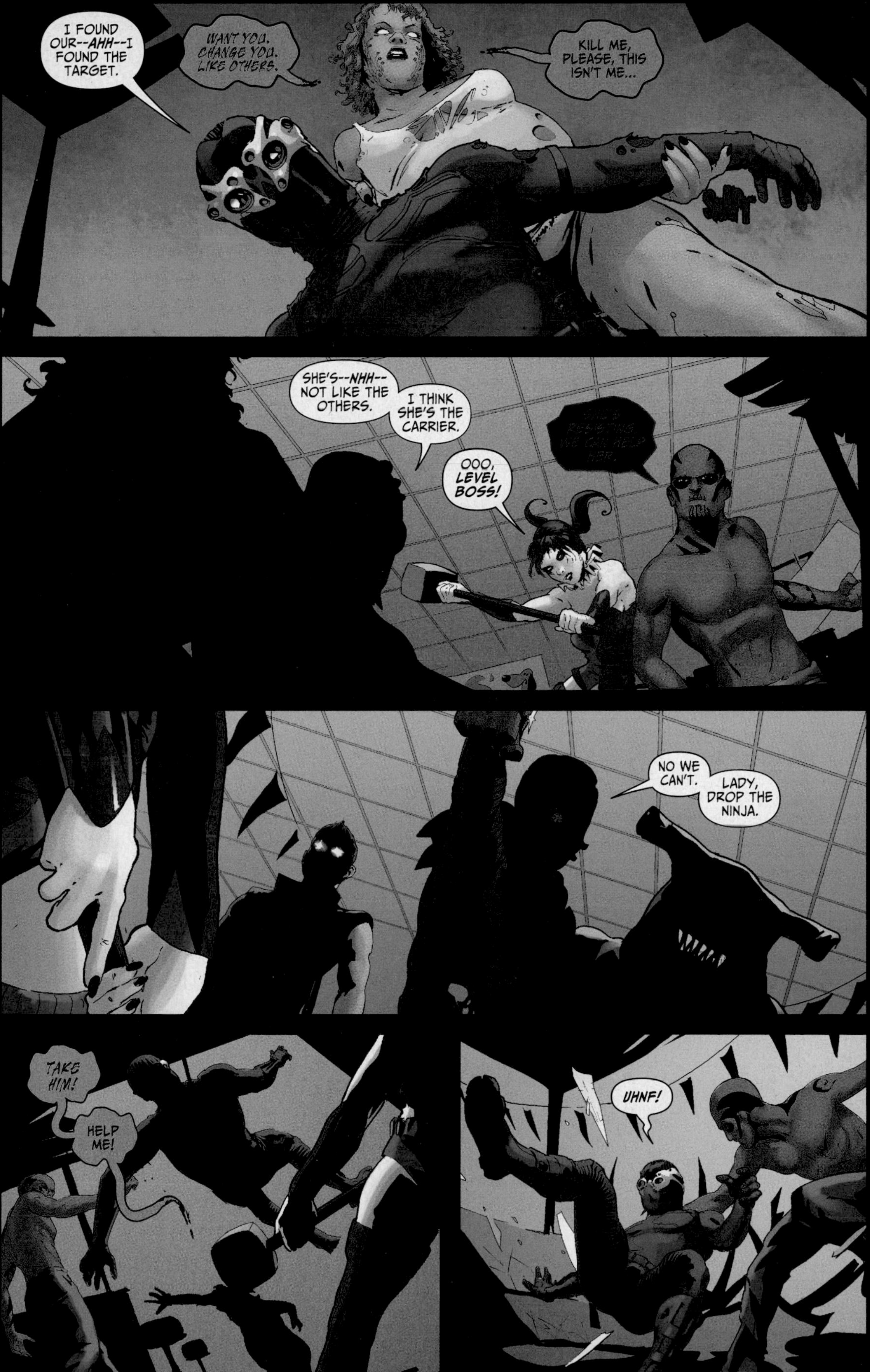
I FOUND OUR--AHH--I FOUND THE TARGET.
WANT YOU. CHANGE YOU. LIKE OTHERS.
KILL ME, PLEASE, THIS ISN'T ME...
SHE'S--NHH--NOT LIKE THE OTHERS.
I THINK SHE'S THE CARRIER.
SHE'S RESISTING WE CAN HELP HER.
OOO, LEVEL BOSS!
NO WE CAN'T.
LADY, DROP THE NINJA.
TAKE HIM!
HELP ME!
UHNF!

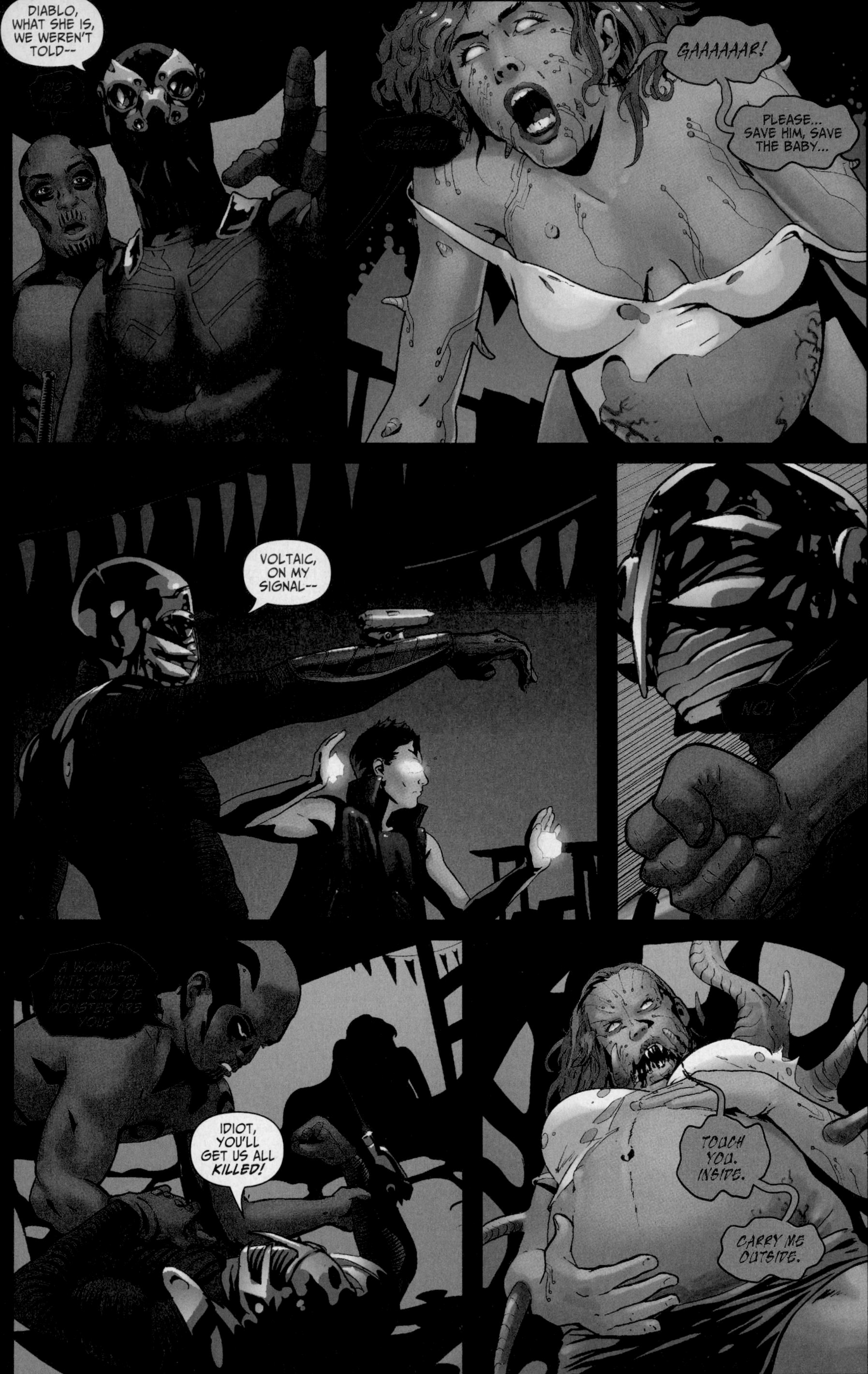
DIABLO, WHAT SHE IS, WE WEREN'T TOLD--
SHE'S PREGNANT!
GAAAAAAR!
PLEASE... SAVE HIM, SAVE THE BABY...
VOLTAIC, ON MY SIGNAL--
NO!
IDIOT, YOU'LL GET US ALL KILLED!
TOUCH YOU. INSIDE.
CARRY ME OUTSIDE.

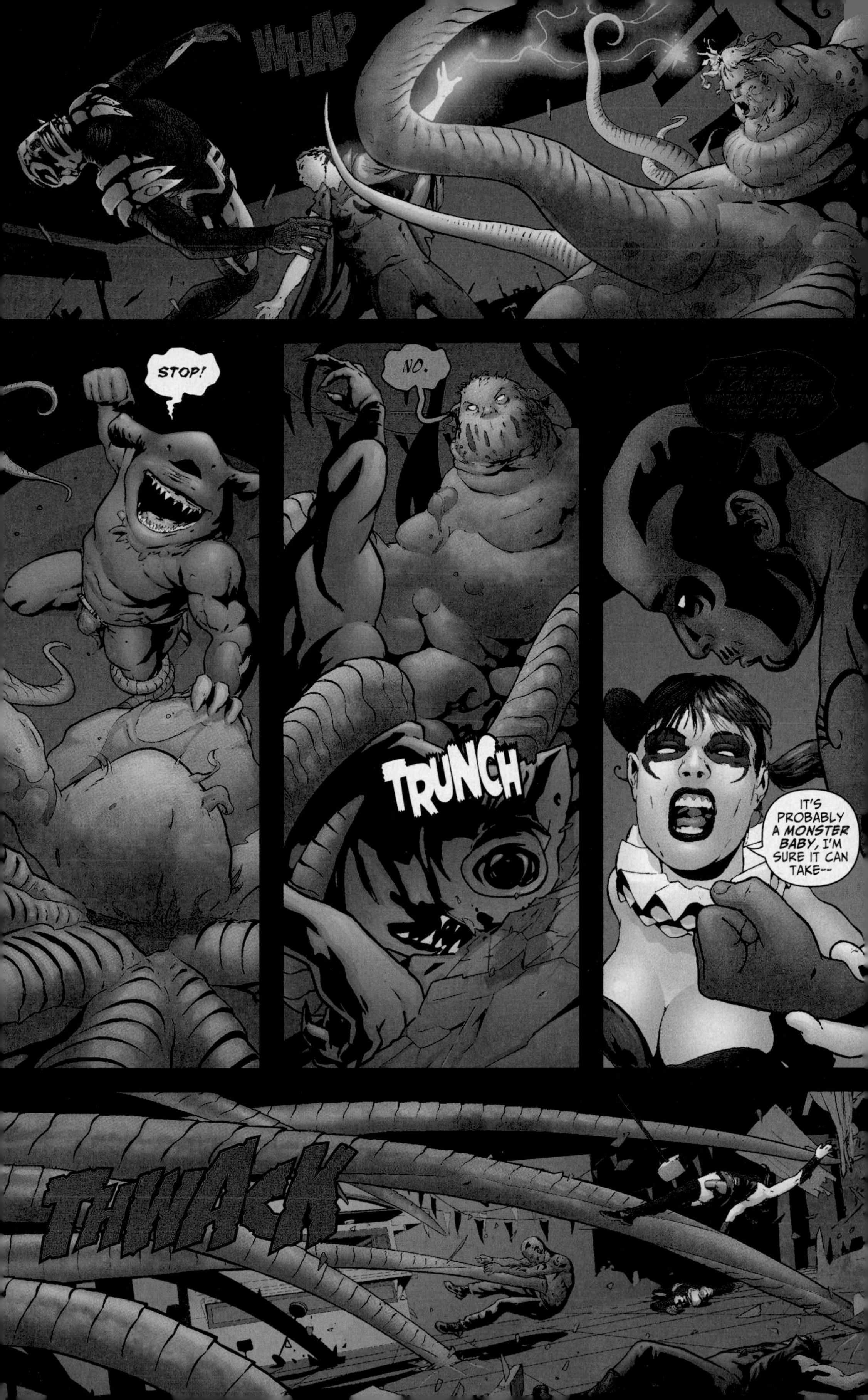
WHAP
STOP!
NO.
TRUNCH
THE CHILD... I CAN'T FIGHT WITHOUT HURTING THE CHILD.
IT'S PROBABLY A MONSTER BABY, I'M SURE IT CAN TAKE--
THWACK

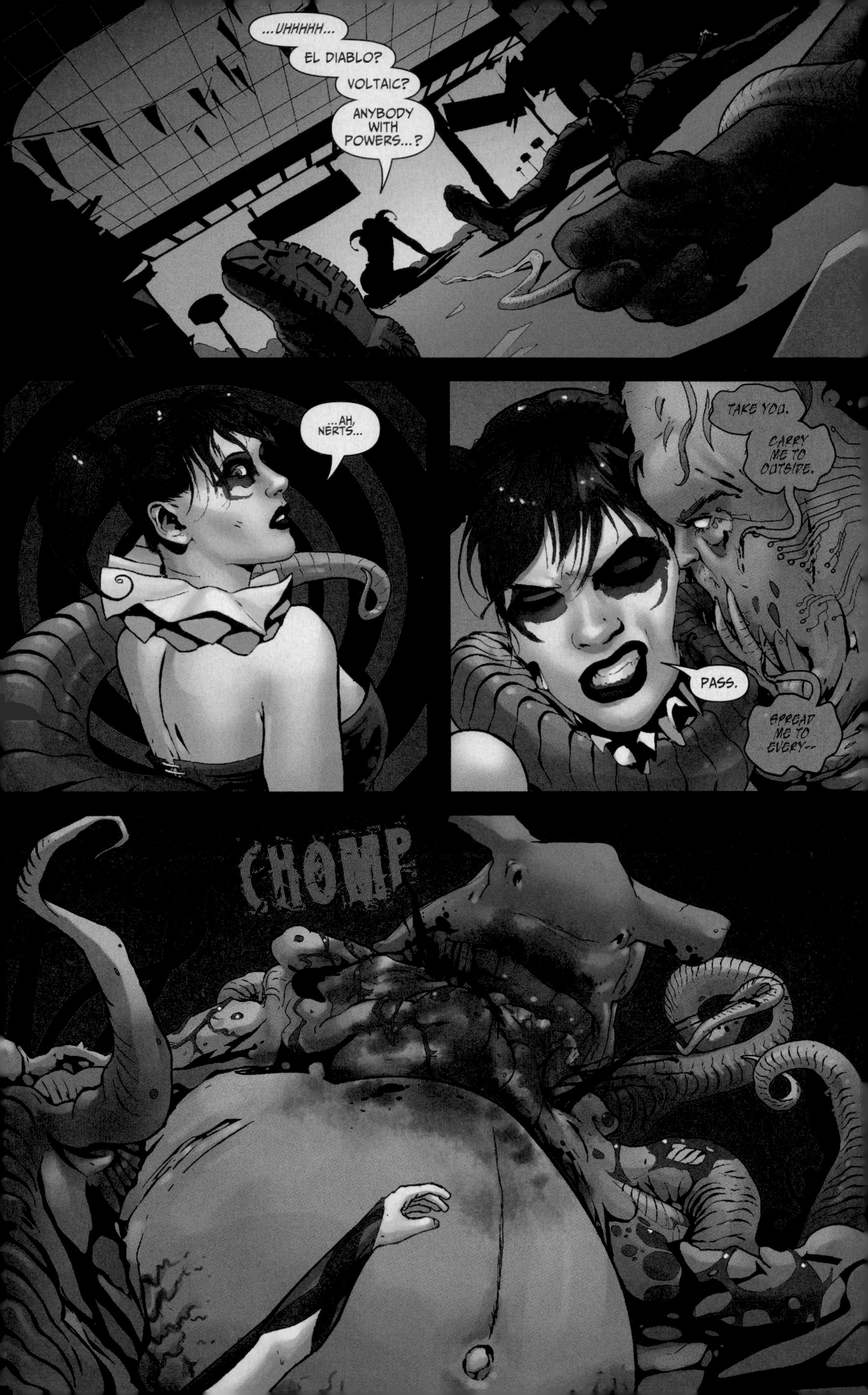
...UHHHHH...
EL DIABLO?
VOLTAIC?
ANYBODY WITH POWERS...?
...AH, NERTS...
TAKE YOU.
CARRY ME TO OUTSIDE.
PASS.
SPREAD ME TO EVERY--
CHOMP

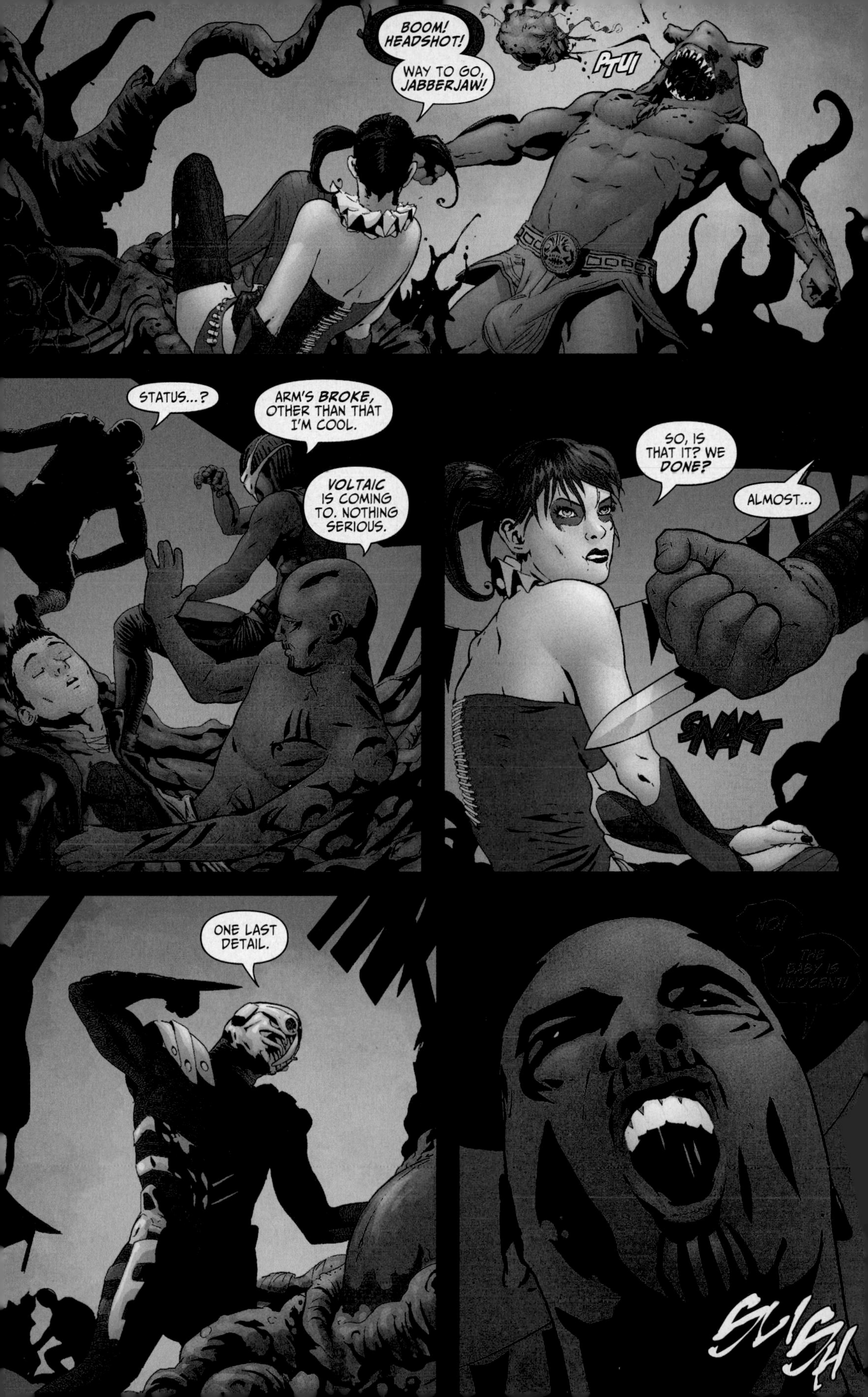
BOOM! HEADSHOT!
WAY TO GO, JABBERJAW!
PTUI
STATUS...?
ARM'S BROKE, OTHER THAN THAT I'M COOL.
VOLTAIC IS COMING TO. NOTHING SERIOUS.
SO, IS THAT IT? WE DONE?
ALMOST...
SNAKT
ONE LAST DETAIL.
NO!
THE BABY IS INNOCENT!
SLISH

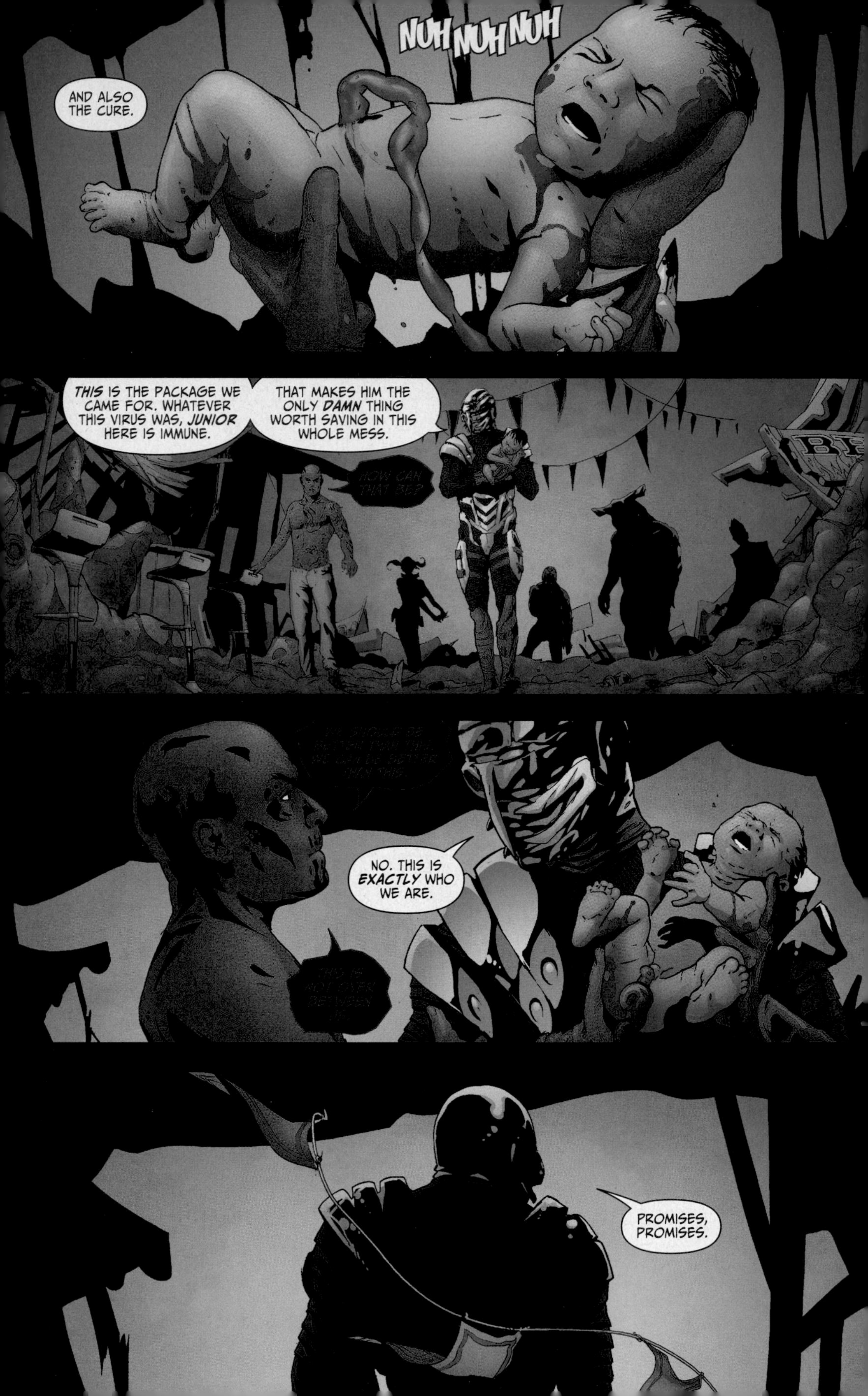
NUH NUH NUH
AND ALSO THE CURE.
THIS IS THE PACKAGE WE CAME FOR. WHATEVER THIS VIRUS WAS, JUNIOR HERE IS IMMUNE.
THAT MAKES HIM THE ONLY DAMN THING WORTH SAVING IN THIS WHOLE MESS.
HOW CAN THAT BE?
WE SHOULD BE BETTER THAN THIS. WE CAN BE BETTER THAN THIS.
NO. THIS IS EXACTLY WHO WE ARE.
THIS IS NOT OVER BETWEEN US.
PROMISES, PROMISES.

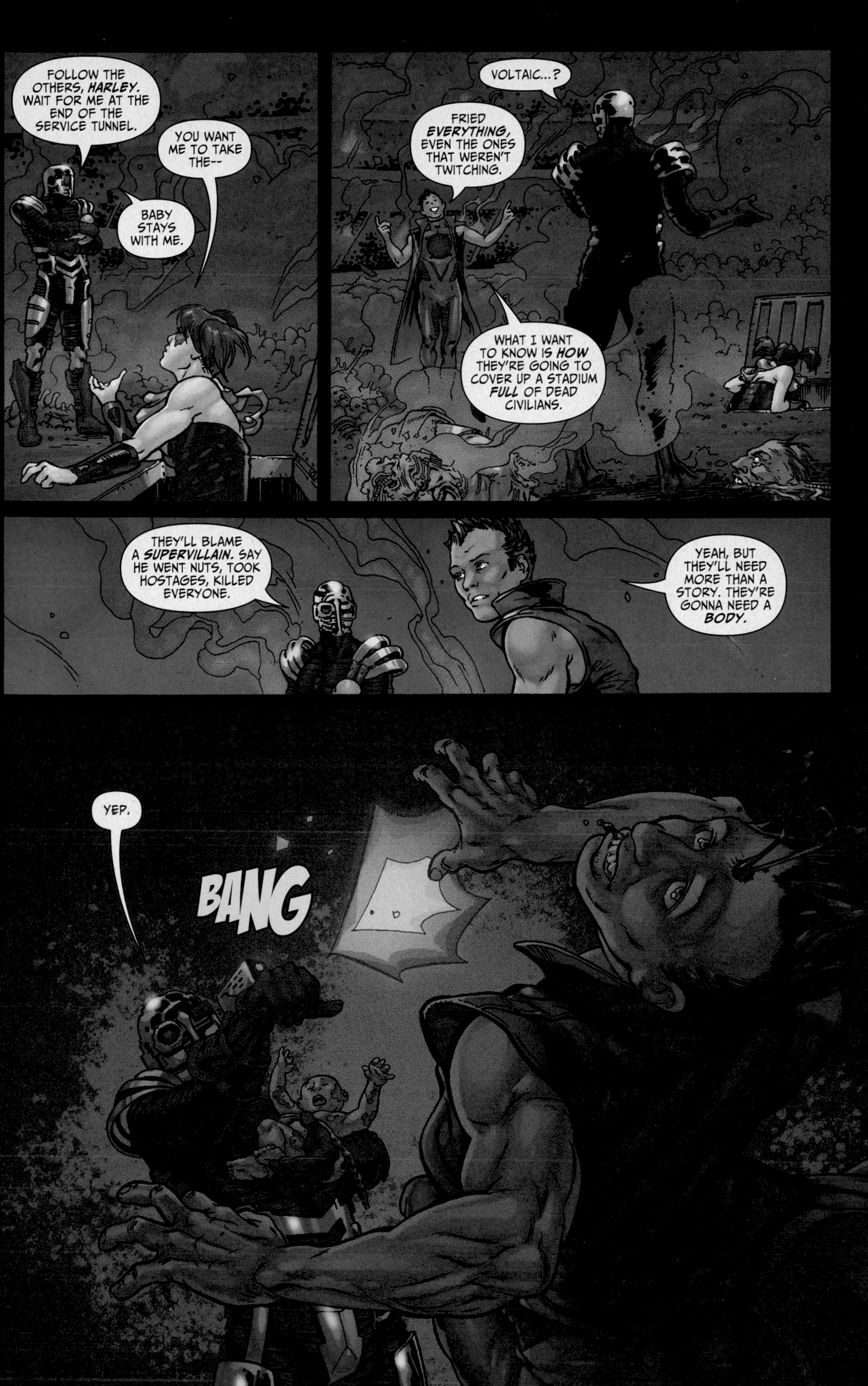
FOLLOW THE OTHERS, **HARLEY.** WAIT FOR ME AT THE END OF THE SERVICE TUNNEL.
YOU WANT ME TO TAKE THE--
BABY STAYS WITH ME.
VOLTAIC...?
FRIED **EVERYTHING,** EVEN THE ONES THAT WEREN'T TWITCHING.
WHAT I WANT TO KNOW IS **HOW** THEY'RE GOING TO COVER UP A STADIUM **FULL** OF DEAD CIVILIANS.
THEY'LL BLAME A **SUPERVILLAIN.** SAY HE WENT NUTS, TOOK HOSTAGES, KILLED EVERYONE.
YEAH, BUT THEY'LL NEED MORE THAN A STORY. THEY'RE GONNA NEED A **BODY.**
YEP.
BANG

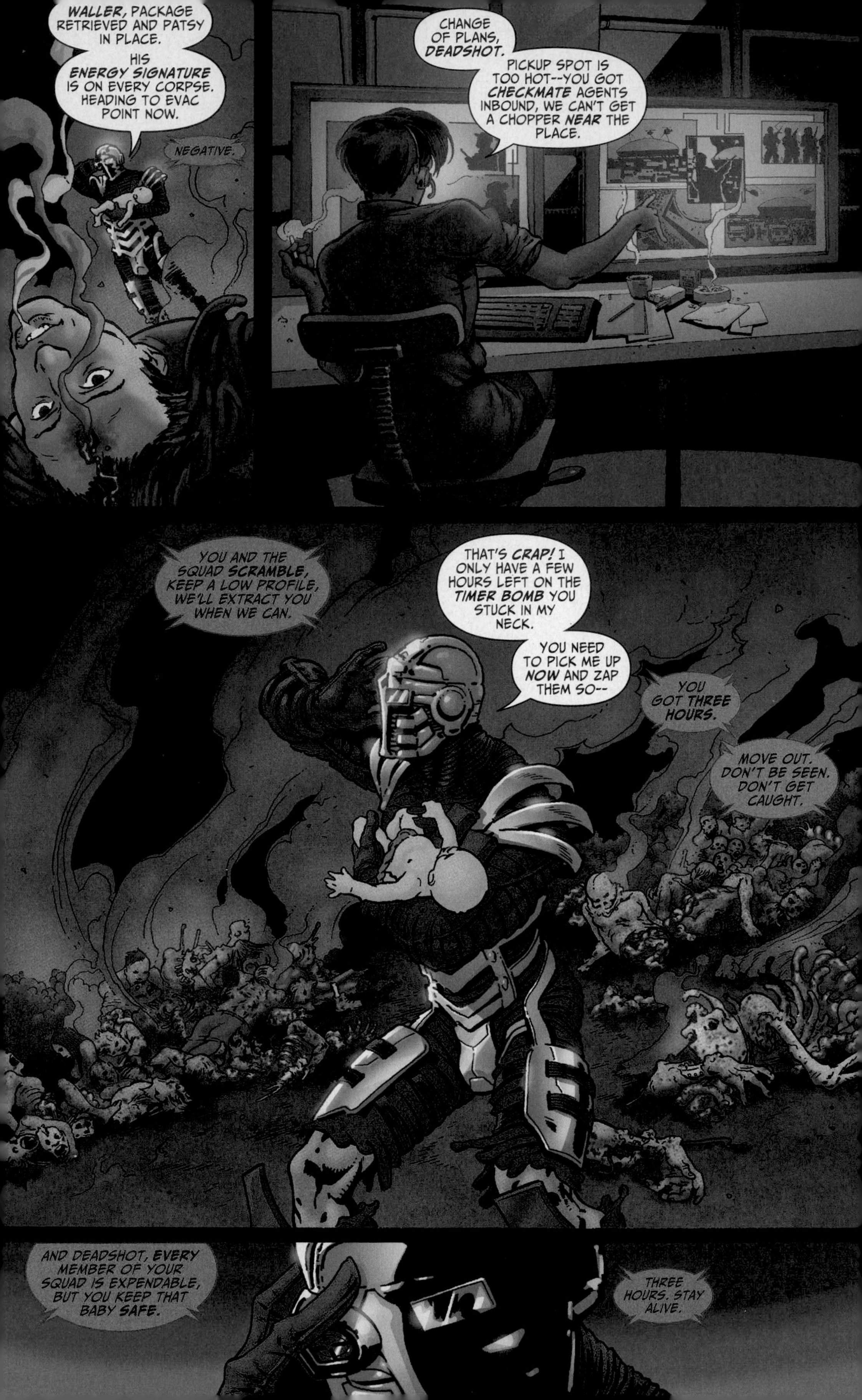

WALLER, PACKAGE RETRIEVED AND PATSY IN PLACE.
HIS ENERGY SIGNATURE IS ON EVERY CORPSE. HEADING TO EVAC POINT NOW.
NEGATIVE.
CHANGE OF PLANS, DEADSHOT.
PICKUP SPOT IS TOO HOT--YOU GOT CHECKMATE AGENTS INBOUND, WE CAN'T GET A CHOPPER NEAR THE PLACE.
YOU AND THE SQUAD SCRAMBLE, KEEP A LOW PROFILE, WE'LL EXTRACT YOU WHEN WE CAN.
THAT'S CRAP! I ONLY HAVE A FEW HOURS LEFT ON THE TIMER BOMB YOU STUCK IN MY NECK.
YOU NEED TO PICK ME UP NOW AND ZAP THEM SO--
YOU GOT THREE HOURS.
MOVE OUT. DON'T BE SEEN. DON'T GET CAUGHT.
AND DEADSHOT, EVERY MEMBER OF YOUR SQUAD IS EXPENDABLE, BUT YOU KEEP THAT BABY SAFE.
THREE HOURS. STAY ALIVE.

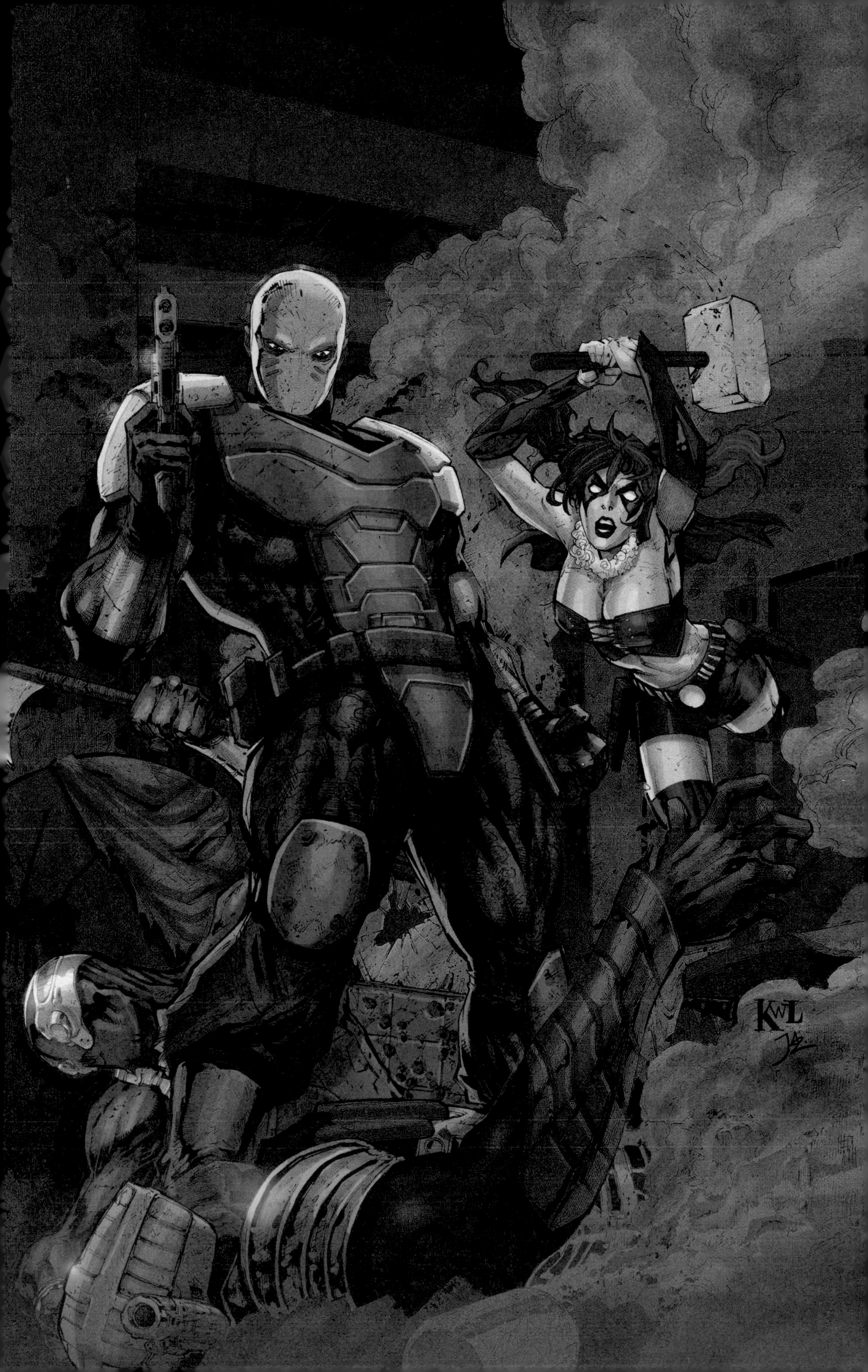

LAST CHANCE

ADAM GLASS
writer

CLIFF RICHARDS
artist

cover art by KEN LASHLEY

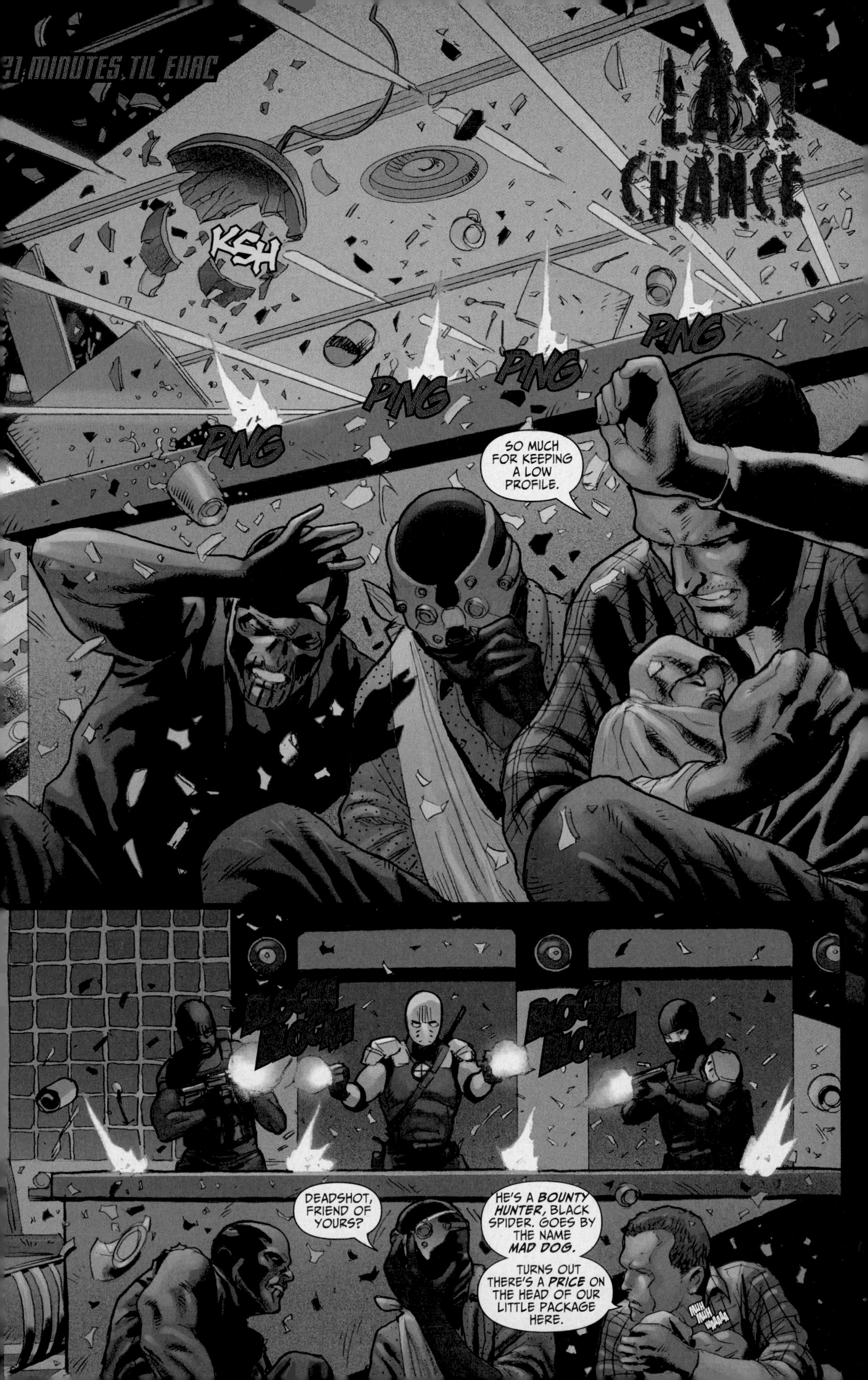
21 MINUTES TIL EVAC
LAST CHANCE
KSH
PING
PING
PING
PING
SO MUCH FOR KEEPING A LOW PROFILE.
DEADSHOT, FRIEND OF YOURS?
HE'S A BOUNTY HUNTER, BLACK SPIDER. GOES BY THE NAME MAD DOG.
TURNS OUT THERE'S A PRICE ON THE HEAD OF OUR LITTLE PACKAGE HERE.

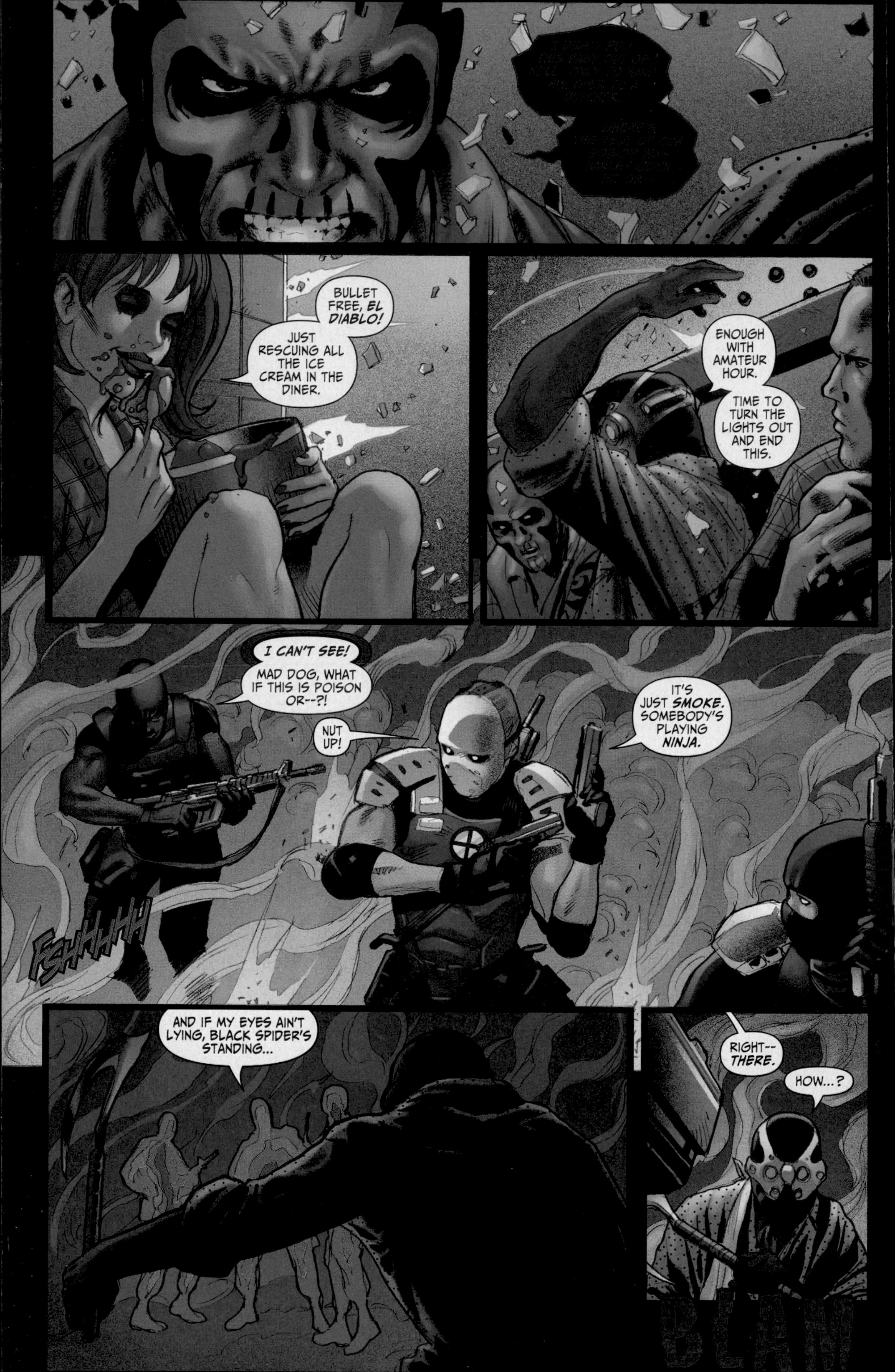
BULLET FREE, *EL DIABLO!*
JUST RESCUING ALL THE ICE CREAM IN THE DINER.
ENOUGH WITH AMATEUR HOUR.
TIME TO TURN THE LIGHTS OUT AND END THIS.
I CAN'T SEE!
MAD DOG, WHAT IF THIS IS POISON OR--?!
NUT UP!
IT'S JUST **SMOKE.** SOMEBODY'S PLAYING ***NINJA.***
FSHHHHH
AND IF MY EYES AIN'T LYING, BLACK SPIDER'S STANDING...
RIGHT-- ***THERE.***
HOW...?

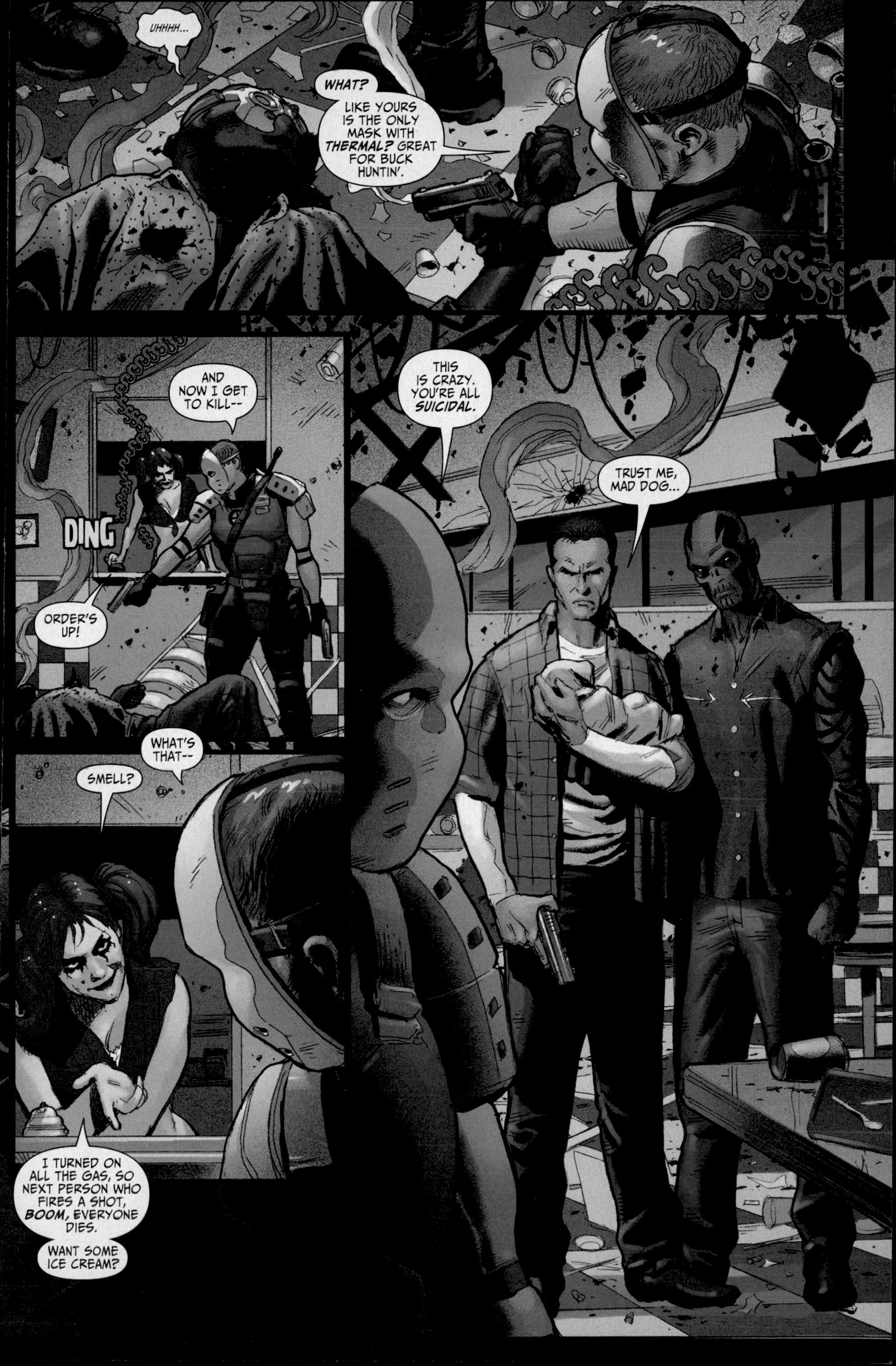
UHHHH...
WHAT? LIKE YOURS IS THE ONLY MASK WITH THERMAL? GREAT FOR BUCK HUNTIN'.
SSSSSSSSSSSSSSSSS
AND NOW I GET TO KILL--
DING
ORDER'S UP!
THIS IS CRAZY. YOU'RE ALL SUICIDAL.
TRUST ME, MAD DOG...
WHAT'S THAT--
SMELL?
I TURNED ON ALL THE GAS, SO NEXT PERSON WHO FIRES A SHOT, BOOM, EVERYONE DIES.
WANT SOME ICE CREAM?

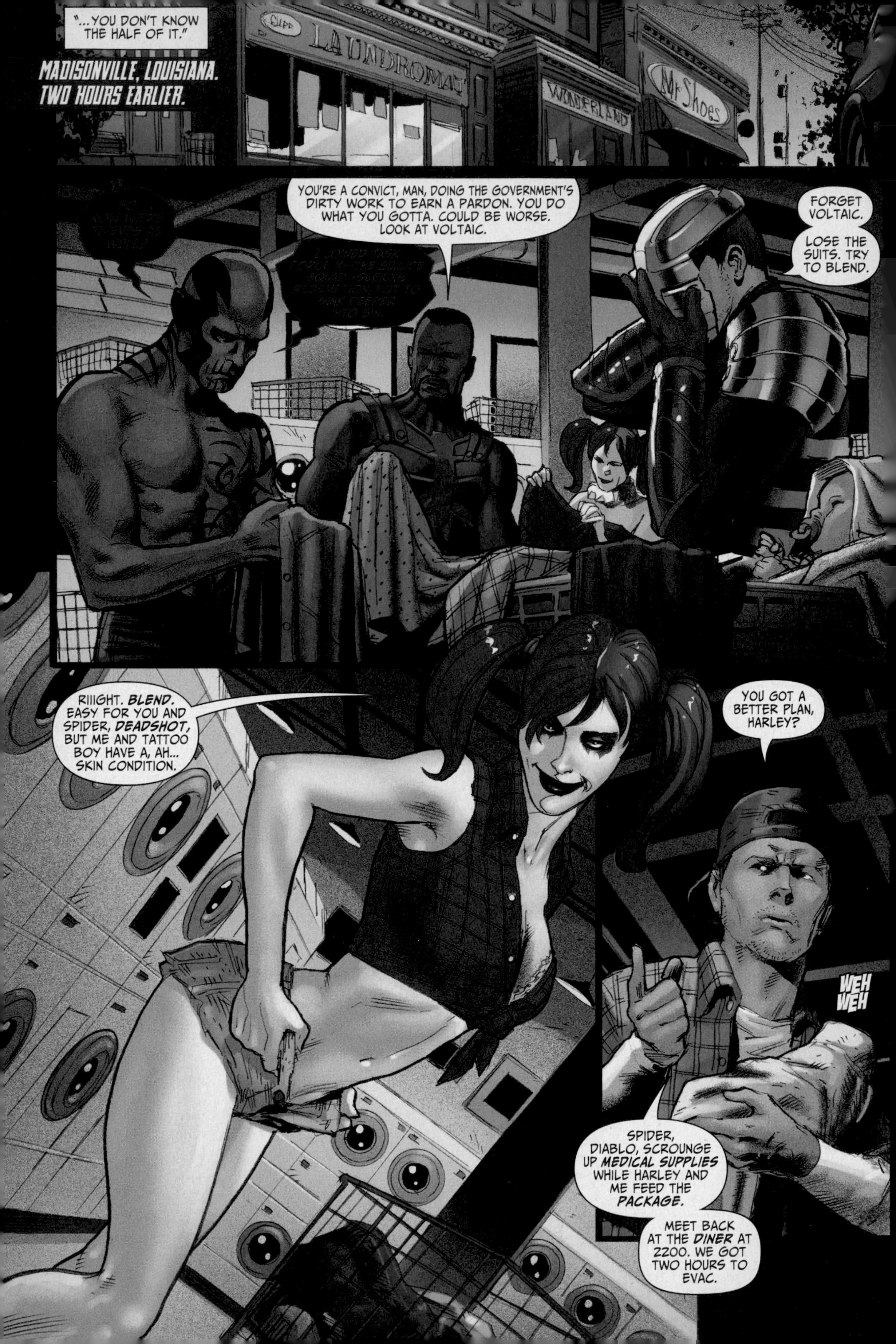

"...YOU DON'T KNOW THE HALF OF IT."
MADISONVILLE, LOUISIANA. TWO HOURS EARLIER.
LAUNDROMAT
WONDERLAND
Mr Shoes
YOU'RE A CONVICT, MAN, DOING THE GOVERNMENT'S DIRTY WORK TO EARN A PARDON. YOU DO WHAT YOU GOTTA. COULD BE WORSE. LOOK AT VOLTAIC.
FORGET VOLTAIC.
LOSE THE SUITS. TRY TO BLEND.
RIIIGHT. BLEND. EASY FOR YOU AND SPIDER, DEADSHOT, BUT ME AND TATTOO BOY HAVE A, AH... SKIN CONDITION.
YOU GOT A BETTER PLAN, HARLEY?
WEH WEH
SPIDER, DIABLO, SCROUNGE UP MEDICAL SUPPLIES WHILE HARLEY AND ME FEED THE PACKAGE.
MEET BACK AT THE DINER AT 2200. WE GOT TWO HOURS TO EVAC.

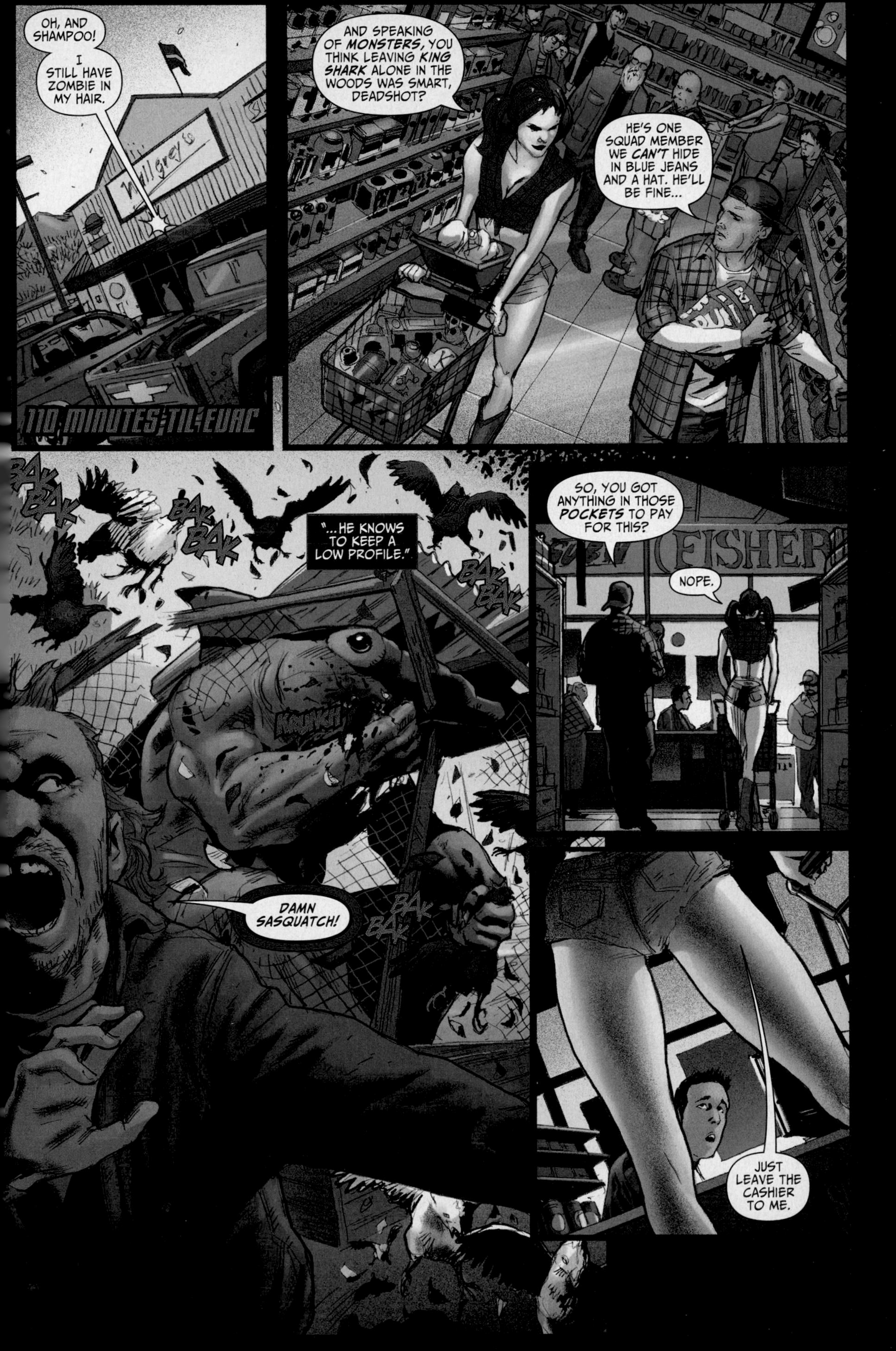
OH, AND SHAMPOO!
I STILL HAVE ZOMBIE IN MY HAIR.
110 MINUTES TIL EVAC
AND SPEAKING OF MONSTERS, YOU THINK LEAVING KING SHARK ALONE IN THE WOODS WAS SMART, DEADSHOT?
HE'S ONE SQUAD MEMBER WE CAN'T HIDE IN BLUE JEANS AND A HAT. HE'LL BE FINE...
BAK BAK
BAK BAK
"...HE KNOWS TO KEEP A LOW PROFILE."
BAK BAK
KRUNCH
DAMN SASQUATCH!
BAK BAK
SO, YOU GOT ANYTHING IN THOSE POCKETS TO PAY FOR THIS?
FISHER
NOPE.
JUST LEAVE THE CASHIER TO ME.

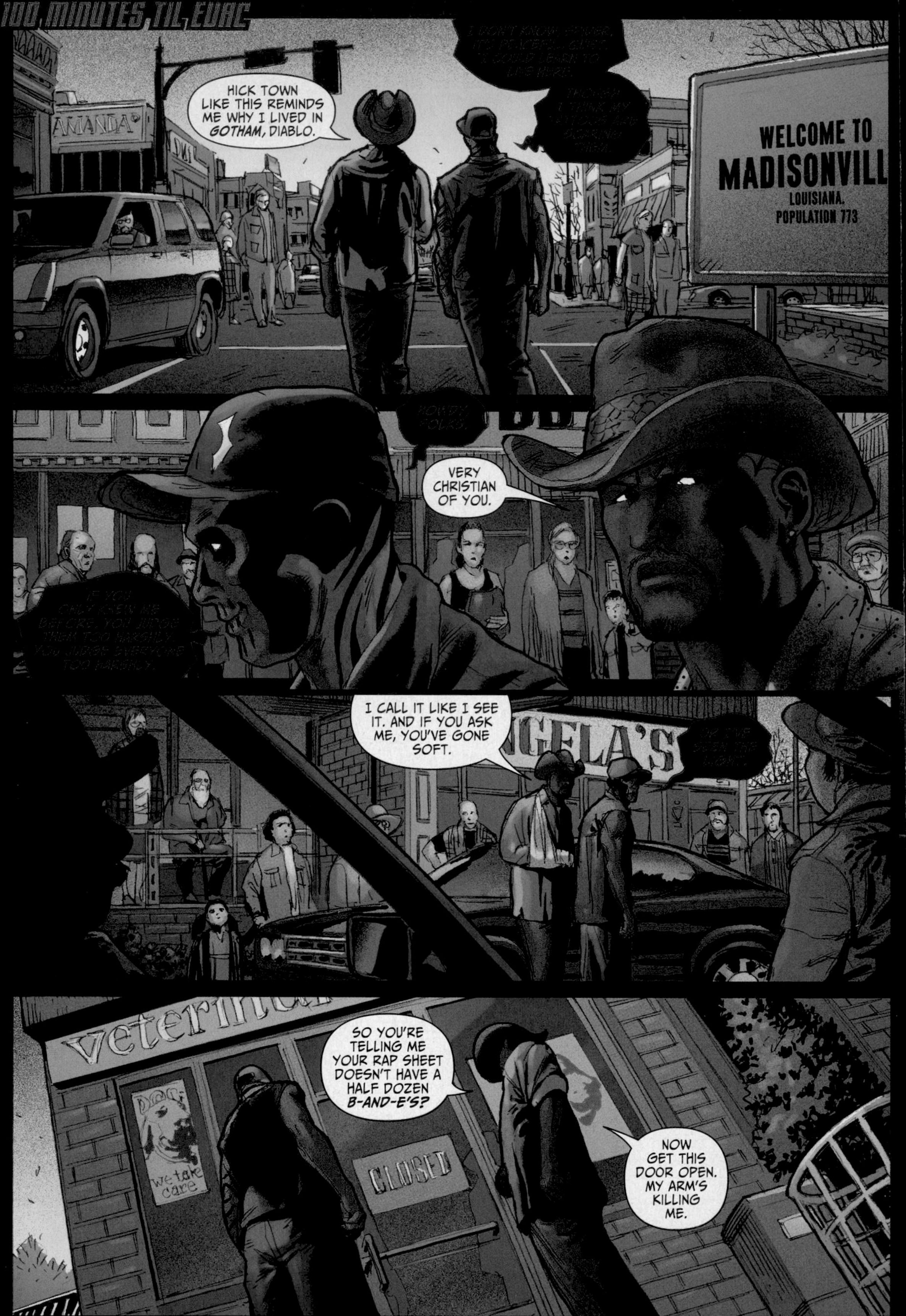
100 MINUTES TIL EVAC
AMANDA
HICK TOWN LIKE THIS REMINDS ME WHY I LIVED IN GOTHAM, DIABLO.
I DON'T KNOW. IT'S PEACEFUL, QUIET. I COULD LEARN TO LIVE HERE.
THOUGH I THINK MY LOOKS ARE SCARING THEM.
WELCOME TO MADISONVILL
LOUISIANA, POPULATION 773
HOWDY, FOLKS!
VERY CHRISTIAN OF YOU.
IF YOU ONLY KNEW ME BEFORE. YOU JUDGE THEM TOO HARSHLY. YOU JUDGE EVERYONE TOO HARSHLY.
I CALL IT LIKE I SEE IT. AND IF YOU ASK ME, YOU'VE GONE SOFT.
OR I'VE SEEN THE LIGHT.
veterinar
we take care
CLOSED
SO YOU'RE TELLING ME YOUR RAP SHEET DOESN'T HAVE A HALF DOZEN B-AND-E'S?
NOW GET THIS DOOR OPEN. MY ARM'S KILLING ME.

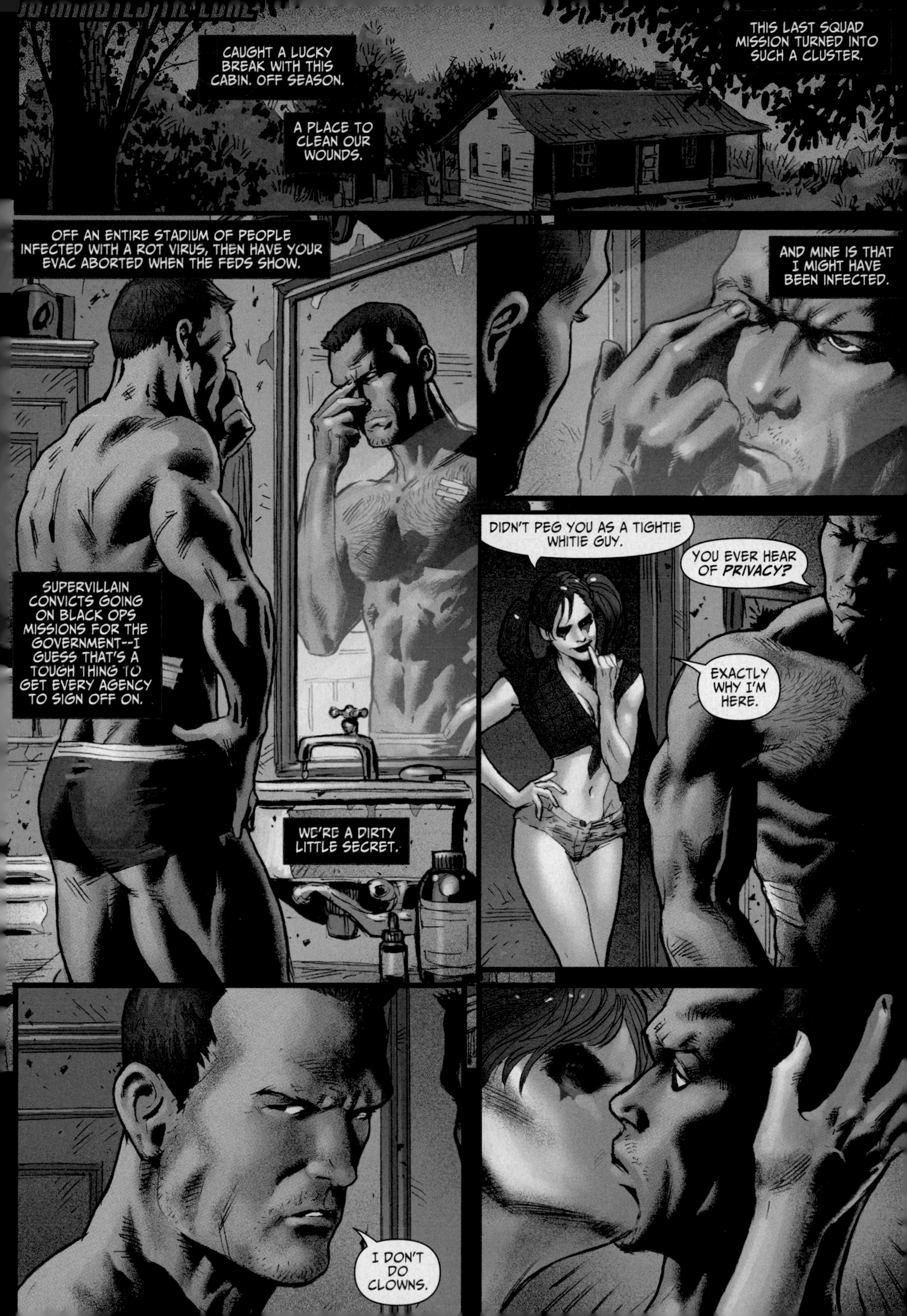
CAUGHT A LUCKY BREAK WITH THIS CABIN. OFF SEASON.
A PLACE TO CLEAN OUR WOUNDS.
THIS LAST SQUAD MISSION TURNED INTO SUCH A CLUSTER.
OFF AN ENTIRE STADIUM OF PEOPLE INFECTED WITH A ROT VIRUS, THEN HAVE YOUR EVAC ABORTED WHEN THE FEDS SHOW.
SUPERVILLAIN CONVICTS GOING ON BLACK OPS MISSIONS FOR THE GOVERNMENT--I GUESS THAT'S A TOUGH THING TO GET EVERY AGENCY TO SIGN OFF ON.
WE'RE A DIRTY LITTLE SECRET.
AND MINE IS THAT I MIGHT HAVE BEEN INFECTED.
DIDN'T PEG YOU AS A TIGHTIE WHITIE GUY.
YOU EVER HEAR OF *PRIVACY?*
EXACTLY WHY I'M HERE.
I DON'T DO CLOWNS.

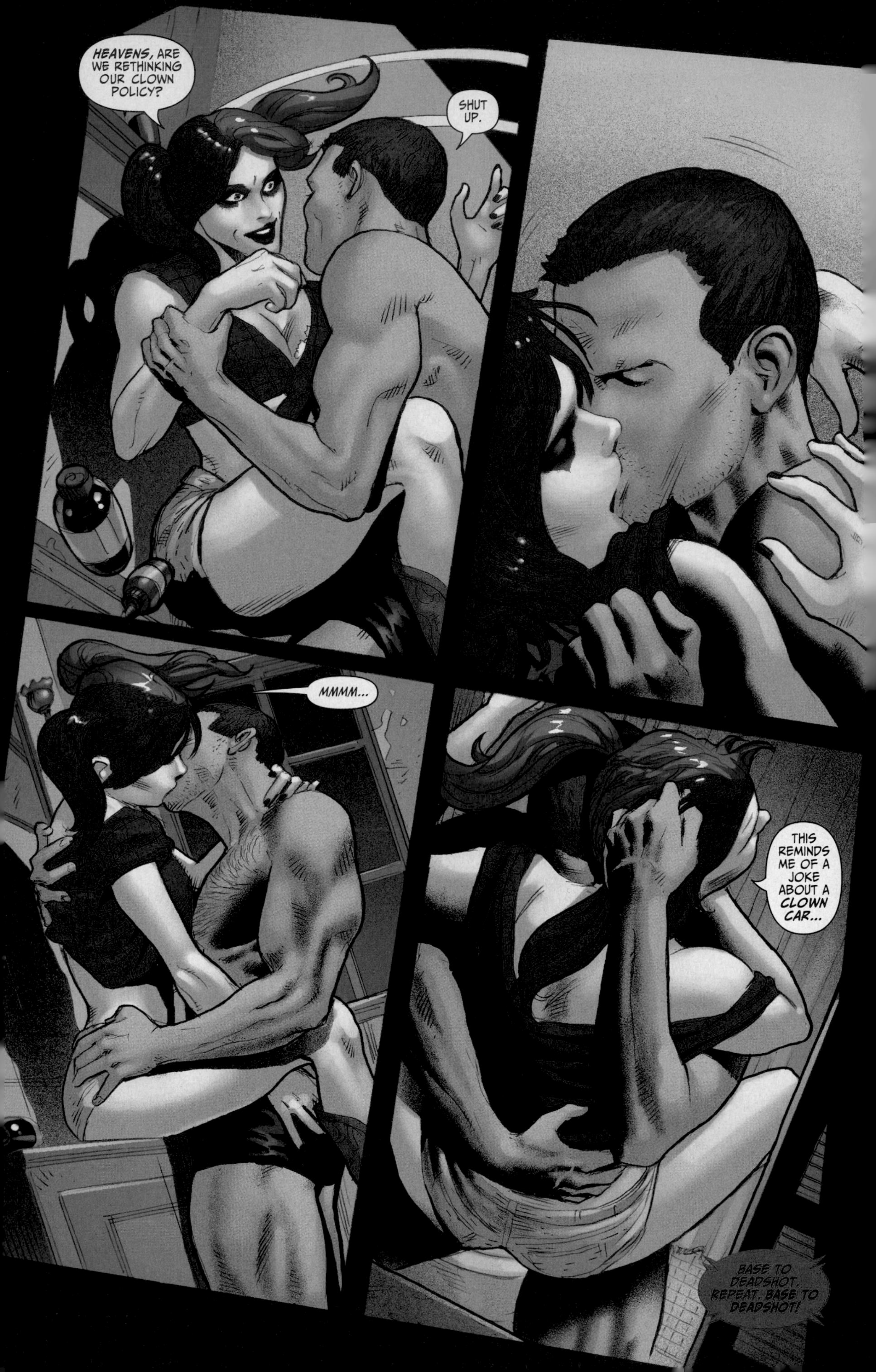
HEAVENS, ARE WE RETHINKING OUR CLOWN POLICY?
SHUT UP.
MMMM...
THIS REMINDS ME OF A JOKE ABOUT A CLOWN CAR...
BASE TO DEADSHOT. REPEAT. BASE TO DEADSHOT!

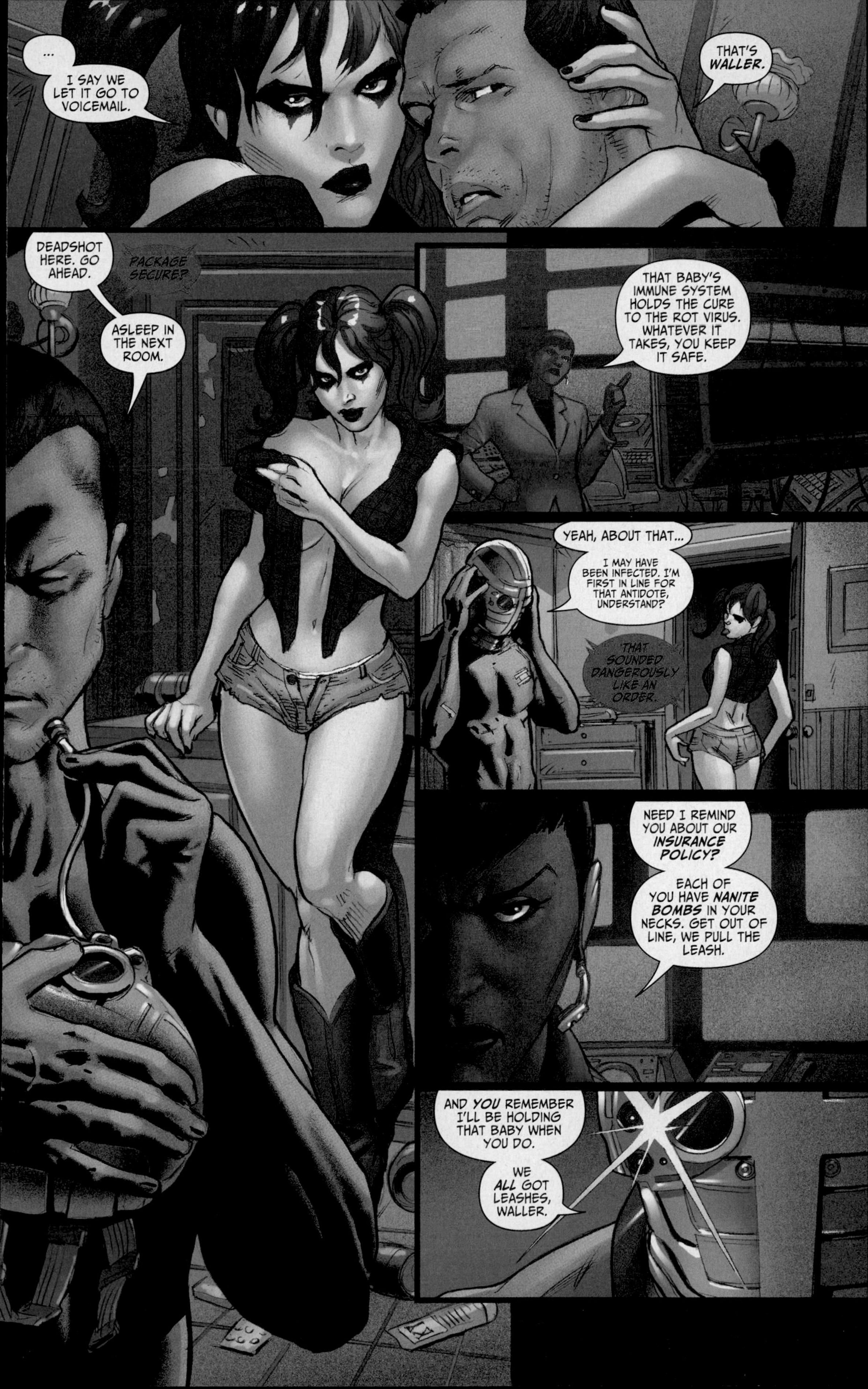
...
I SAY WE LET IT GO TO VOICEMAIL.
THAT'S WALLER.
DEADSHOT HERE. GO AHEAD.
PACKAGE SECURE?
ASLEEP IN THE NEXT ROOM.
THAT BABY'S IMMUNE SYSTEM HOLDS THE CURE TO THE ROT VIRUS. WHATEVER IT TAKES, YOU KEEP IT SAFE.
YEAH, ABOUT THAT...
I MAY HAVE BEEN INFECTED. I'M FIRST IN LINE FOR THAT ANTIDOTE, UNDERSTAND?
THAT SOUNDED DANGEROUSLY LIKE AN ORDER.
NEED I REMIND YOU ABOUT OUR INSURANCE POLICY?
EACH OF YOU HAVE NANITE BOMBS IN YOUR NECKS. GET OUT OF LINE, WE PULL THE LEASH.
AND YOU REMEMBER I'LL BE HOLDING THAT BABY WHEN YOU DO.
WE ALL GOT LEASHES, WALLER.

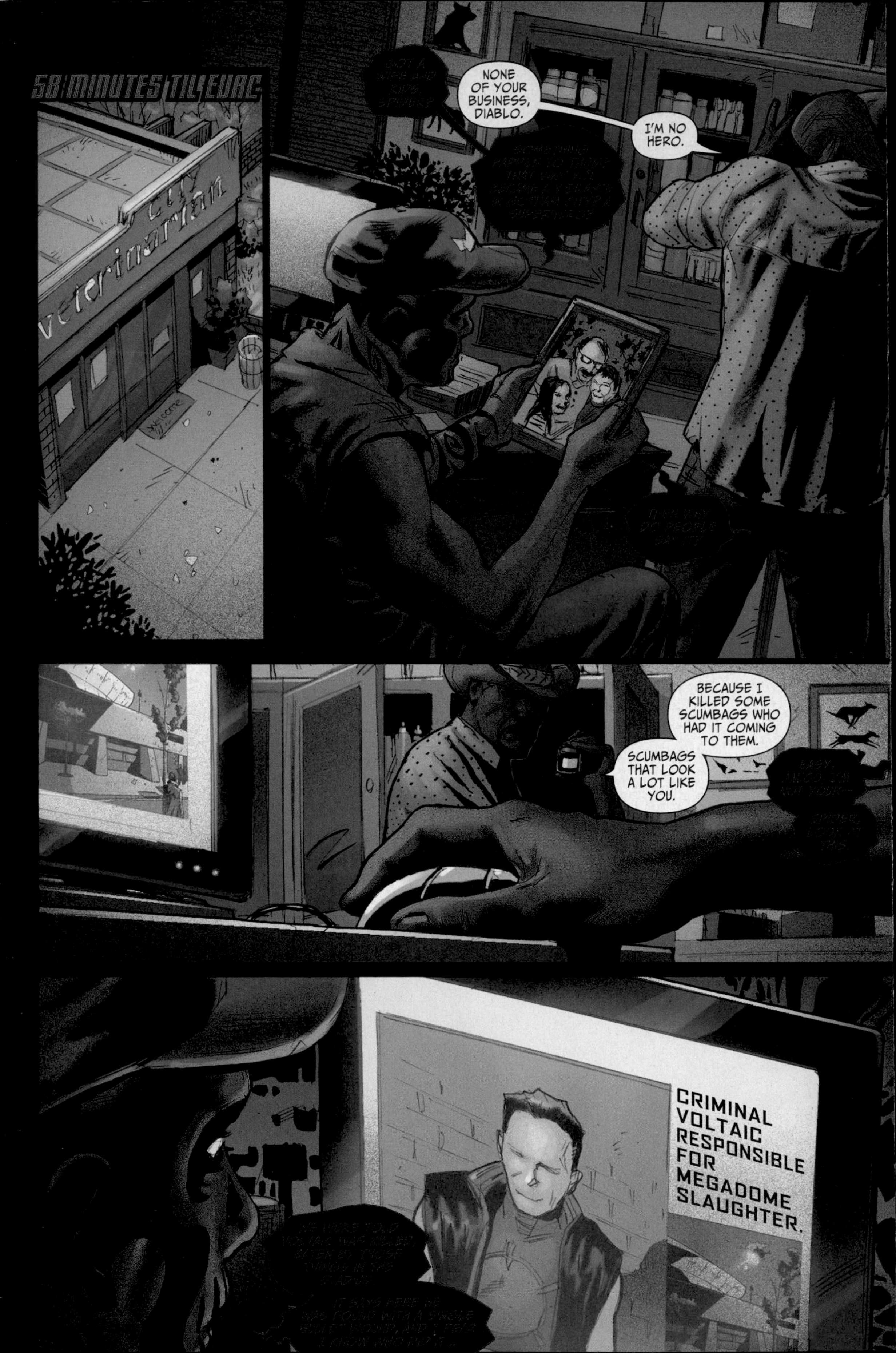
58 MINUTES TIL EVAC
City Veterinarian
NONE OF YOUR BUSINESS, DIABLO.
I'M NO HERO.
BECAUSE I KILLED SOME SCUMBAGS WHO HAD IT COMING TO THEM.
SCUMBAGS THAT LOOK A LOT LIKE YOU.
CRIMINAL VOLTAIC RESPONSIBLE FOR MEGADOME SLAUGHTER.

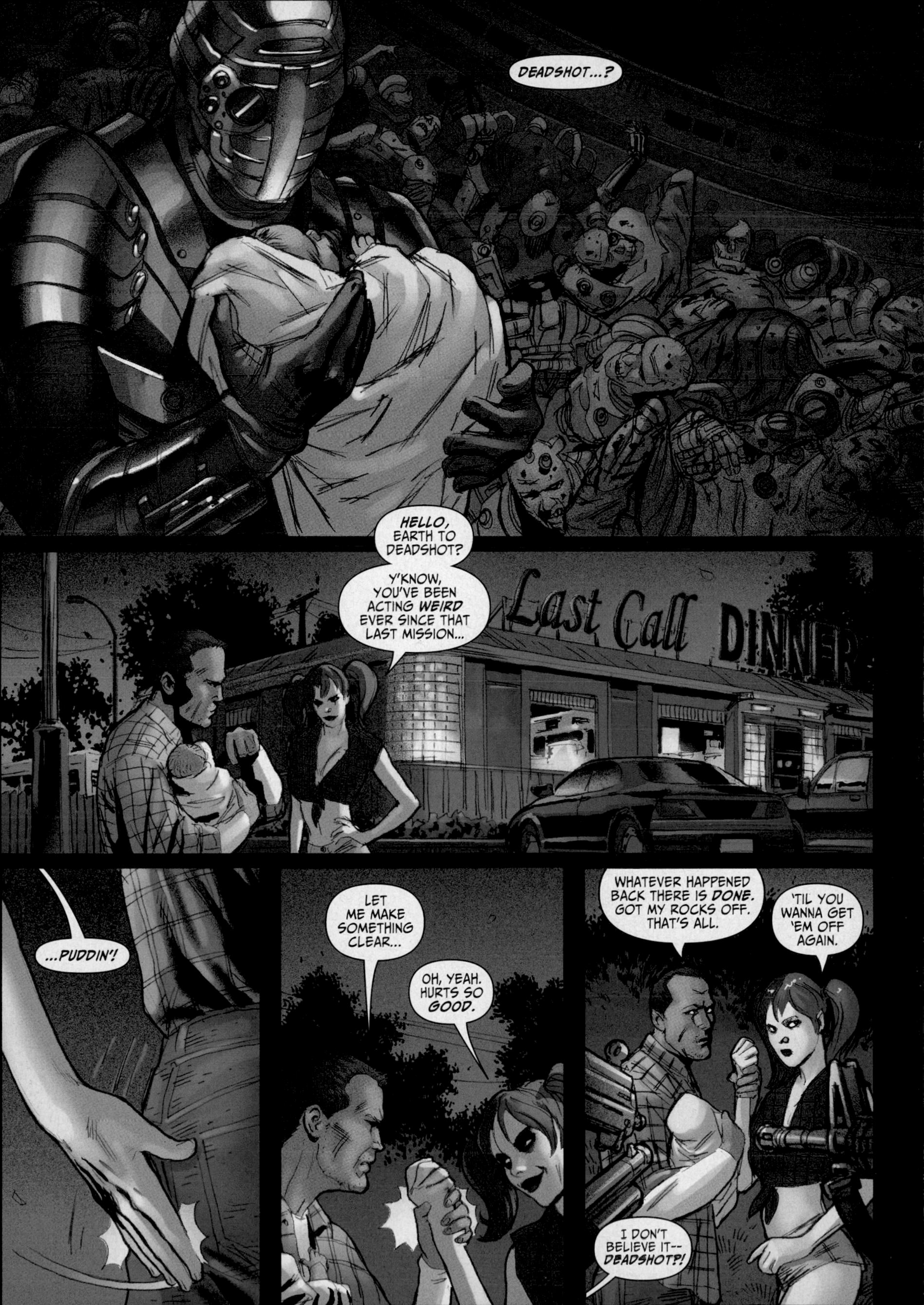
DEADSHOT...?
HELLO, EARTH TO DEADSHOT?
Y'KNOW, YOU'VE BEEN ACTING WEIRD EVER SINCE THAT LAST MISSION...
Last Call DINNER
...PUDDIN'!
LET ME MAKE SOMETHING CLEAR...
OH, YEAH. HURTS SO GOOD.
WHATEVER HAPPENED BACK THERE IS DONE. GOT MY ROCKS OFF. THAT'S ALL.
'TIL YOU WANNA GET 'EM OFF AGAIN.
I DON'T BELIEVE IT-- DEADSHOT?!

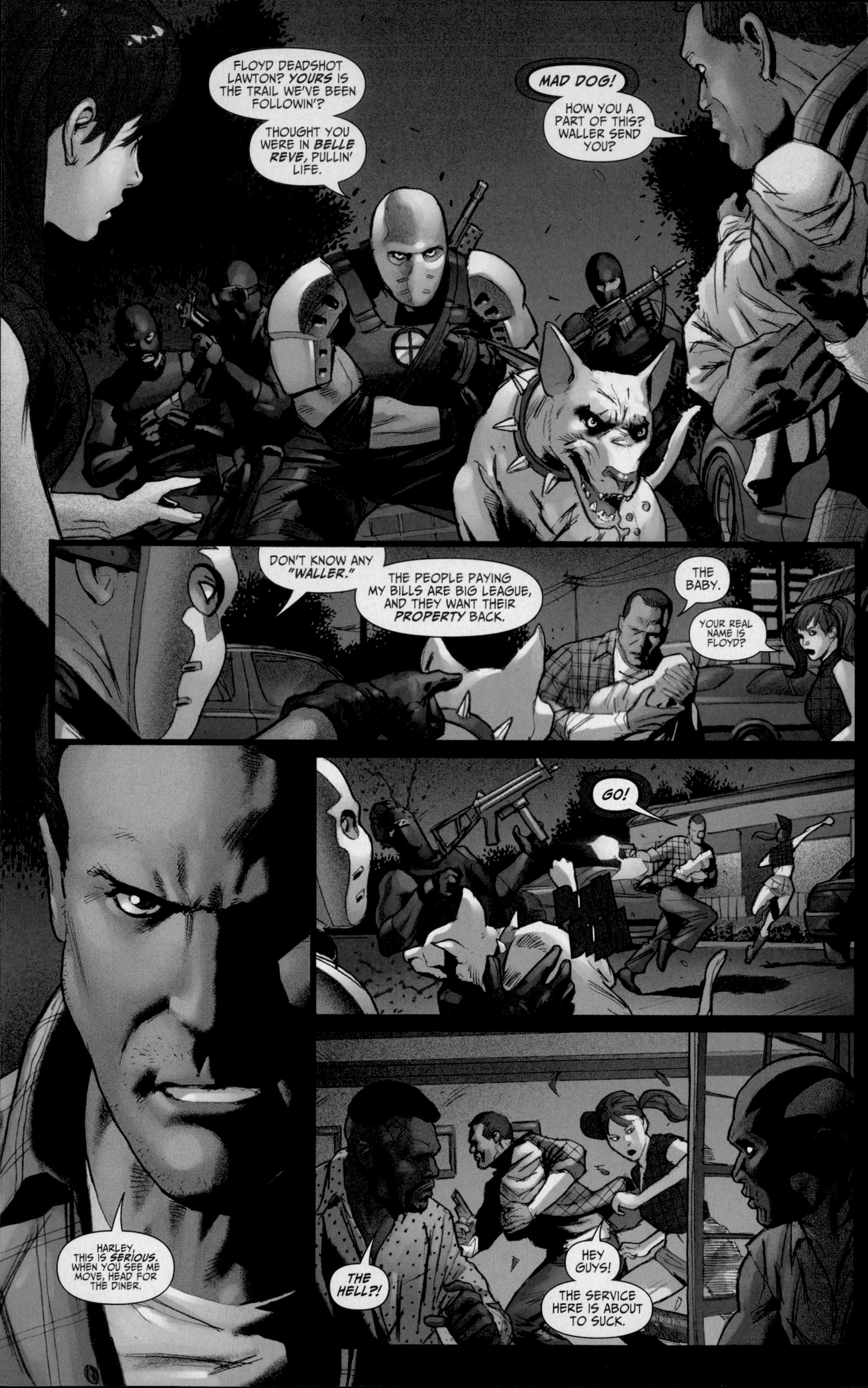
FLOYD DEADSHOT LAWTON? YOURS IS THE TRAIL WE'VE BEEN FOLLOWIN'?
THOUGHT YOU WERE IN BELLE REVE, PULLIN' LIFE.
MAD DOG!
HOW YOU A PART OF THIS? WALLER SEND YOU?
DON'T KNOW ANY "WALLER."
THE PEOPLE PAYING MY BILLS ARE BIG LEAGUE, AND THEY WANT THEIR PROPERTY BACK.
THE BABY.
YOUR REAL NAME IS FLOYD?
HARLEY, THIS IS SERIOUS. WHEN YOU SEE ME MOVE, HEAD FOR THE DINER.
GO!
THE HELL?!
HEY GUYS!
THE SERVICE HERE IS ABOUT TO SUCK.

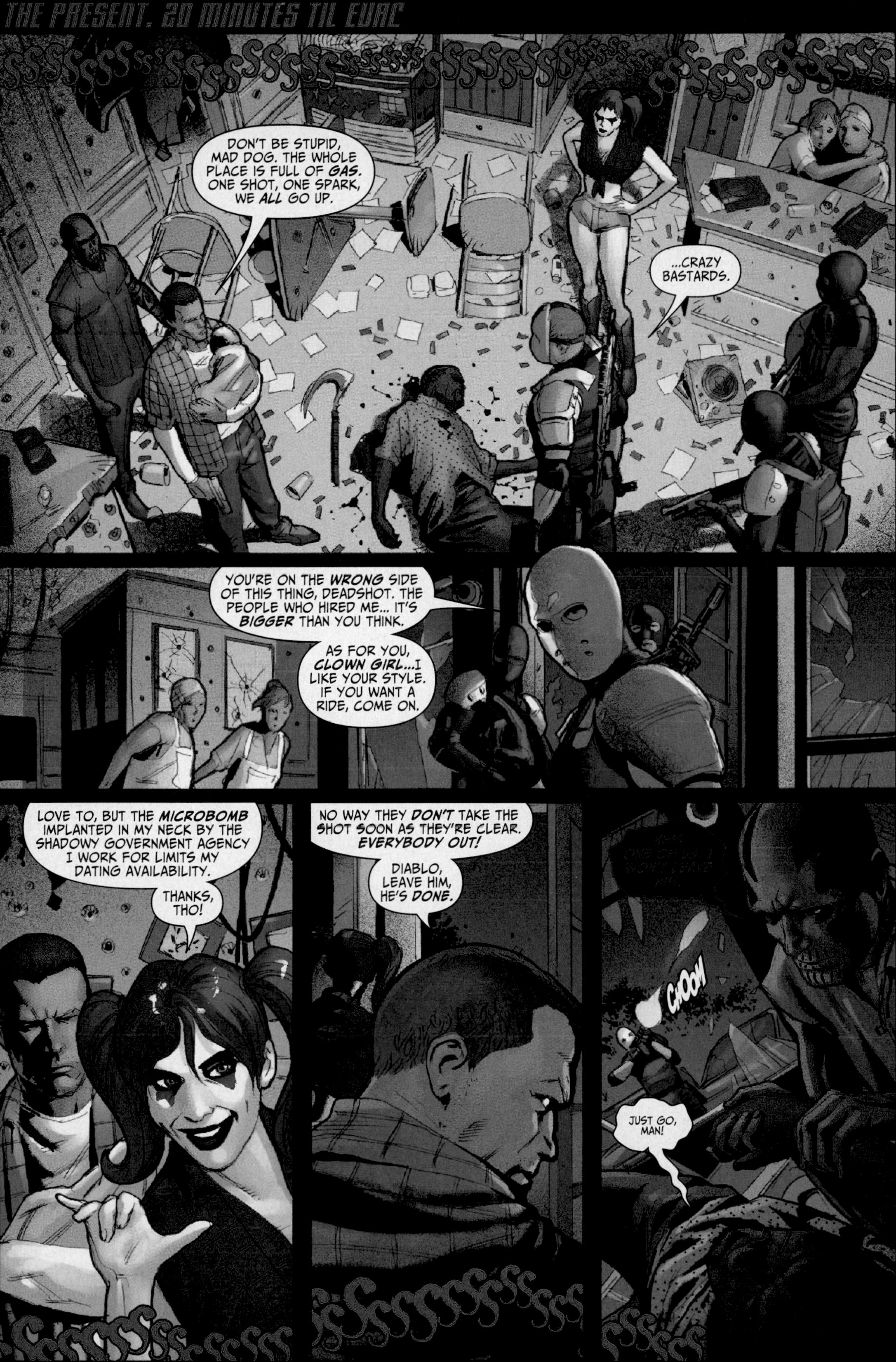
THE PRESENT. 20 MINUTES TIL EVAC
DON'T BE STUPID, MAD DOG. THE WHOLE PLACE IS FULL OF GAS. ONE SHOT, ONE SPARK, WE ALL GO UP.
...CRAZY BASTARDS.
YOU'RE ON THE WRONG SIDE OF THIS THING, DEADSHOT. THE PEOPLE WHO HIRED ME... IT'S BIGGER THAN YOU THINK.
AS FOR YOU, CLOWN GIRL...I LIKE YOUR STYLE. IF YOU WANT A RIDE, COME ON.
LOVE TO, BUT THE MICROBOMB IMPLANTED IN MY NECK BY THE SHADOWY GOVERNMENT AGENCY I WORK FOR LIMITS MY DATING AVAILABILITY.
THANKS, THO!
NO WAY THEY DON'T TAKE THE SHOT SOON AS THEY'RE CLEAR. EVERYBODY OUT!
DIABLO, LEAVE HIM, HE'S DONE.
CHOOM
JUST GO, MAN!

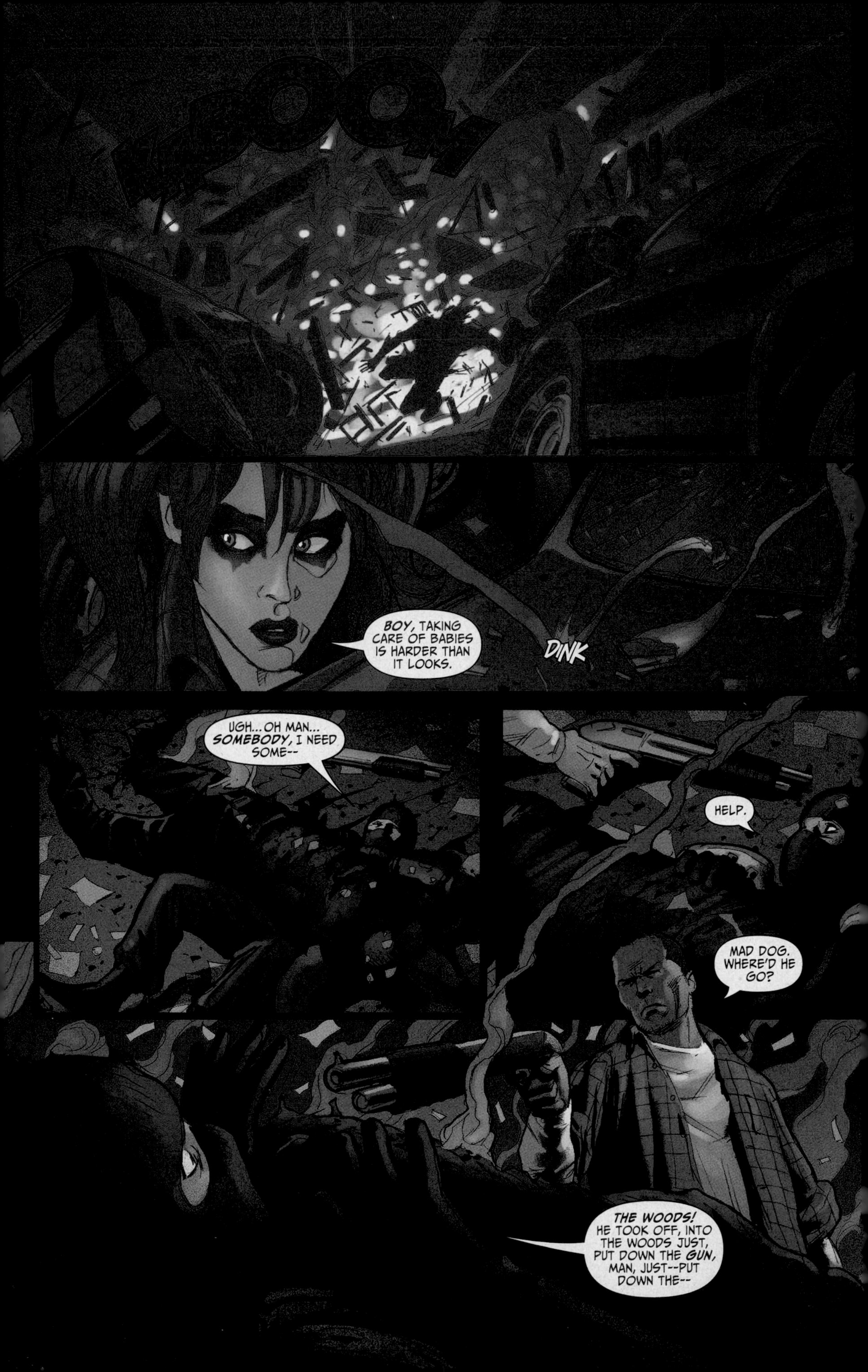
BOY, TAKING CARE OF BABIES IS HARDER THAN IT LOOKS.
DINK
UGH...OH MAN... SOMEBODY, I NEED SOME--
HELP.
MAD DOG. WHERE'D HE GO?
THE WOODS! HE TOOK OFF, INTO THE WOODS JUST, PUT DOWN THE GUN, MAN, JUST--PUT DOWN THE--

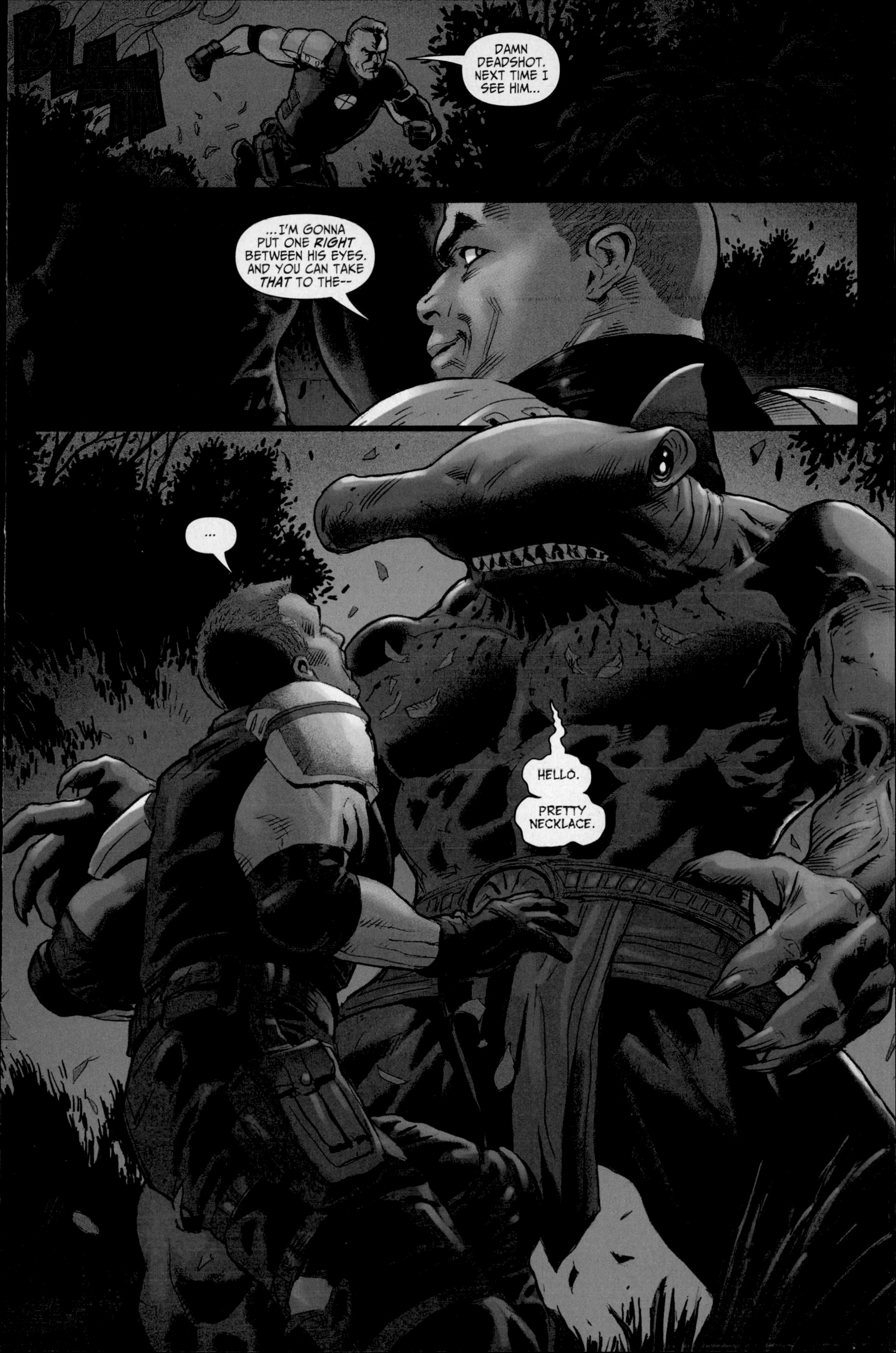
DAMN DEADSHOT. NEXT TIME I SEE HIM...
...I'M GONNA PUT ONE *RIGHT* BETWEEN HIS EYES. AND YOU CAN TAKE *THAT* TO THE--
...
HELLO.
PRETTY NECKLACE.

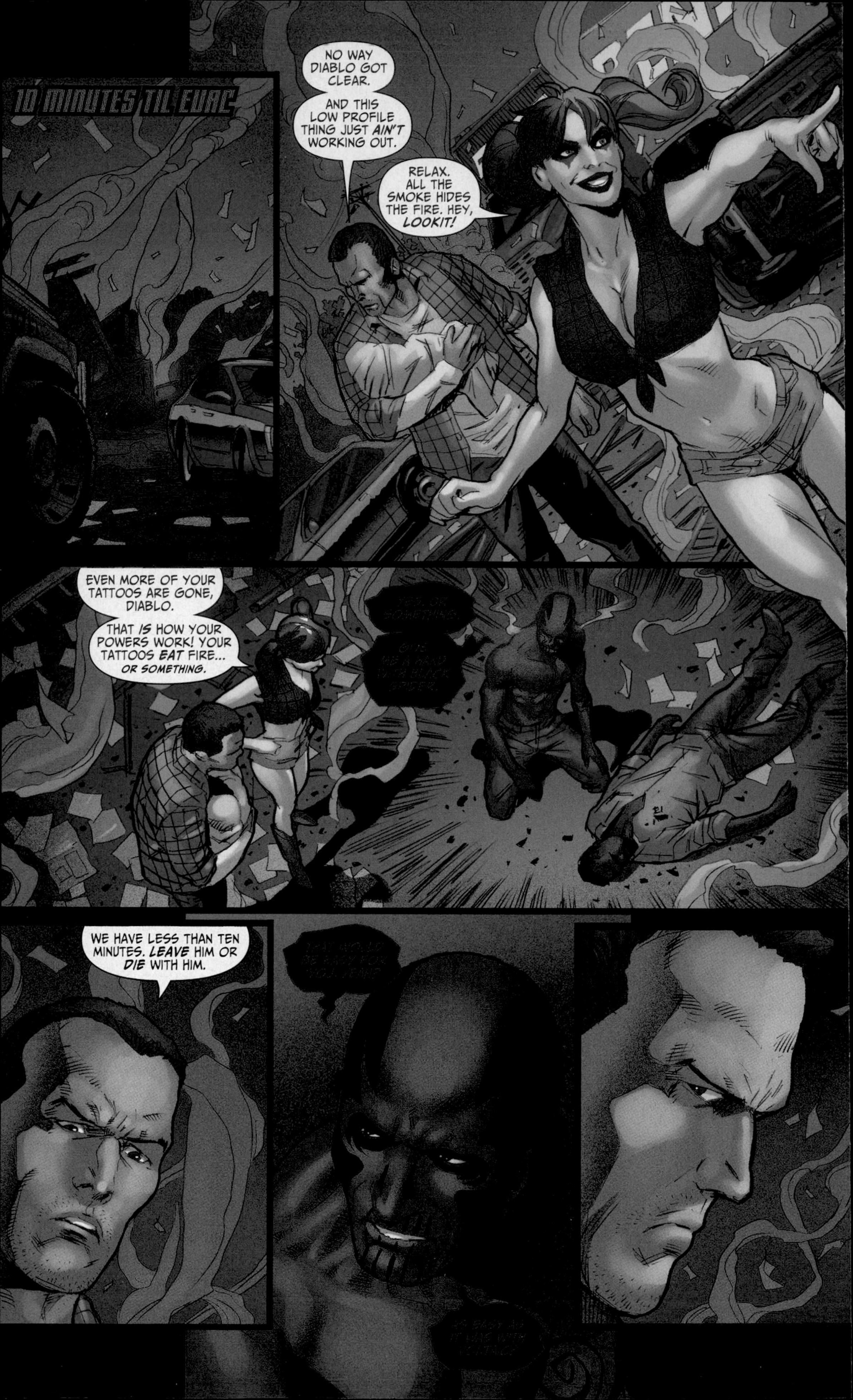
10 MINUTES TIL EVAC
NO WAY DIABLO GOT CLEAR.
AND THIS LOW PROFILE THING JUST AIN'T WORKING OUT.
RELAX. ALL THE SMOKE HIDES THE FIRE. HEY, LOOKIT!
EVEN MORE OF YOUR TATTOOS ARE GONE, DIABLO.
THAT IS HOW YOUR POWERS WORK! YOUR TATTOOS EAT FIRE... OR SOMETHING.
YES. OR SOMETHING.
GIVE ME A HAND WITH BLACK SPIDER.
WE HAVE LESS THAN TEN MINUTES. LEAVE HIM OR DIE WITH HIM.

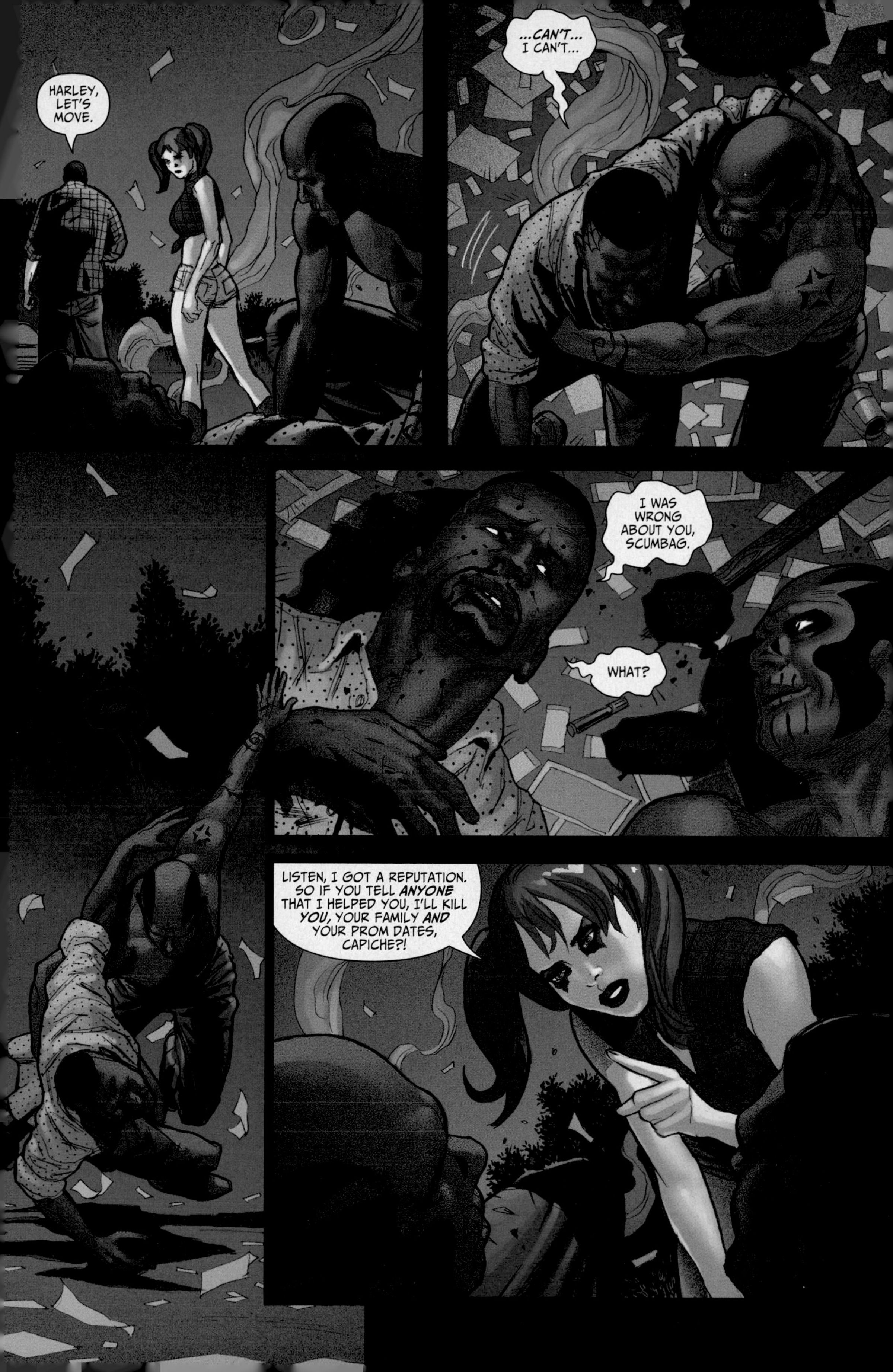
HARLEY, LET'S MOVE.
...CAN'T... I CAN'T...
I WAS WRONG ABOUT YOU, SCUMBAG.
WHAT?
LISTEN, I GOT A REPUTATION. SO IF YOU TELL ANYONE THAT I HELPED YOU, I'LL KILL YOU, YOUR FAMILY AND YOUR PROM DATES, CAPICHE?!

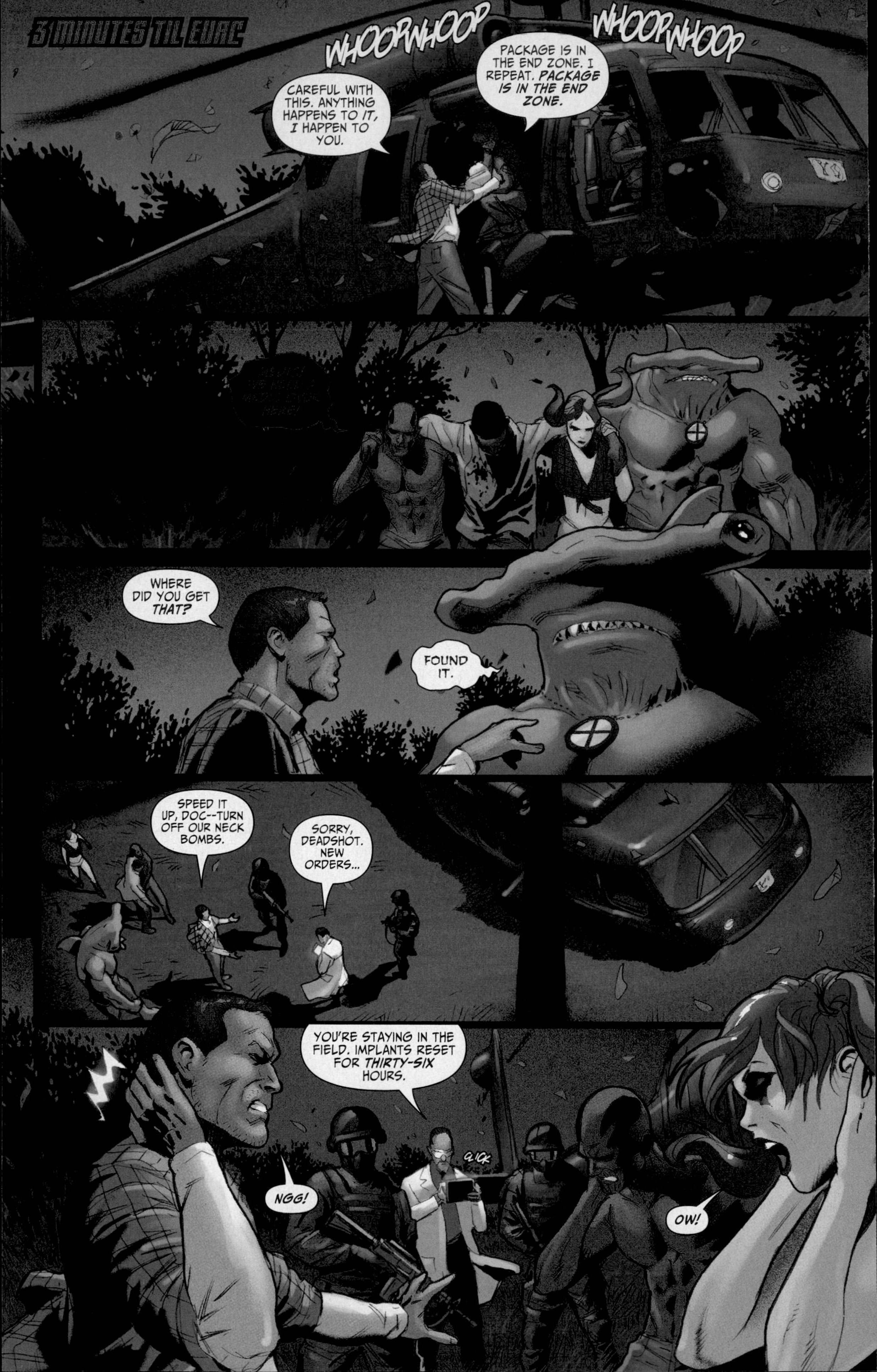
3 MINUTES TIL EVAC
WHOOPWHOOP
CAREFUL WITH THIS. ANYTHING HAPPENS TO *IT*, *I* HAPPEN TO YOU.
WHOOPWHOOP
PACKAGE IS IN THE END ZONE. I REPEAT. *PACKAGE IS IN THE END ZONE.*
WHERE DID YOU GET *THAT?*
FOUND IT.
SPEED IT UP, DOC--TURN OFF OUR NECK BOMBS.
SORRY, DEADSHOT. NEW ORDERS...
YOU'RE STAYING IN THE FIELD. IMPLANTS RESET FOR *THIRTY-SIX* HOURS.
CLICK
NGG!
OW!

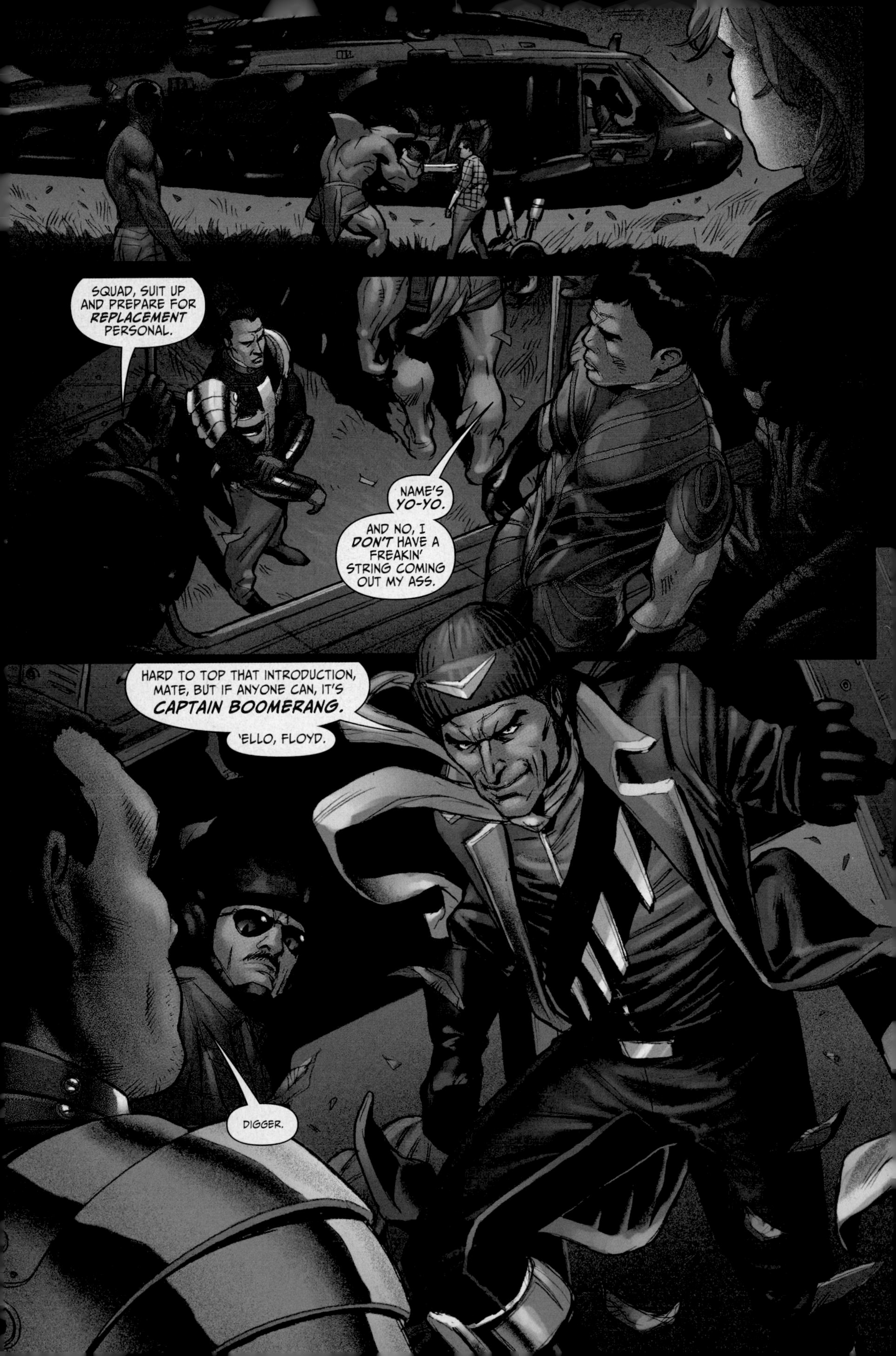
SQUAD, SUIT UP AND PREPARE FOR REPLACEMENT PERSONAL.
NAME'S YO-YO.
AND NO, I DON'T HAVE A FREAKIN' STRING COMING OUT MY ASS.
HARD TO TOP THAT INTRODUCTION, MATE, BUT IF ANYONE CAN, IT'S CAPTAIN BOOMERANG.
'ELLO, FLOYD.
DIGGER.

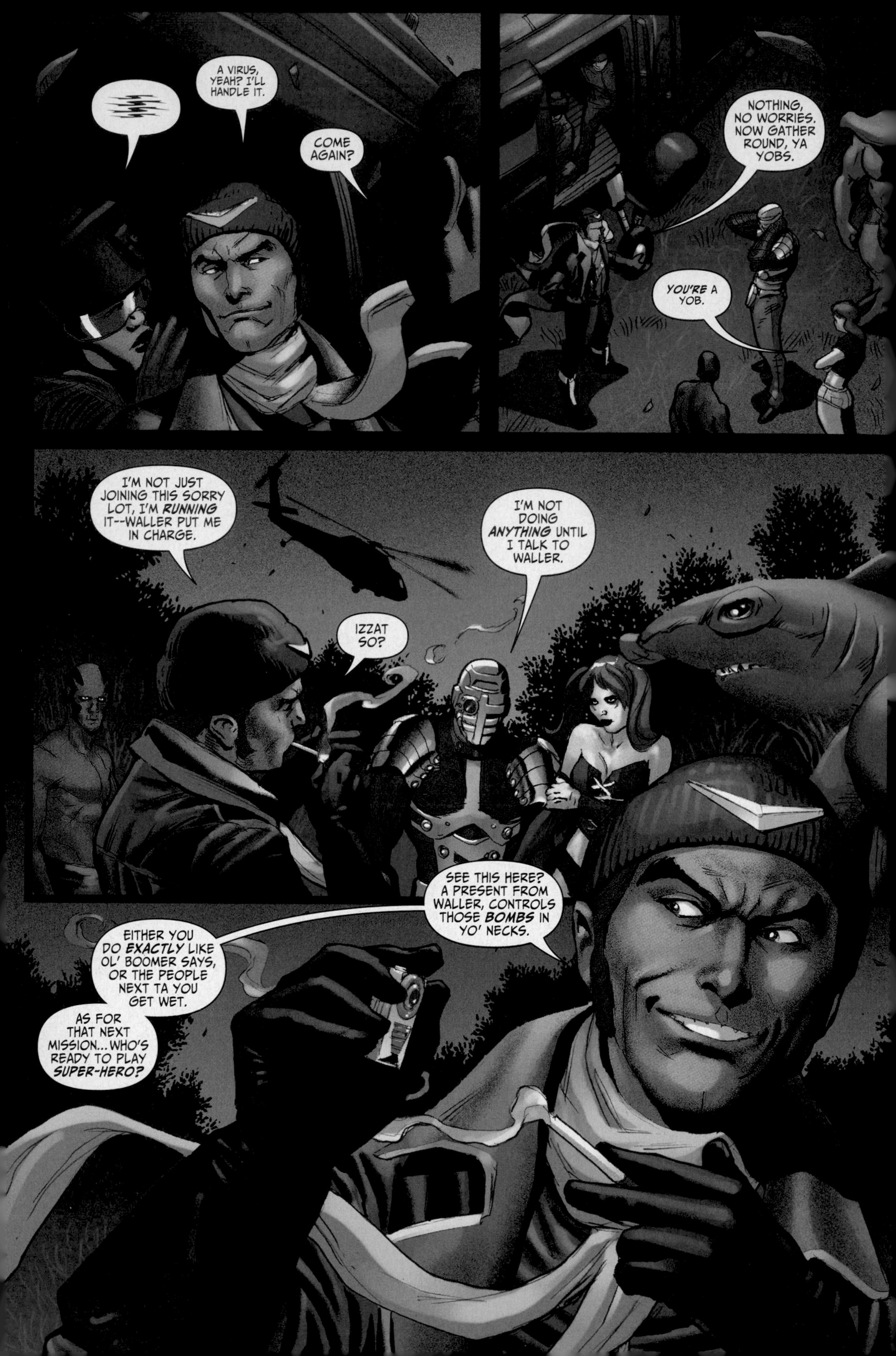

A VIRUS, YEAH? I'LL HANDLE IT.
COME AGAIN?
NOTHING, NO WORRIES. NOW GATHER ROUND, YA YOBS.
YOU'RE A YOB.
I'M NOT JUST JOINING THIS SORRY LOT, I'M RUNNING IT--WALLER PUT ME IN CHARGE.
I'M NOT DOING ANYTHING UNTIL I TALK TO WALLER.
IZZAT SO?
SEE THIS HERE? A PRESENT FROM WALLER, CONTROLS THOSE BOMBS IN YO' NECKS.
EITHER YOU DO EXACTLY LIKE OL' BOOMER SAYS, OR THE PEOPLE NEXT TA YOU GET WET.
AS FOR THAT NEXT MISSION... WHO'S READY TO PLAY SUPER-HERO?

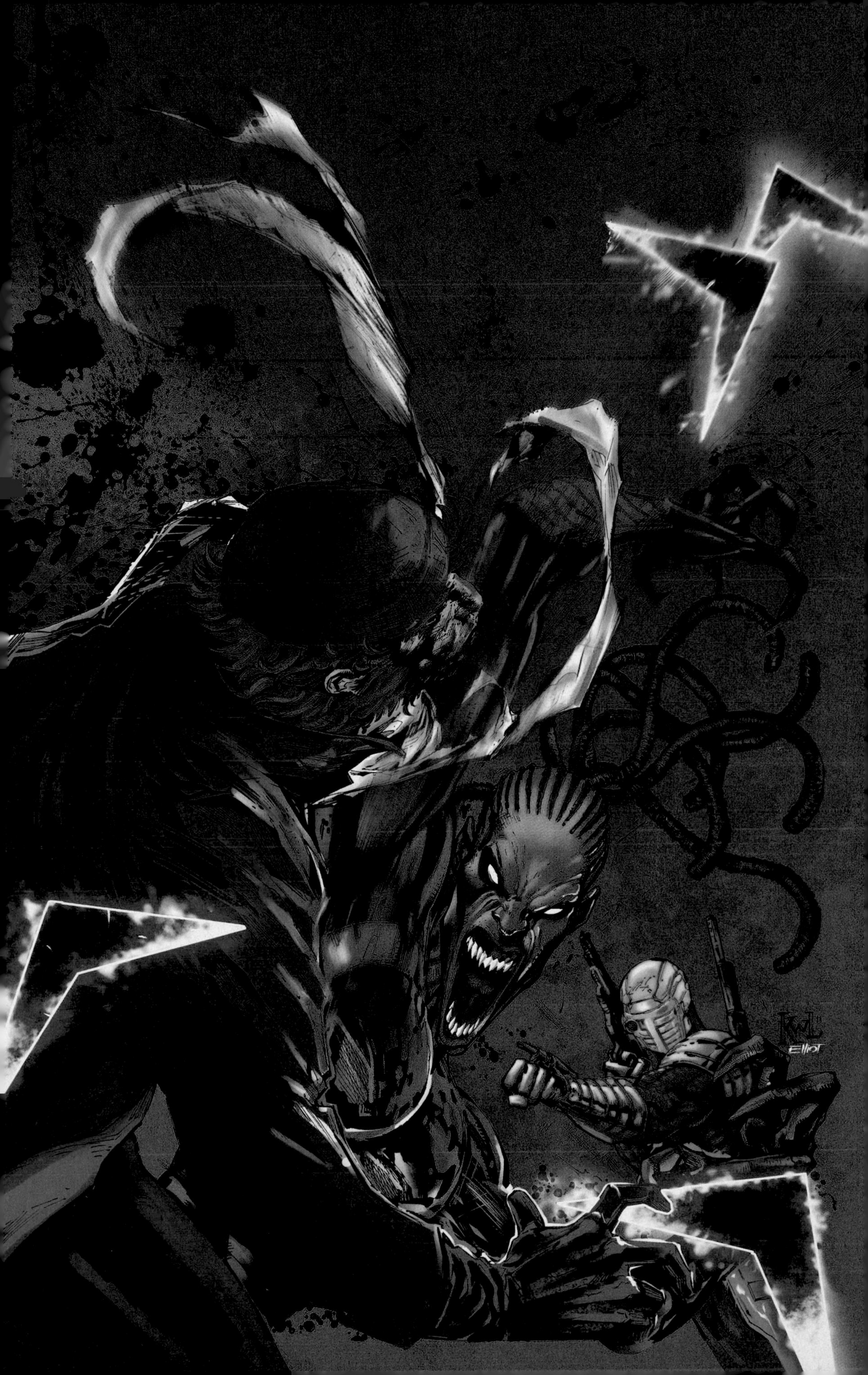

BAD COMPANY

ADAM GLASS
writer

FEDERICO DALLOCCHIO
artist

cover art by KEN LASHLEY

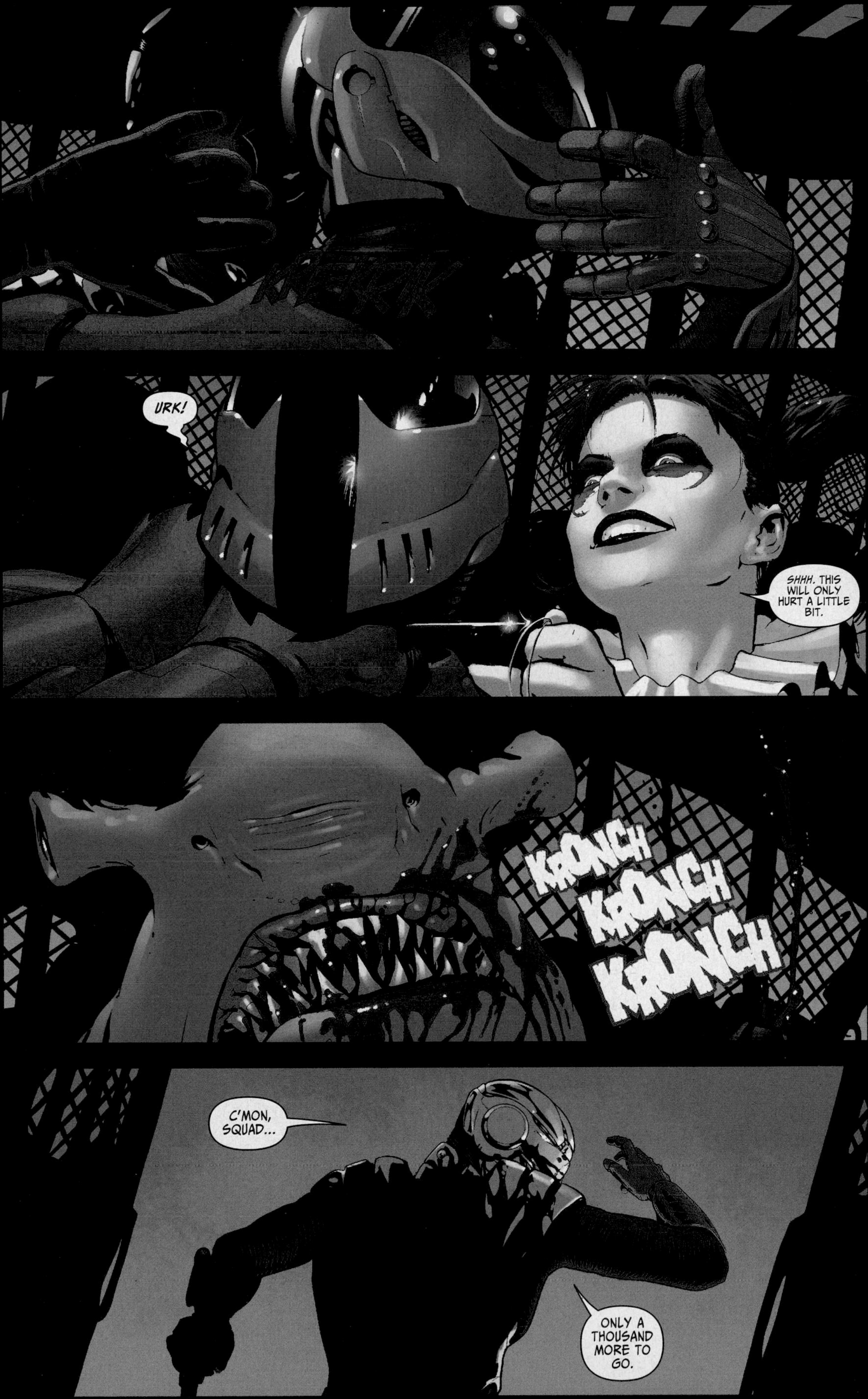
URK!
SHHH. THIS WILL ONLY HURT A LITTLE BIT.
KRONCH
KRONCH
KRONCH
C'MON, SQUAD...
ONLY A THOUSAND MORE TO GO.

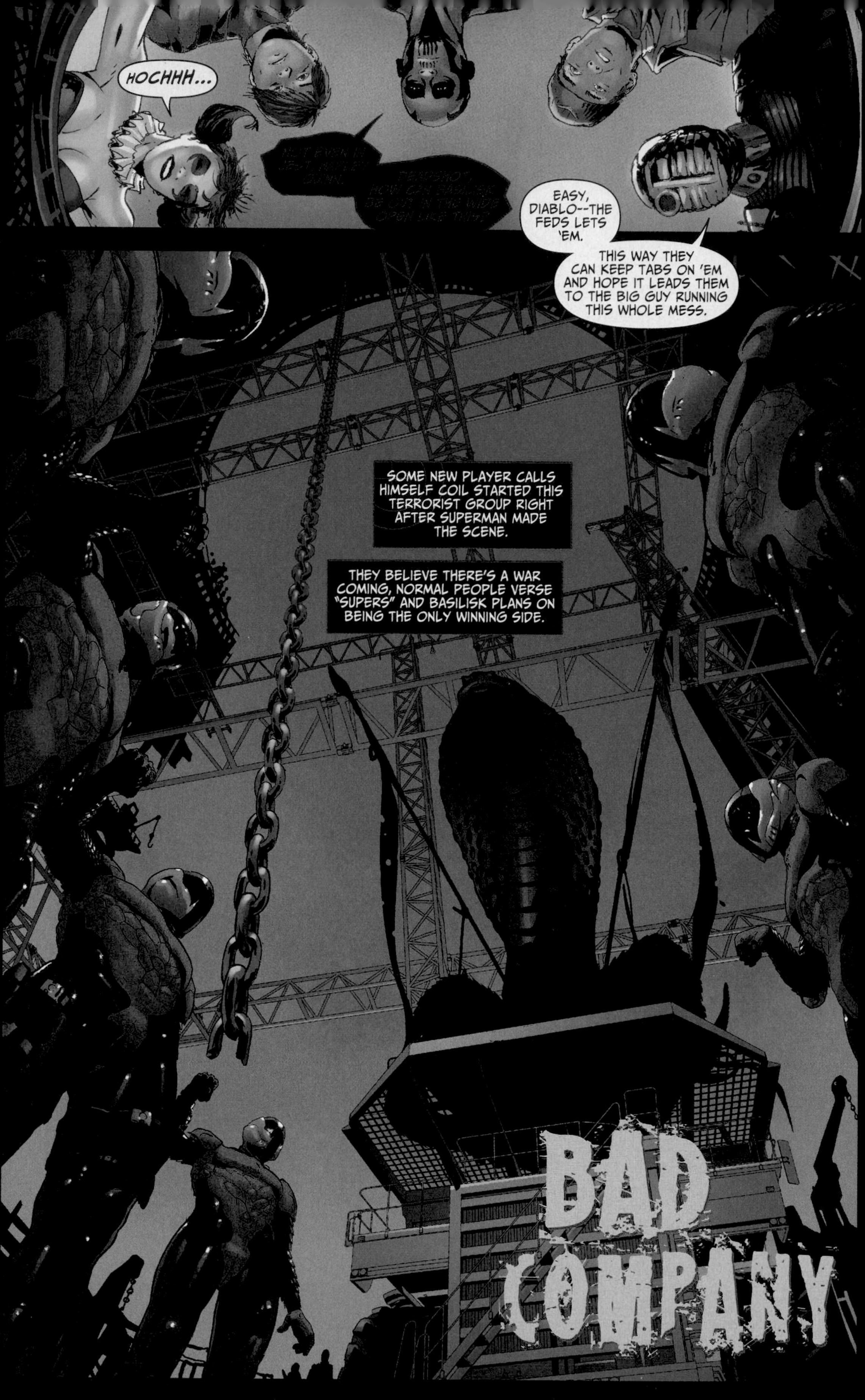
HOCHHH...
NOT EVEN IN JEST, HARLEY QUINN.
DEADSHOT, HOW CAN BASILISK BE OUT IN THE WIDE OPEN LIKE THIS?
EASY, DIABLO--THE FEDS LETS 'EM.
THIS WAY THEY CAN KEEP TABS ON 'EM AND HOPE IT LEADS THEM TO THE BIG GUY RUNNING THIS WHOLE MESS.
SOME NEW PLAYER CALLS HIMSELF COIL STARTED THIS TERRORIST GROUP RIGHT AFTER SUPERMAN MADE THE SCENE.
THEY BELIEVE THERE'S A WAR COMING, NORMAL PEOPLE VERSE "SUPERS" AND BASILISK PLANS ON BEING THE ONLY WINNING SIDE.
BAD COMPANY

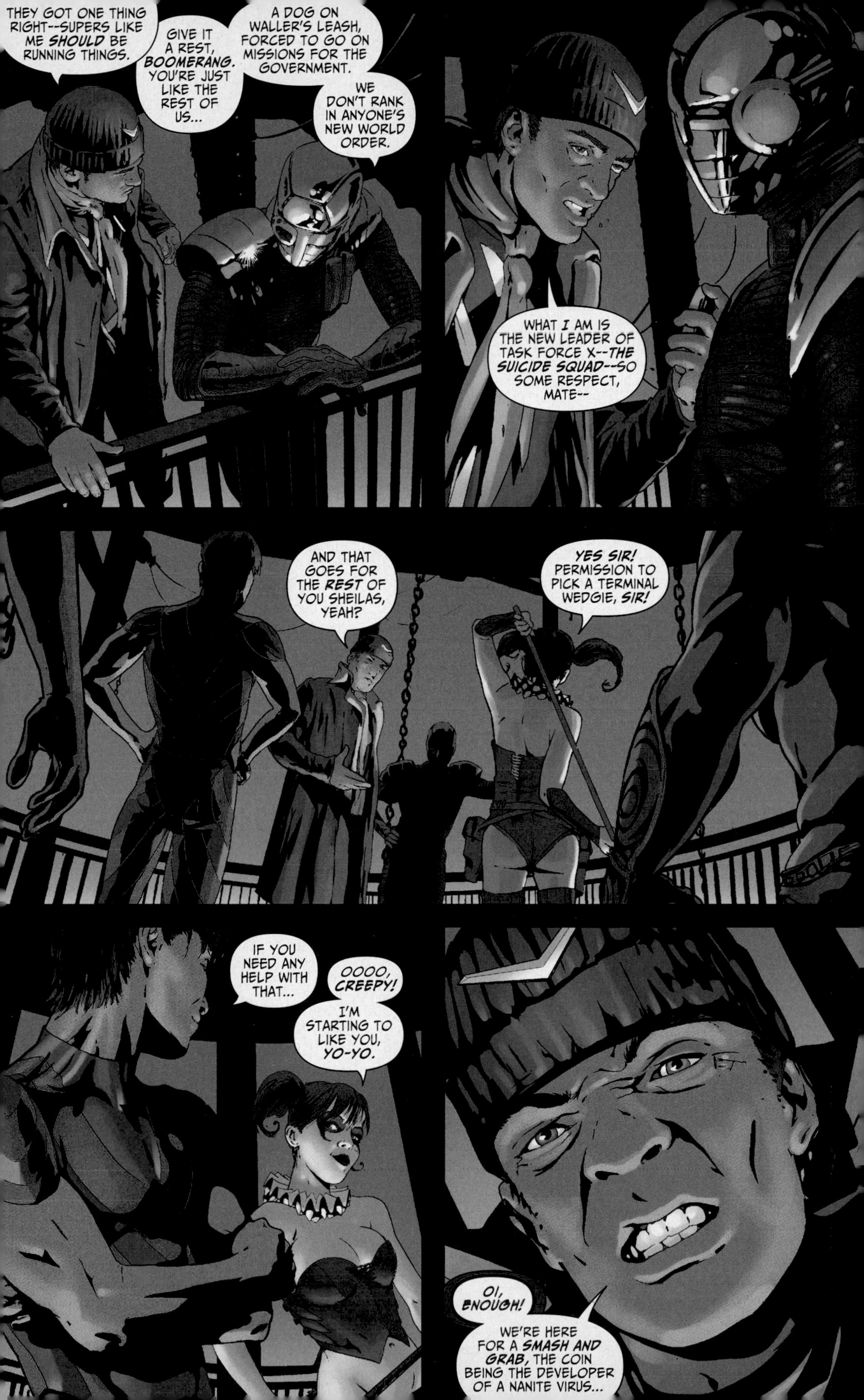
THEY GOT ONE THING RIGHT--SUPERS LIKE ME *SHOULD* BE RUNNING THINGS.
GIVE IT A REST, *BOOMERANG*. YOU'RE JUST LIKE THE REST OF US...
A DOG ON WALLER'S LEASH, FORCED TO GO ON MISSIONS FOR THE GOVERNMENT.
WE DON'T RANK IN ANYONE'S NEW WORLD ORDER.
WHAT *I* AM IS THE NEW LEADER OF TASK FORCE X--*THE SUICIDE SQUAD*--SO SOME RESPECT, MATE--
AND THAT GOES FOR THE *REST* OF YOU SHEILAS, YEAH?
YES SIR! PERMISSION TO PICK A TERMINAL WEDGIE, *SIR!*
IF YOU NEED ANY HELP WITH THAT...
OOOO, *CREEPY!*
I'M STARTING TO LIKE YOU, *YO-YO.*
OI, *ENOUGH!*
WE'RE HERE FOR A *SMASH AND GRAB*, THE COIN BEING THE DEVELOPER OF A NANITE VIRUS...

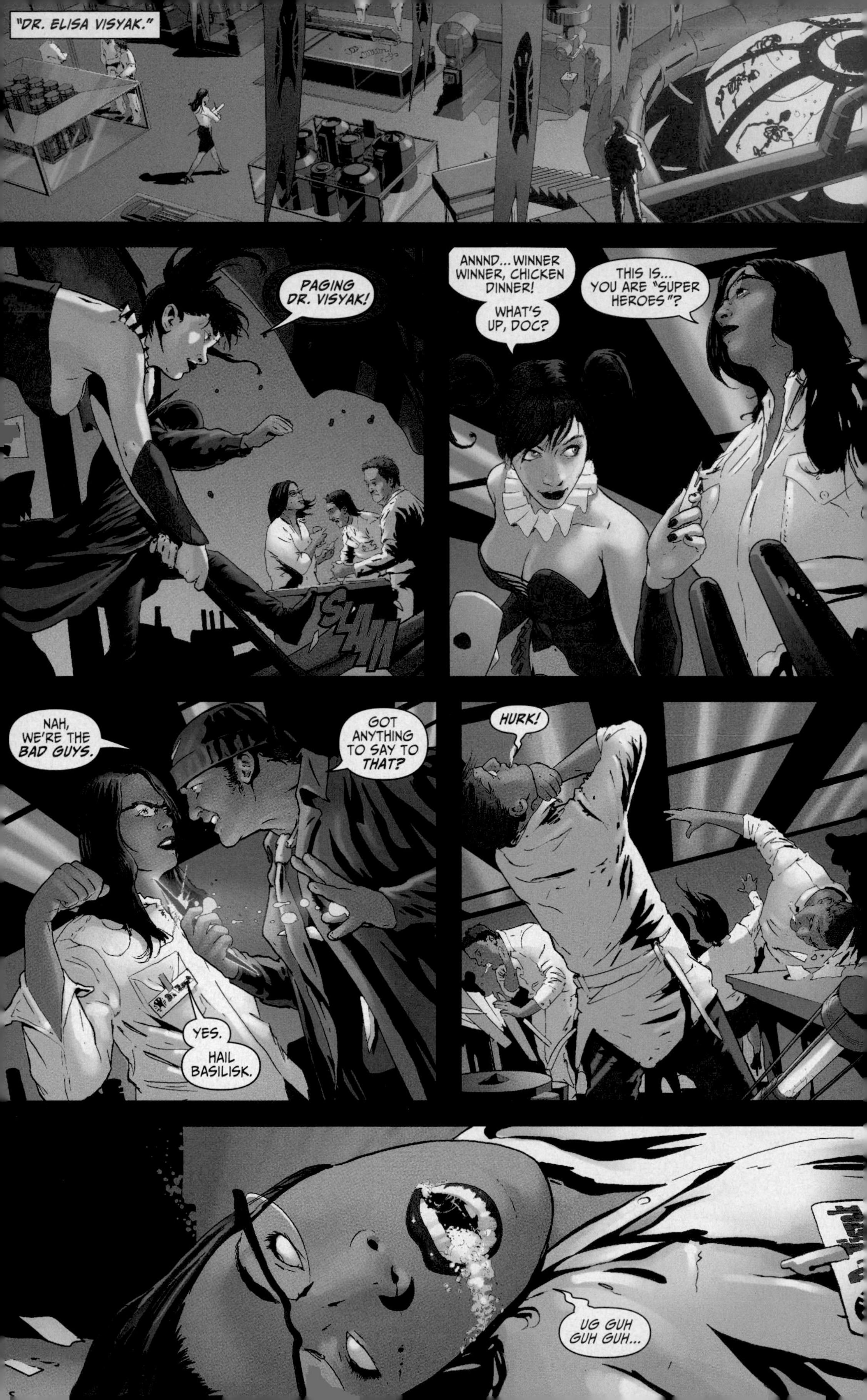
"DR. ELISA VISYAK."
PAGING DR. VISYAK!
SLAM
ANNND... WINNER WINNER, CHICKEN DINNER!
WHAT'S UP, DOC?
THIS IS... YOU ARE "SUPER HEROES"?
NAH, WE'RE THE BAD GUYS.
GOT ANYTHING TO SAY TO THAT?
YES.
HAIL BASILISK.
HURK!
UG GUH GUH GUH...

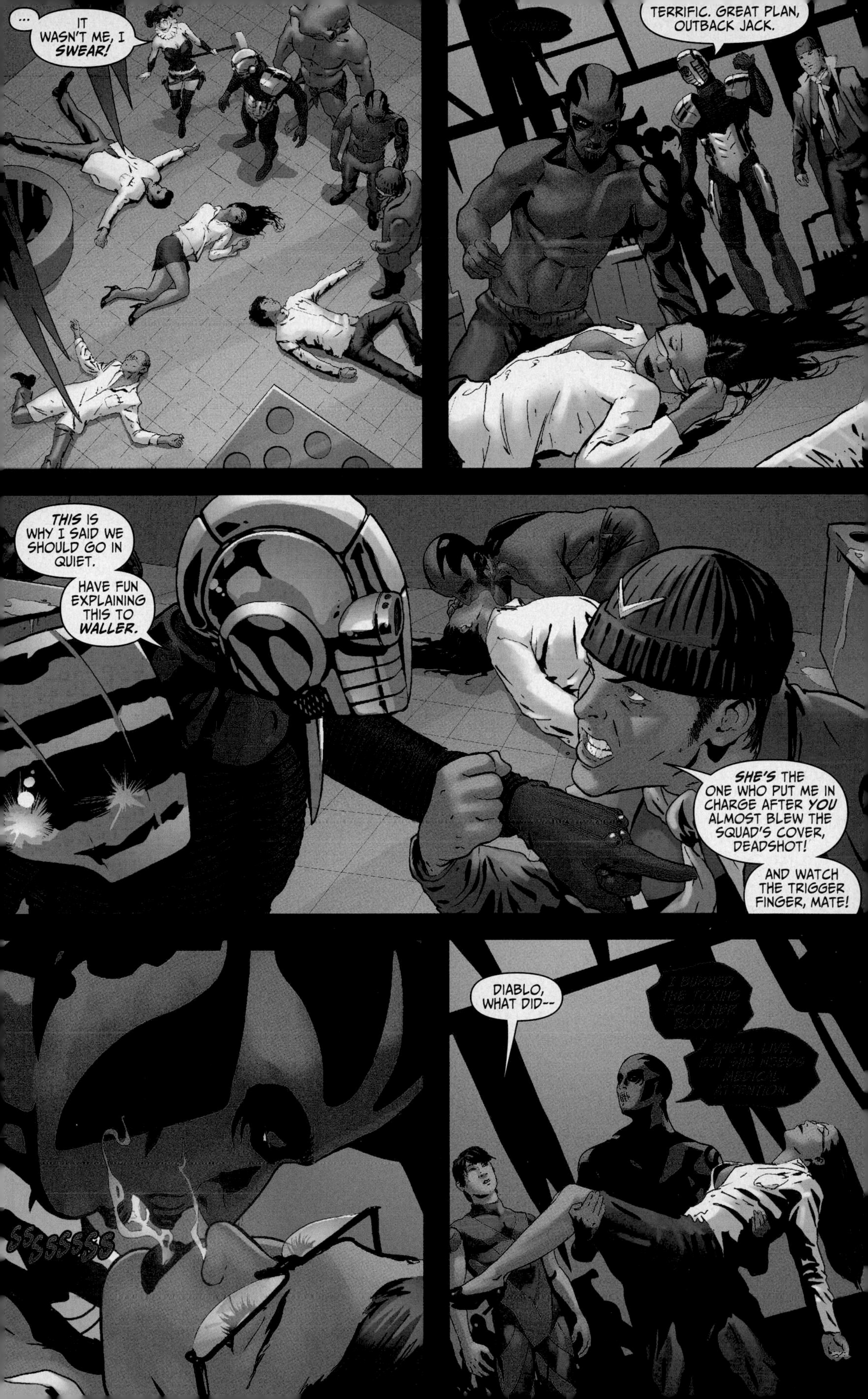
...
IT WASN'T ME, I SWEAR!
TERRIFIC. GREAT PLAN, OUTBACK JACK.
THIS IS WHY I SAID WE SHOULD GO IN QUIET.
HAVE FUN EXPLAINING THIS TO WALLER.
SHE'S THE ONE WHO PUT ME IN CHARGE AFTER YOU ALMOST BLEW THE SQUAD'S COVER, DEADSHOT!
AND WATCH THE TRIGGER FINGER, MATE!
SSSSSSSS
DIABLO, WHAT DID--
I BURNED THE TOXINS FROM HER BLOOD.
SHE'LL LIVE, BUT SHE NEEDS MEDICAL ATTENTION.

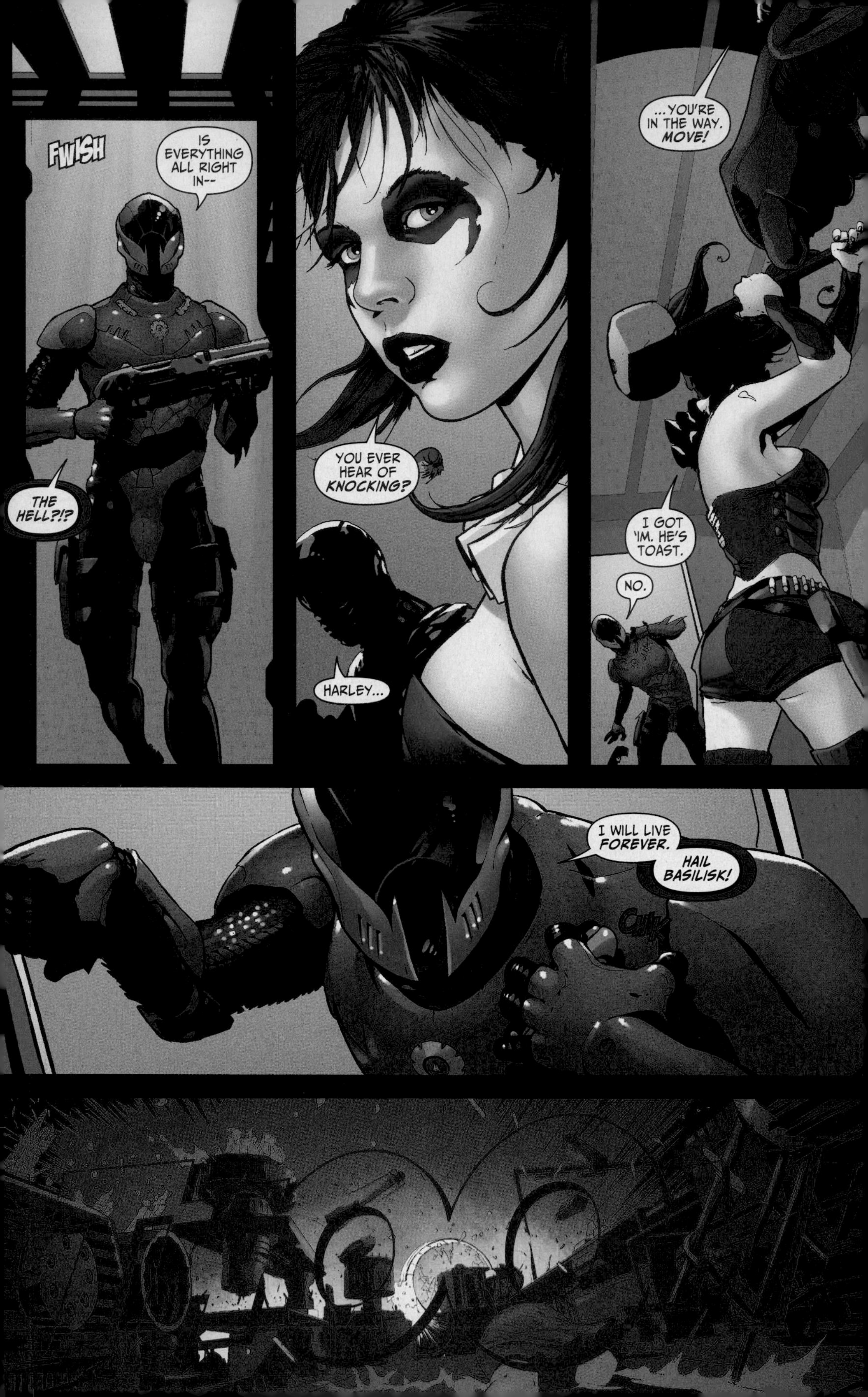
FWISH
IS EVERYTHING ALL RIGHT IN--
THE HELL?!?
YOU EVER HEAR OF KNOCKING?
HARLEY...
...YOU'RE IN THE WAY. MOVE!
I GOT 'IM. HE'S TOAST.
NO.
I WILL LIVE FOREVER.
HAIL BASILISK!
CHAK

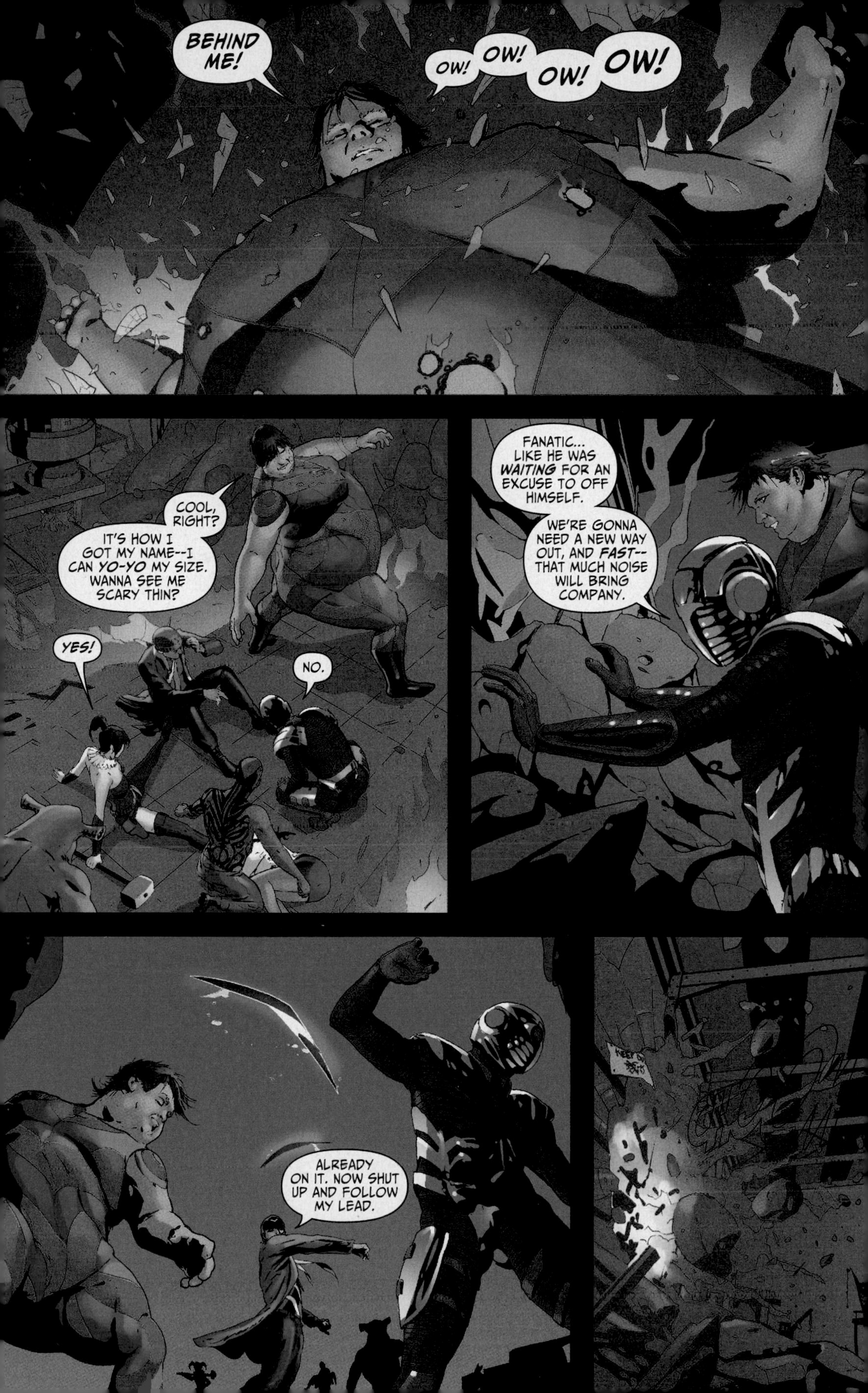
BEHIND ME!
OW! OW! OW! OW!
COOL, RIGHT?
IT'S HOW I GOT MY NAME--I CAN *YO-YO* MY SIZE. WANNA SEE ME SCARY THIN?
YES!
NO.
FANATIC... LIKE HE WAS *WAITING* FOR AN EXCUSE TO OFF HIMSELF.
WE'RE GONNA NEED A NEW WAY OUT, AND *FAST*--THAT MUCH NOISE WILL BRING COMPANY.
ALREADY ON IT. NOW SHUT UP AND FOLLOW MY LEAD.

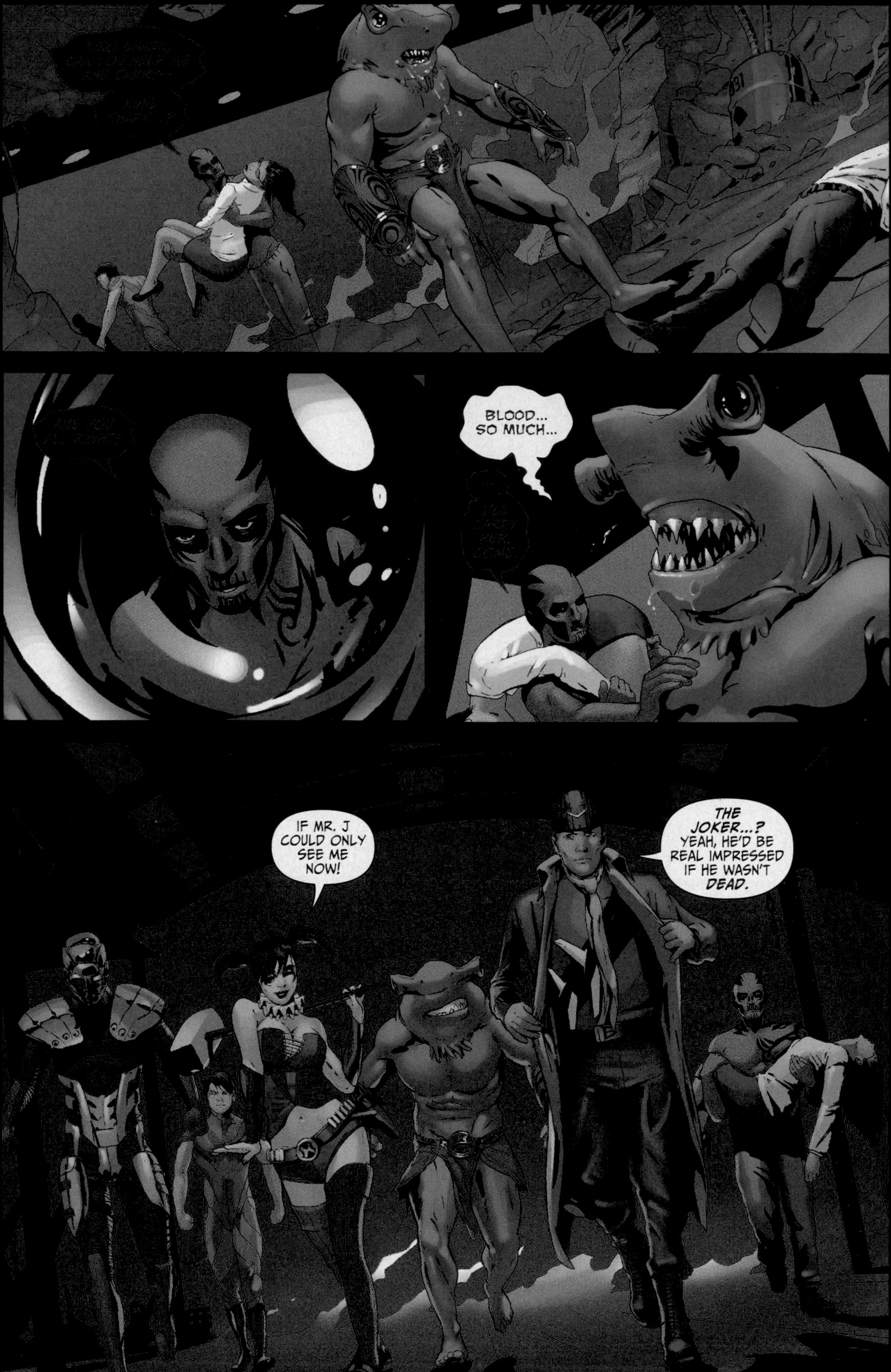
BLOOD... SO MUCH...
IF MR. J COULD ONLY SEE ME NOW!
THE JOKER...? YEAH, HE'D BE REAL IMPRESSED IF HE WASN'T DEAD.

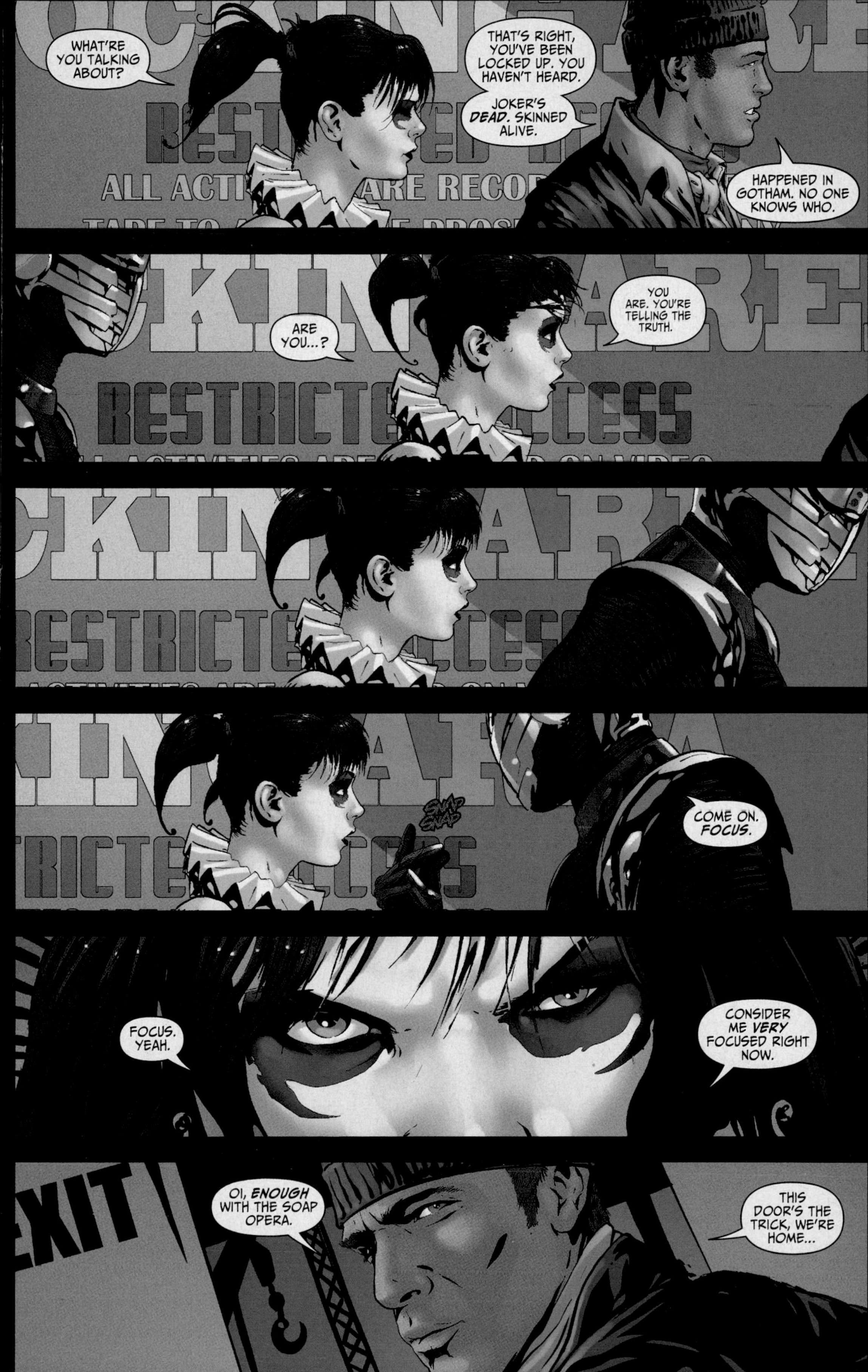
WHAT'RE YOU TALKING ABOUT?
THAT'S RIGHT, YOU'VE BEEN LOCKED UP. YOU HAVEN'T HEARD.
JOKER'S DEAD. SKINNED ALIVE.
HAPPENED IN GOTHAM. NO ONE KNOWS WHO.
ARE YOU...?
YOU ARE. YOU'RE TELLING THE TRUTH.
SNAP SNAP
COME ON. FOCUS.
FOCUS. YEAH.
CONSIDER ME VERY FOCUSED RIGHT NOW.
EXIT
OI, ENOUGH WITH THE SOAP OPERA.
THIS DOOR'S THE TRICK, WE'RE HOME...

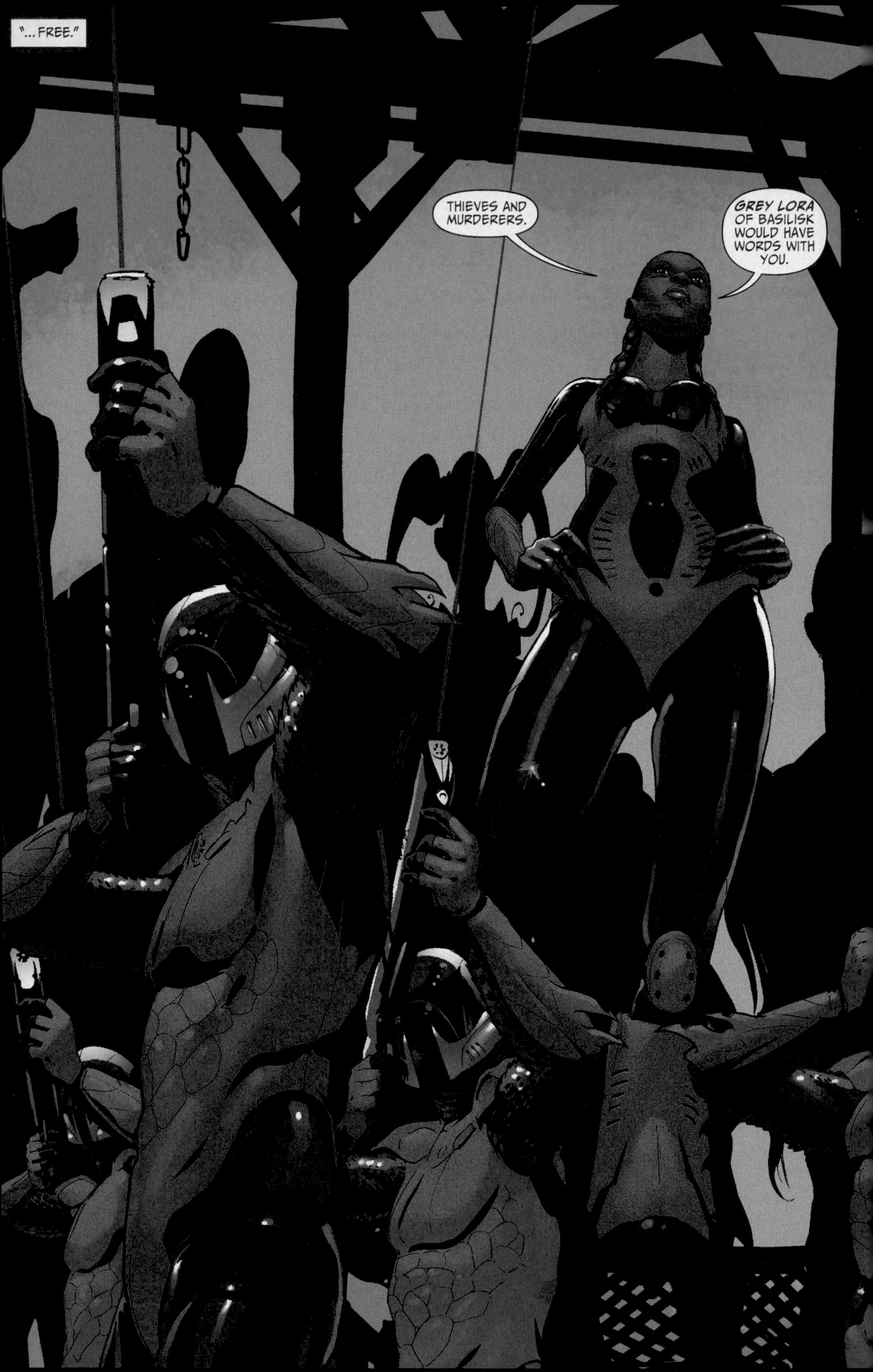
"...FREE."
THIEVES AND MURDERERS.
GREY LORA OF BASILISK WOULD HAVE WORDS WITH YOU.

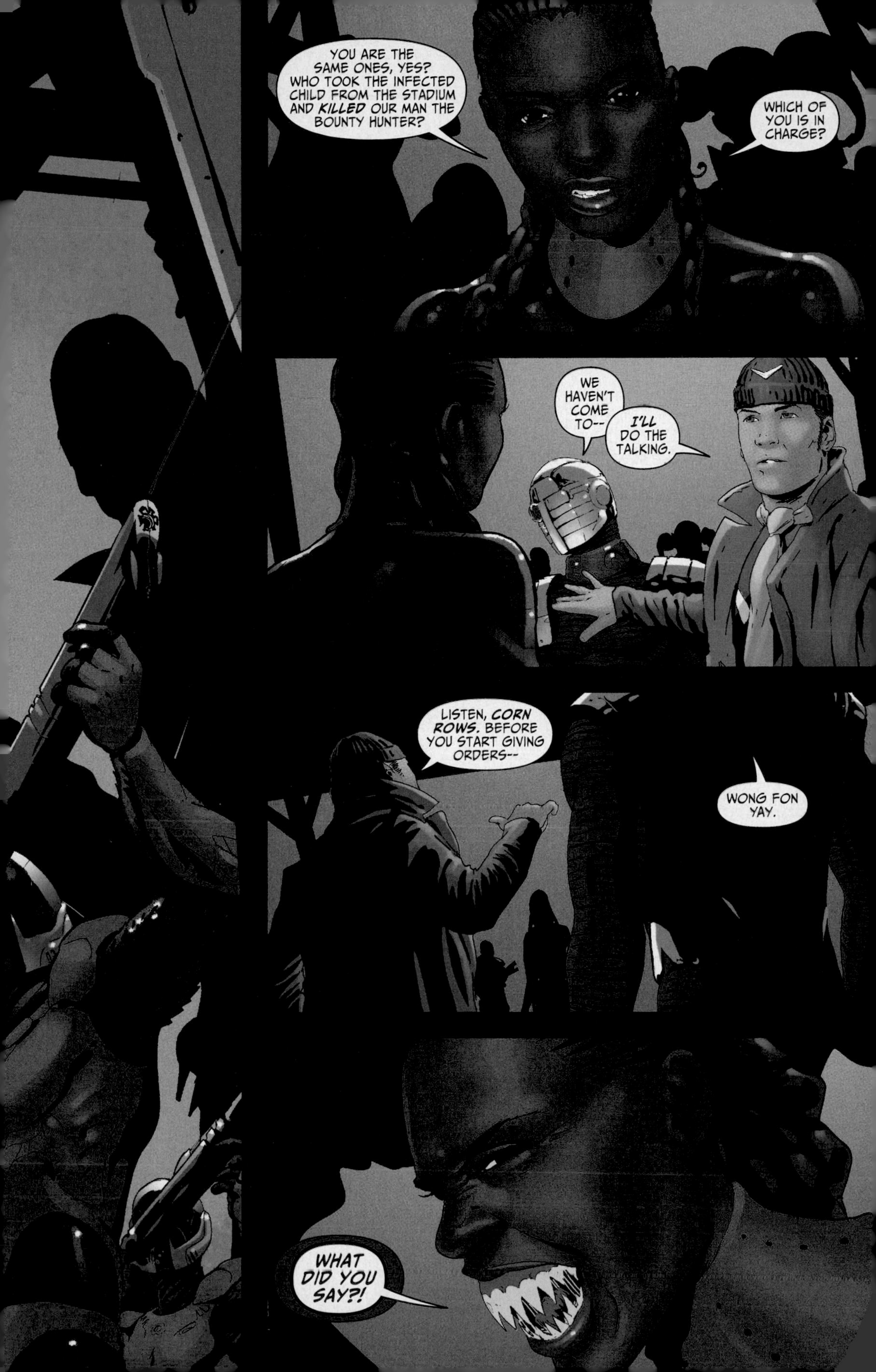
YOU ARE THE SAME ONES, YES? WHO TOOK THE INFECTED CHILD FROM THE STADIUM AND *KILLED* OUR MAN THE BOUNTY HUNTER?
WHICH OF YOU IS IN CHARGE?
WE HAVEN'T COME TO--
I'LL DO THE TALKING.
LISTEN, *CORN ROWS.* BEFORE YOU START GIVING ORDERS--
WONG FON YAY.
WHAT DID YOU SAY?!

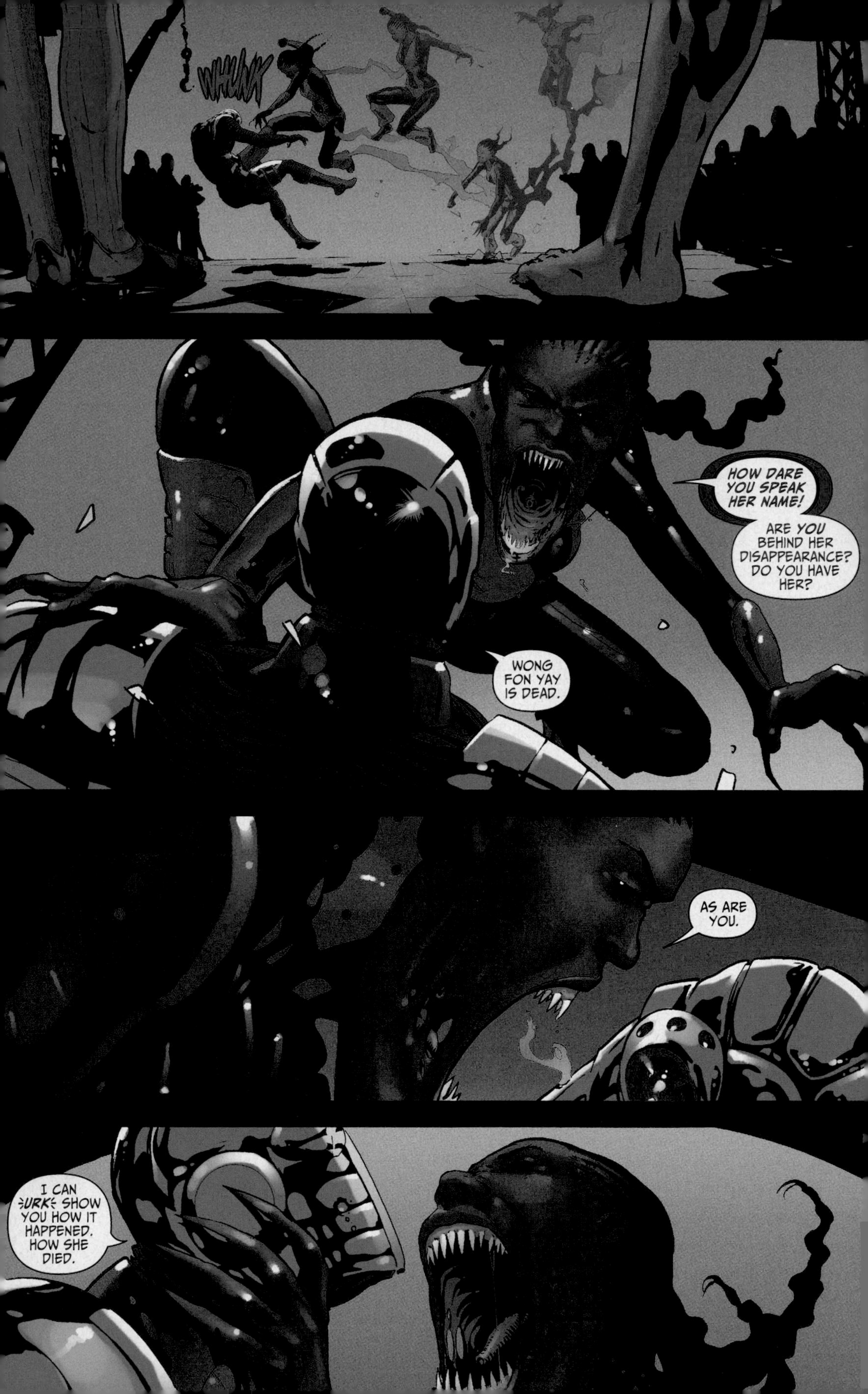
WHUNK
HOW DARE YOU SPEAK HER NAME!
ARE YOU BEHIND HER DISAPPEARANCE? DO YOU HAVE HER?
WONG FON YAY IS DEAD.
AS ARE YOU.
I CAN URK SHOW YOU HOW IT HAPPENED. HOW SHE DIED.

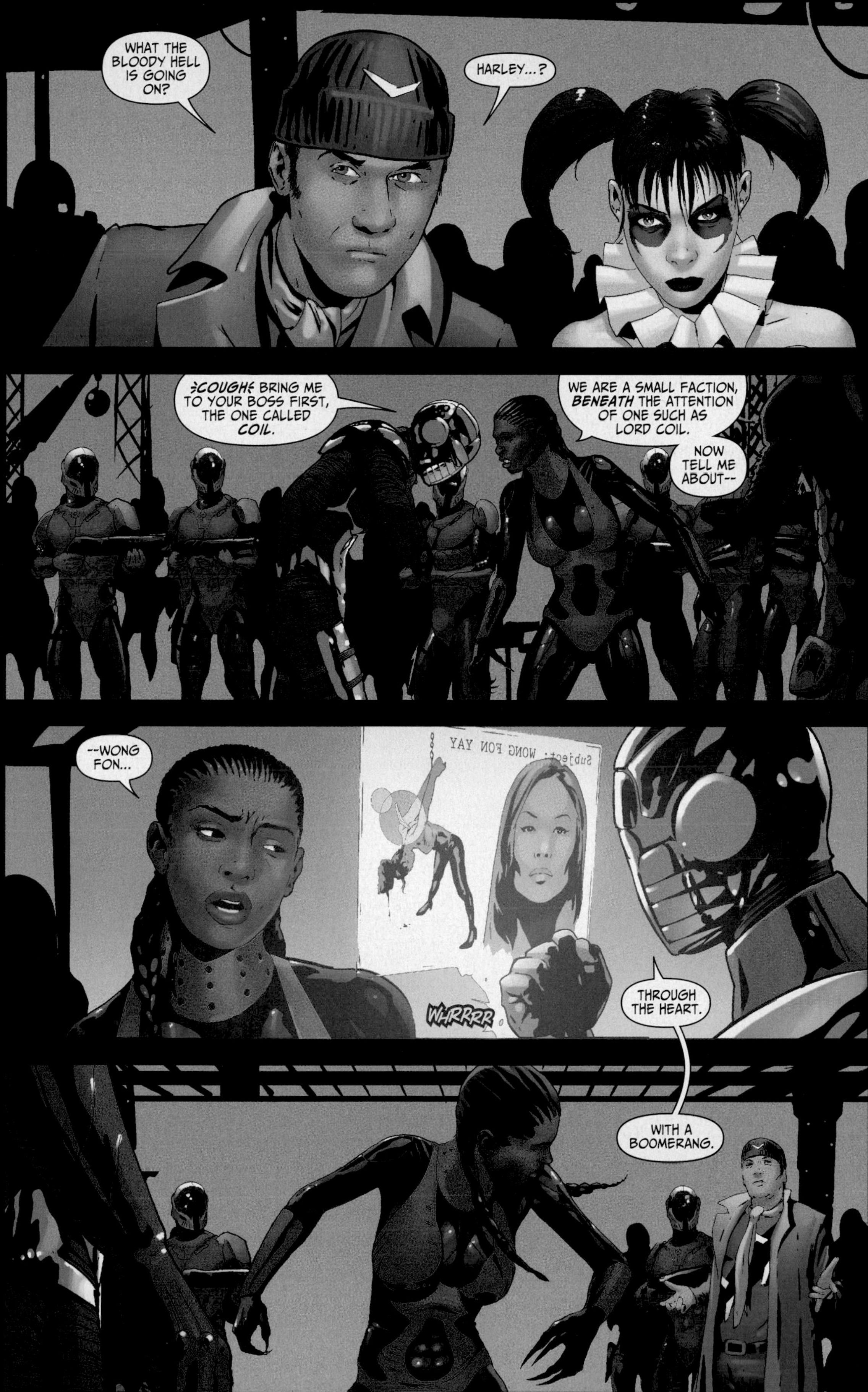
WHAT THE BLOODY HELL IS GOING ON?
HARLEY...?
COUGH BRING ME TO YOUR BOSS FIRST, THE ONE CALLED COIL.
WE ARE A SMALL FACTION, BENEATH THE ATTENTION OF ONE SUCH AS LORD COIL.
NOW TELL ME ABOUT--
--WONG FON...
Subject: WONG FON YAY
WHRRRR
THROUGH THE HEART.
WITH A BOOMERANG.

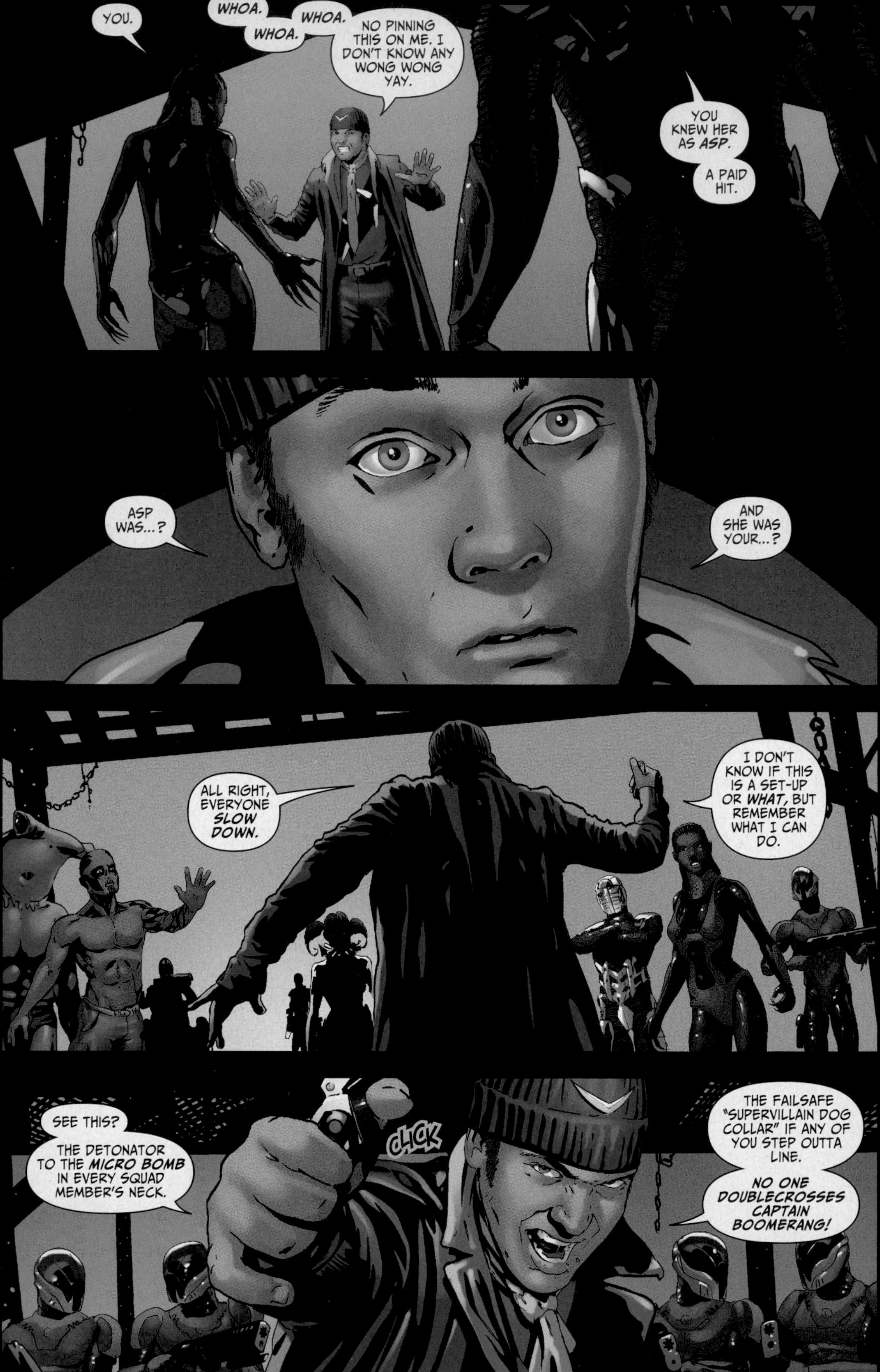
YOU.
WHOA. WHOA. WHOA.
NO PINNING THIS ON ME. I DON'T KNOW ANY WONG WONG YAY.
YOU KNEW HER AS ASP.
A PAID HIT.
ASP WAS...?
AND SHE WAS YOUR...?
ALL RIGHT, EVERYONE SLOW DOWN.
I DON'T KNOW IF THIS IS A SET-UP OR WHAT, BUT REMEMBER WHAT I CAN DO.
SEE THIS?
THE DETONATOR TO THE MICRO BOMB IN EVERY SQUAD MEMBER'S NECK.
CLICK
THE FAILSAFE "SUPERVILLAIN DOG COLLAR" IF ANY OF YOU STEP OUTTA LINE.
NO ONE DOUBLECROSSES CAPTAIN BOOMERANG!

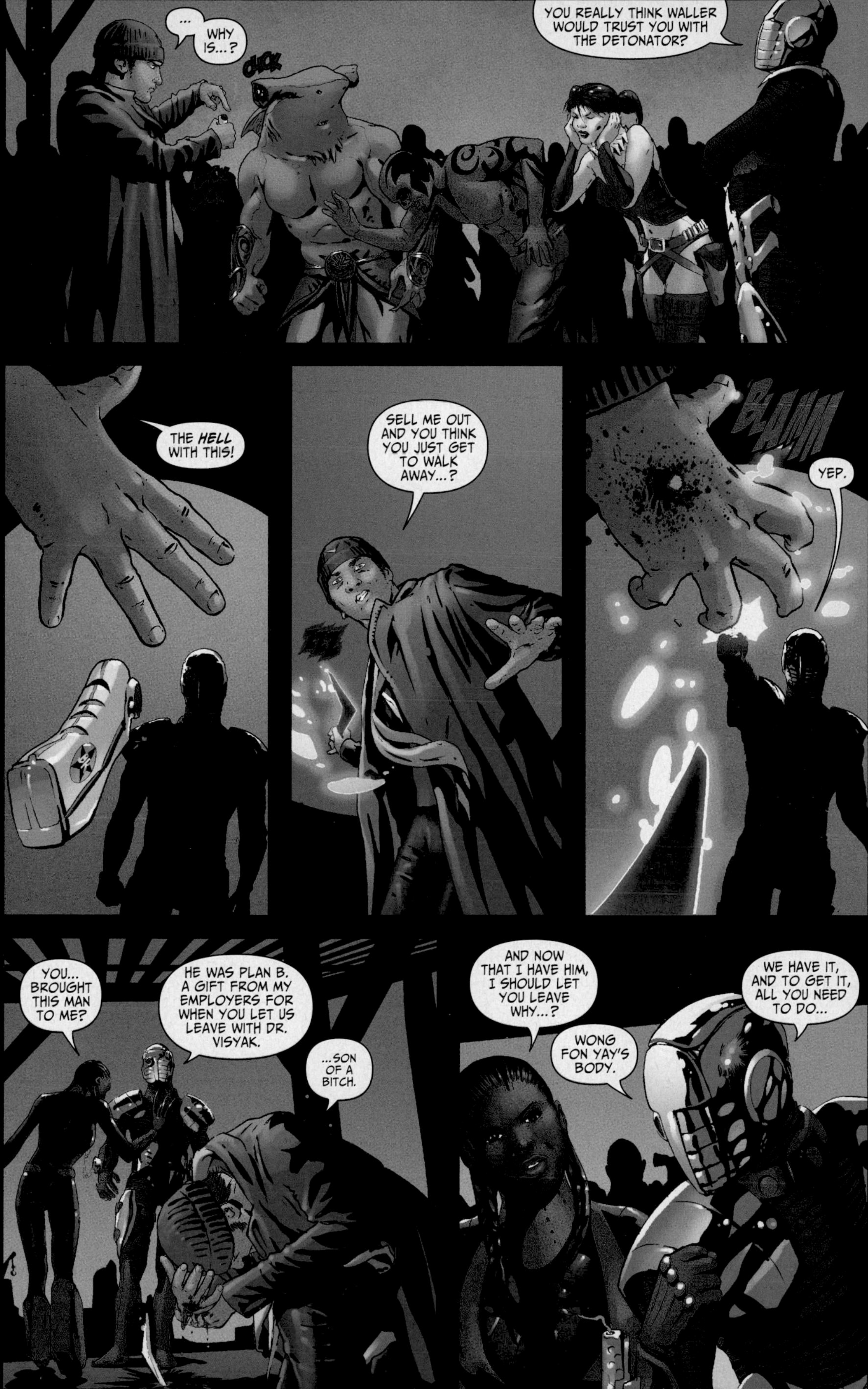

... WHY IS...?
CLICK
YOU REALLY THINK WALLER WOULD TRUST YOU WITH THE DETONATOR?
THE HELL WITH THIS!
SELL ME OUT AND YOU THINK YOU JUST GET TO WALK AWAY...?
BLAMM
YEP.
YOU... BROUGHT THIS MAN TO ME?
HE WAS PLAN B. A GIFT FROM MY EMPLOYERS FOR WHEN YOU LET US LEAVE WITH DR. VISYAK.
...SON OF A BITCH.
AND NOW THAT I HAVE HIM, I SHOULD LET YOU LEAVE WHY...?
WONG FON YAY'S BODY.
WE HAVE IT, AND TO GET IT, ALL YOU NEED TO DO...

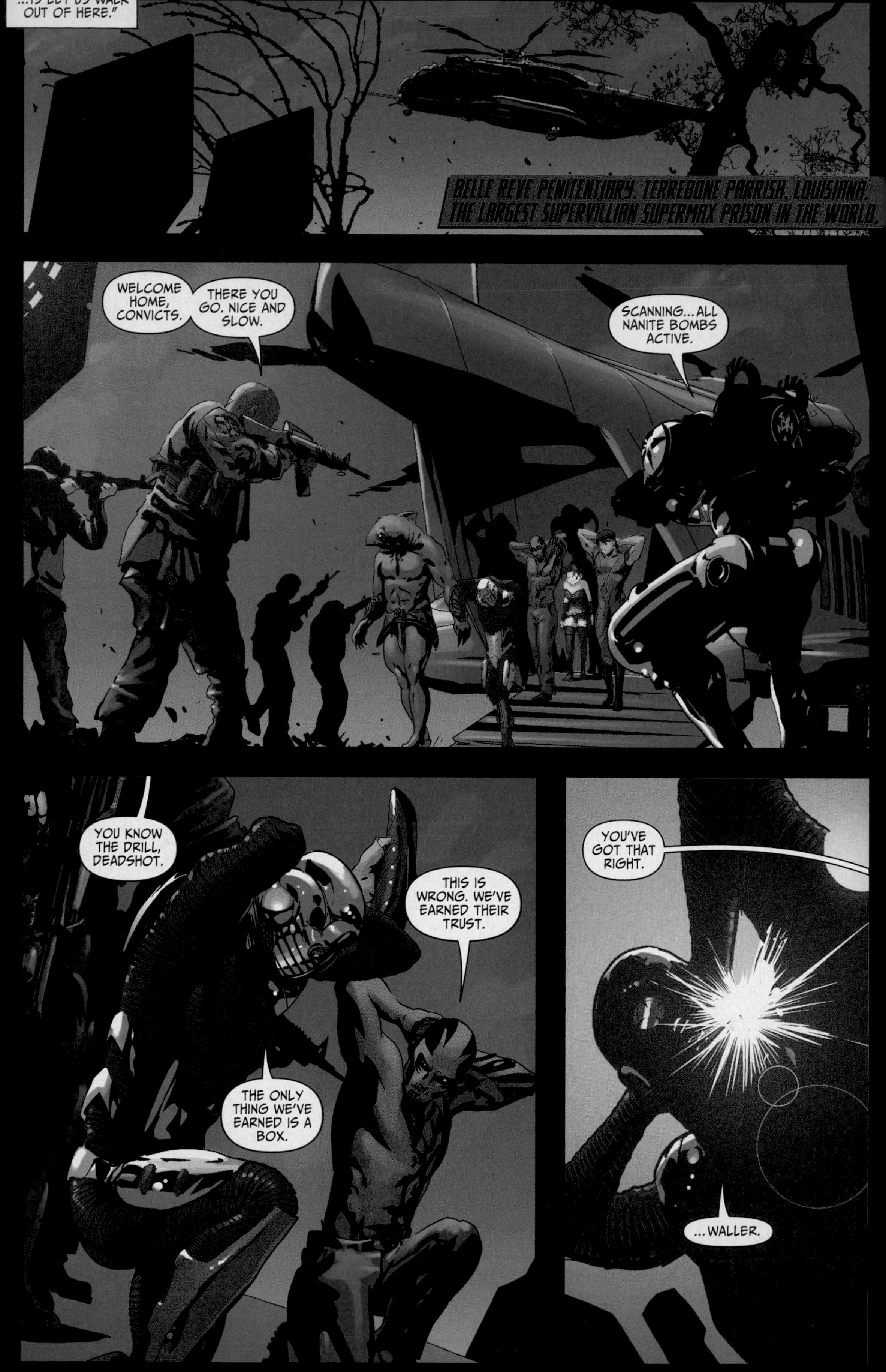
"...IS LET US WALK OUT OF HERE."
BELLE REVE PENITENTIARY. TERREBONE PARRISH, LOUISIANA. THE LARGEST SUPERVILLIAN SUPERMAX PRISON IN THE WORLD.
WELCOME HOME, CONVICTS.
THERE YOU GO. NICE AND SLOW.
SCANNING...ALL NANITE BOMBS ACTIVE.
YOU KNOW THE DRILL, DEADSHOT.
THIS IS WRONG. WE'VE EARNED THEIR TRUST.
THE ONLY THING WE'VE EARNED IS A BOX.
YOU'VE GOT THAT RIGHT.
...WALLER.

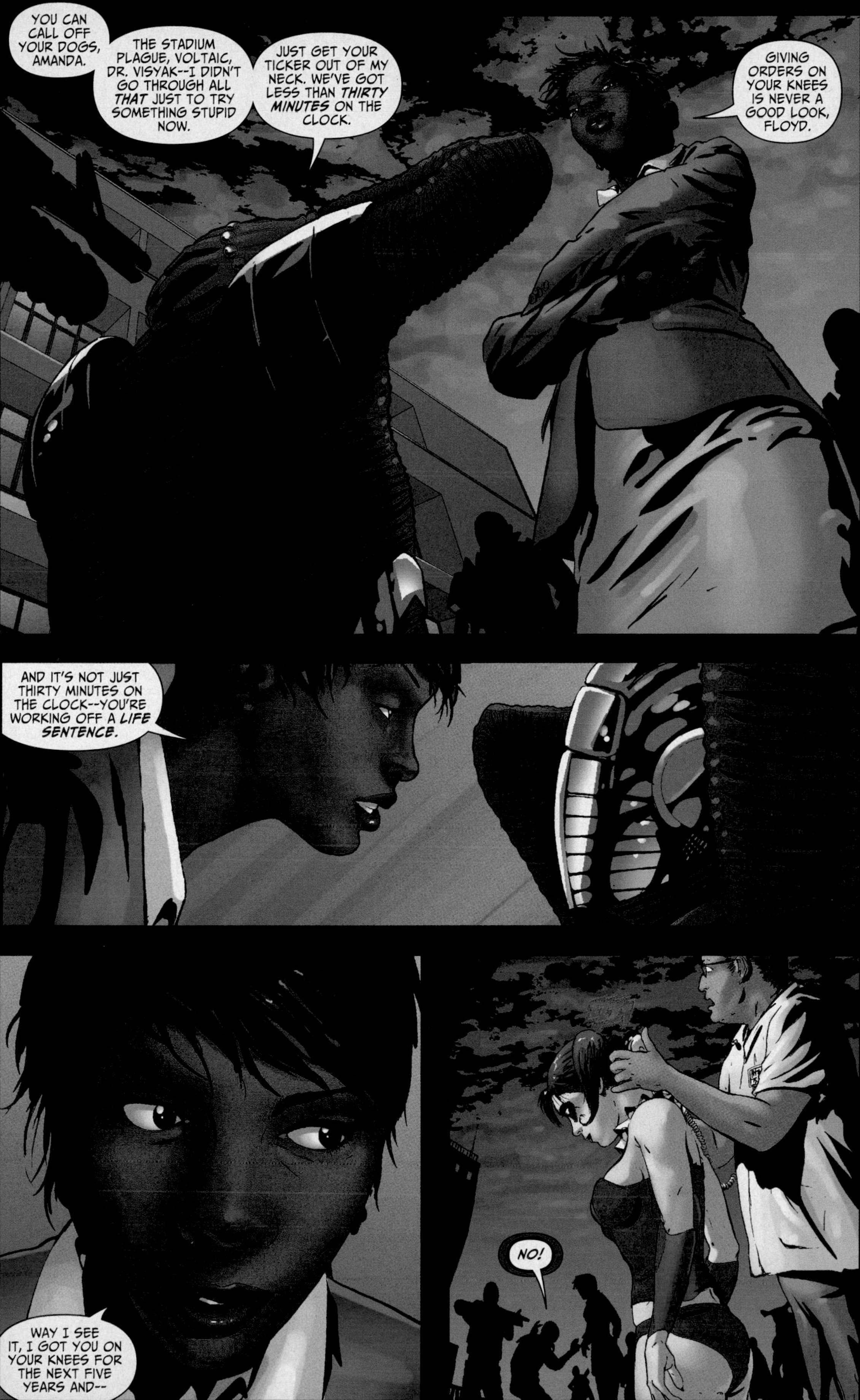
YOU CAN CALL OFF YOUR DOGS, AMANDA.
THE STADIUM PLAGUE, VOLTAIC, DR. VISYAK--I DIDN'T GO THROUGH ALL *THAT* JUST TO TRY SOMETHING STUPID NOW.
JUST GET YOUR TICKER OUT OF MY NECK. WE'VE GOT LESS THAN *THIRTY MINUTES* ON THE CLOCK.
GIVING ORDERS ON YOUR KNEES IS NEVER A GOOD LOOK, FLOYD.
AND IT'S NOT JUST THIRTY MINUTES ON THE CLOCK--YOU'RE WORKING OFF A *LIFE SENTENCE.*
WAY I SEE IT, I GOT YOU ON YOUR KNEES FOR THE NEXT FIVE YEARS AND--
NO!

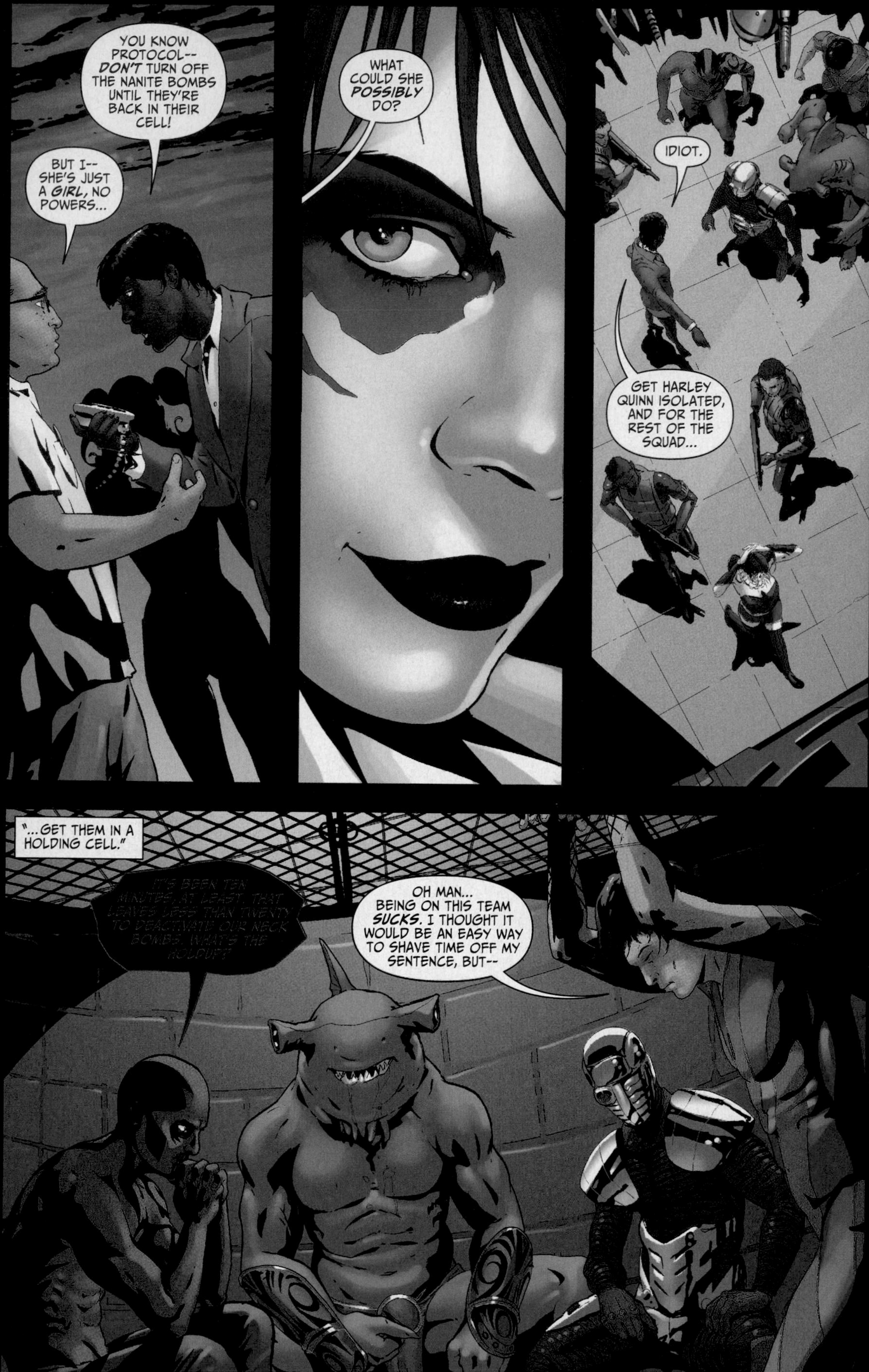

YOU KNOW PROTOCOL-- DON'T TURN OFF THE NANITE BOMBS UNTIL THEY'RE BACK IN THEIR CELL!
BUT I-- SHE'S JUST A GIRL, NO POWERS...
WHAT COULD SHE POSSIBLY DO?
IDIOT.
GET HARLEY QUINN ISOLATED, AND FOR THE REST OF THE SQUAD...
"...GET THEM IN A HOLDING CELL."
IT'S BEEN TEN MINUTES, AT LEAST. THAT LEAVES LESS THAN TWENTY TO DEACTIVATE OUR NECK BOMBS. WHAT'S THE HOLDUP?
OH MAN... BEING ON THIS TEAM SUCKS. I THOUGHT IT WOULD BE AN EASY WAY TO SHAVE TIME OFF MY SENTENCE, BUT--

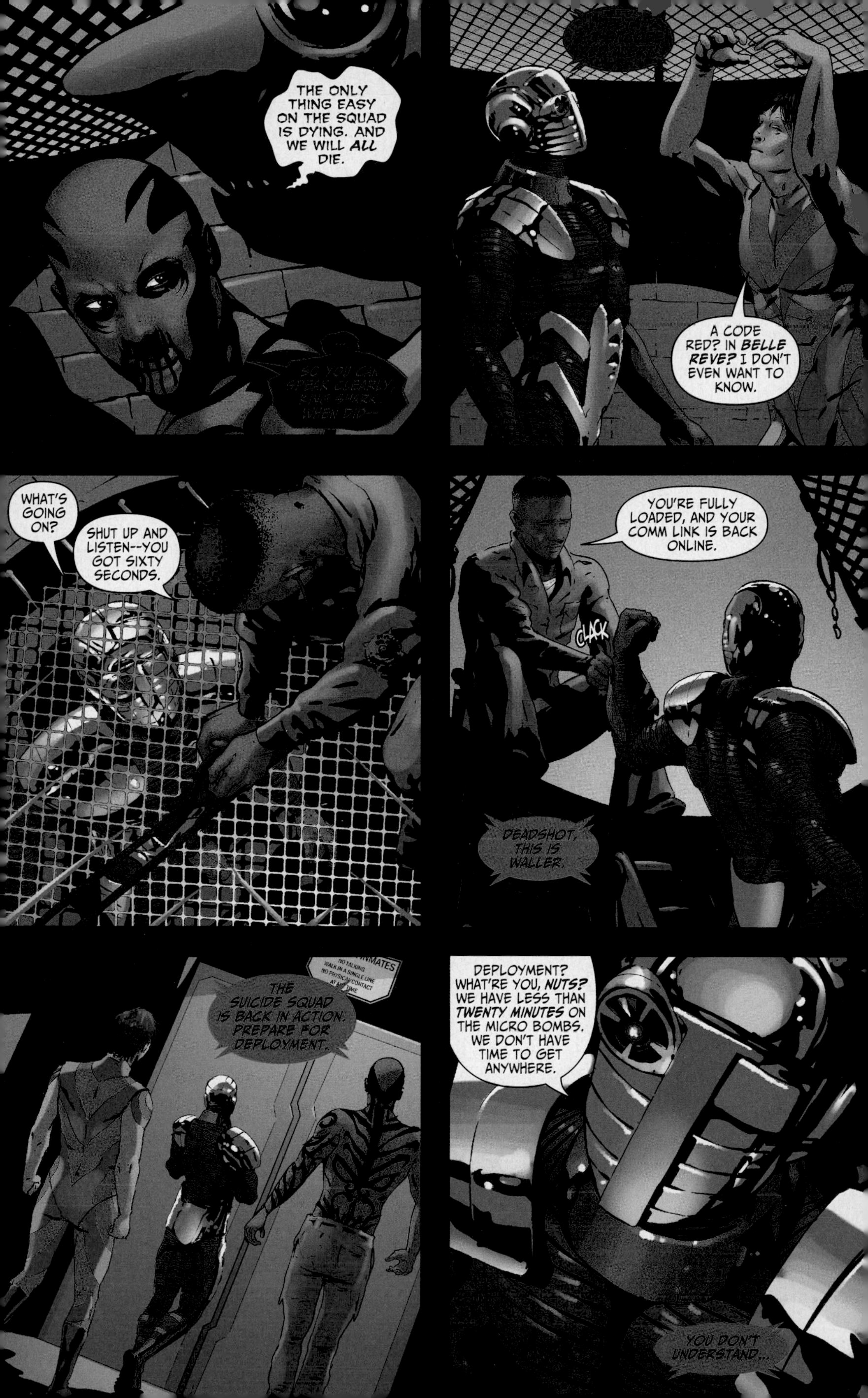
THE ONLY THING EASY ON THE SQUAD IS DYING. AND WE WILL ALL DIE.
SO YOU CAN SPEAK CLEARLY, KING SHARK. WHEN DID--
A CODE RED? IN BELLE REVE? I DON'T EVEN WANT TO KNOW.
WHAT'S GOING ON?
SHUT UP AND LISTEN--YOU GOT SIXTY SECONDS.
YOU'RE FULLY LOADED, AND YOUR COMM LINK IS BACK ONLINE.
CLACK
DEADSHOT, THIS IS WALLER.
INMATES
NO TALKING
WALK IN A SINGLE LINE
NO PHYSICAL CONTACT
TIME
THE SUICIDE SQUAD IS BACK IN ACTION. PREPARE FOR DEPLOYMENT.
DEPLOYMENT? WHAT'RE YOU, NUTS? WE HAVE LESS THAN TWENTY MINUTES ON THE MICRO BOMBS. WE DON'T HAVE TIME TO GET ANYWHERE.
YOU DON'T UNDERSTAND...

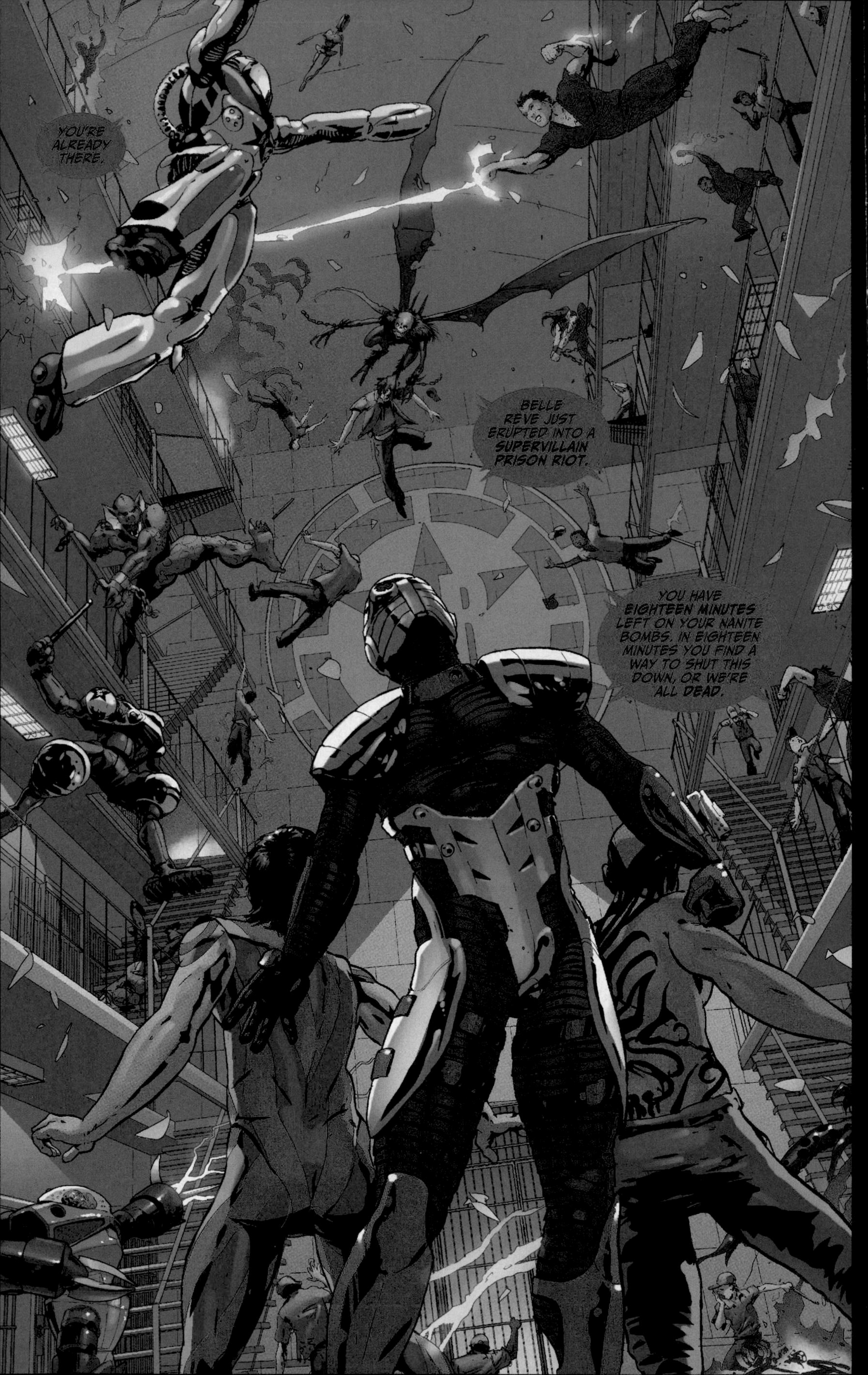
YOU'RE ALREADY THERE.
BELLE REVE JUST ERUPTED INTO A SUPERVILLAIN PRISON RIOT.
YOU HAVE EIGHTEEN MINUTES LEFT ON YOUR NANITE BOMBS. IN EIGHTEEN MINUTES YOU FIND A WAY TO SHUT THIS DOWN, OR WE'RE ALL DEAD.

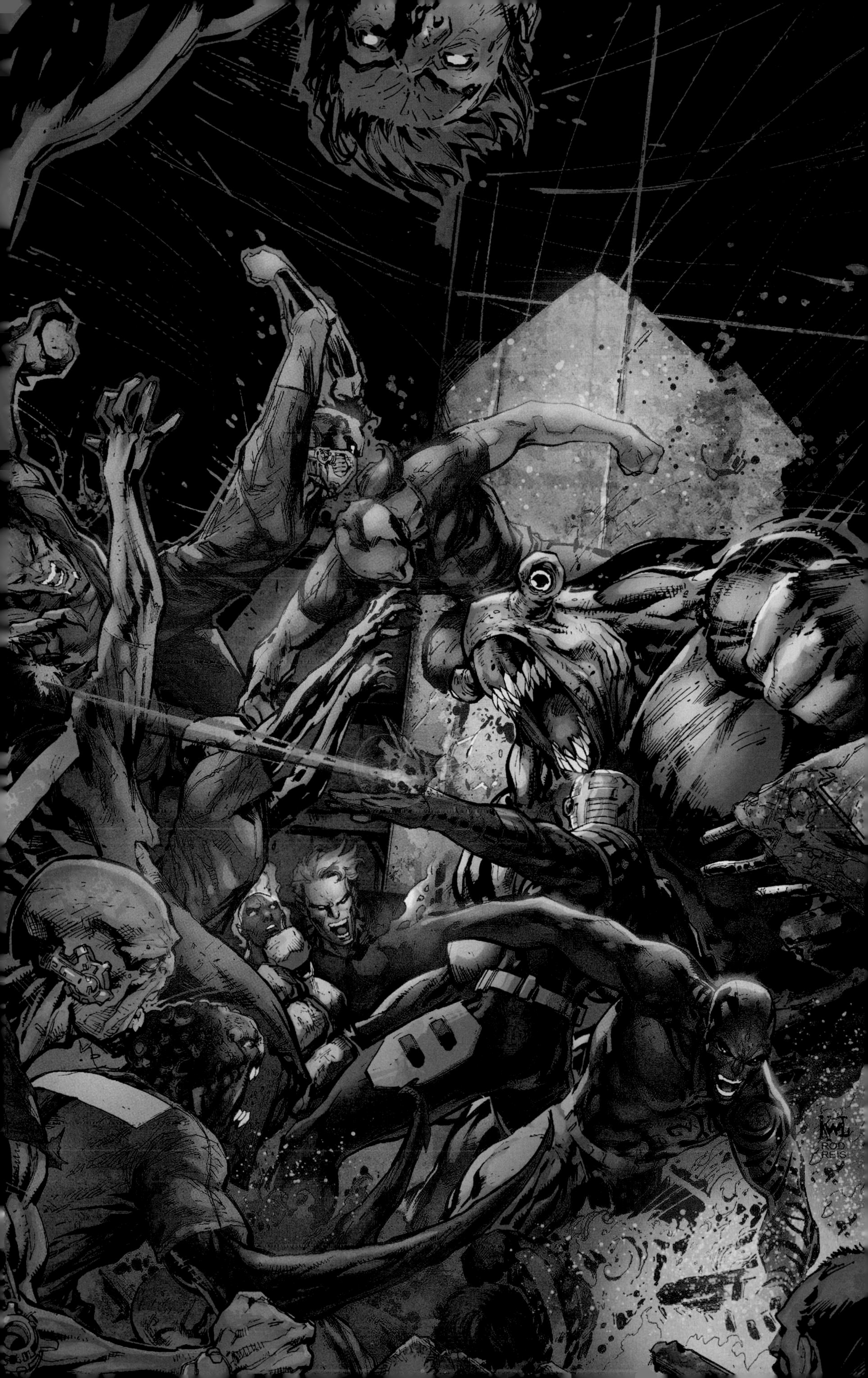
ROD REIS

ABANDON ALL HOPE

ADAM GLASS
writer

FEDERICO DALLOCCHIO
artist

cover art by KEN LASHLEY & ROD REIS

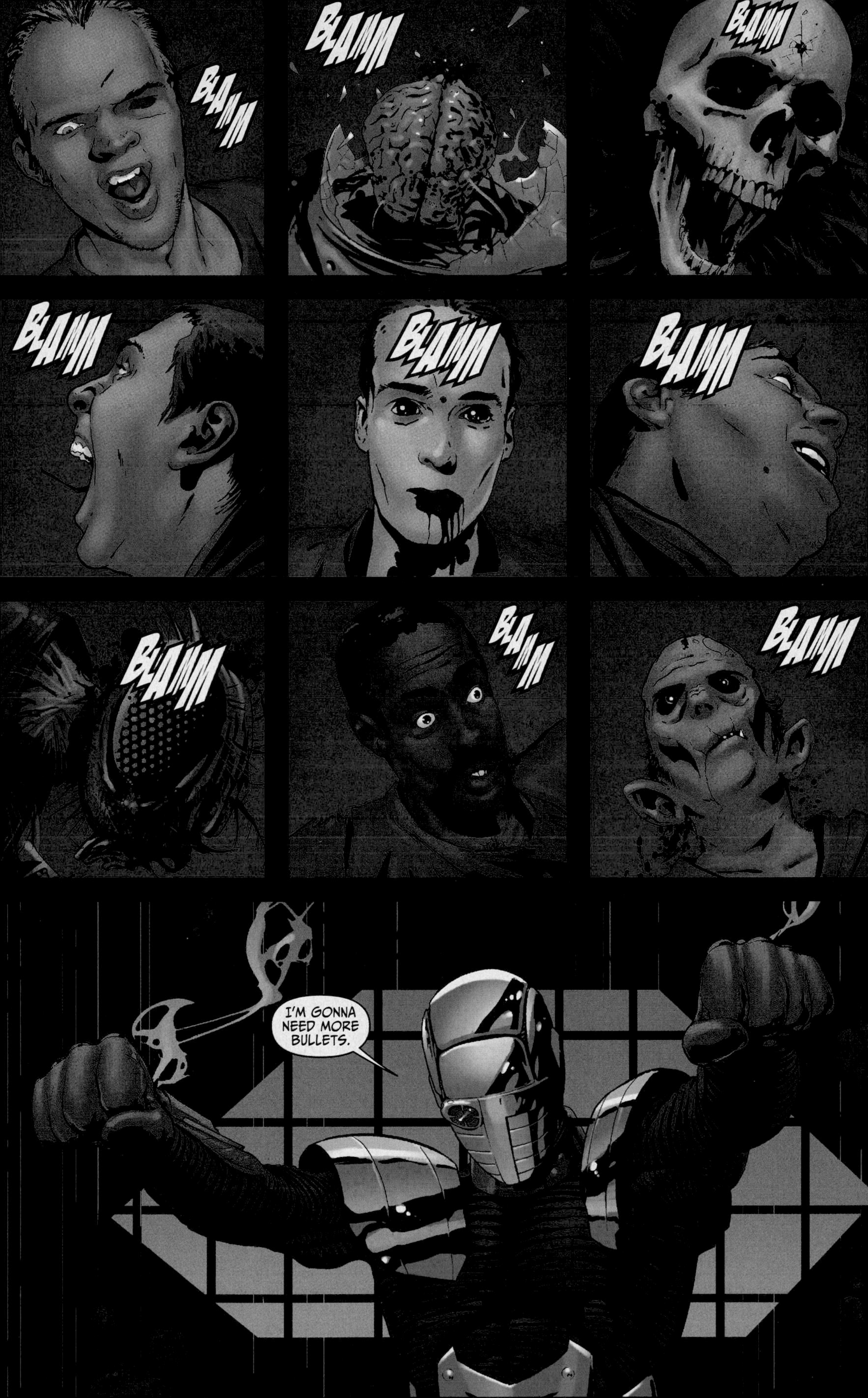
BLAMM
BLAMM
BLAMM
BLAMM
BLAMM
BLAMM
BLAMM
BLAMM
BLAMM
I'M GONNA NEED MORE BULLETS.

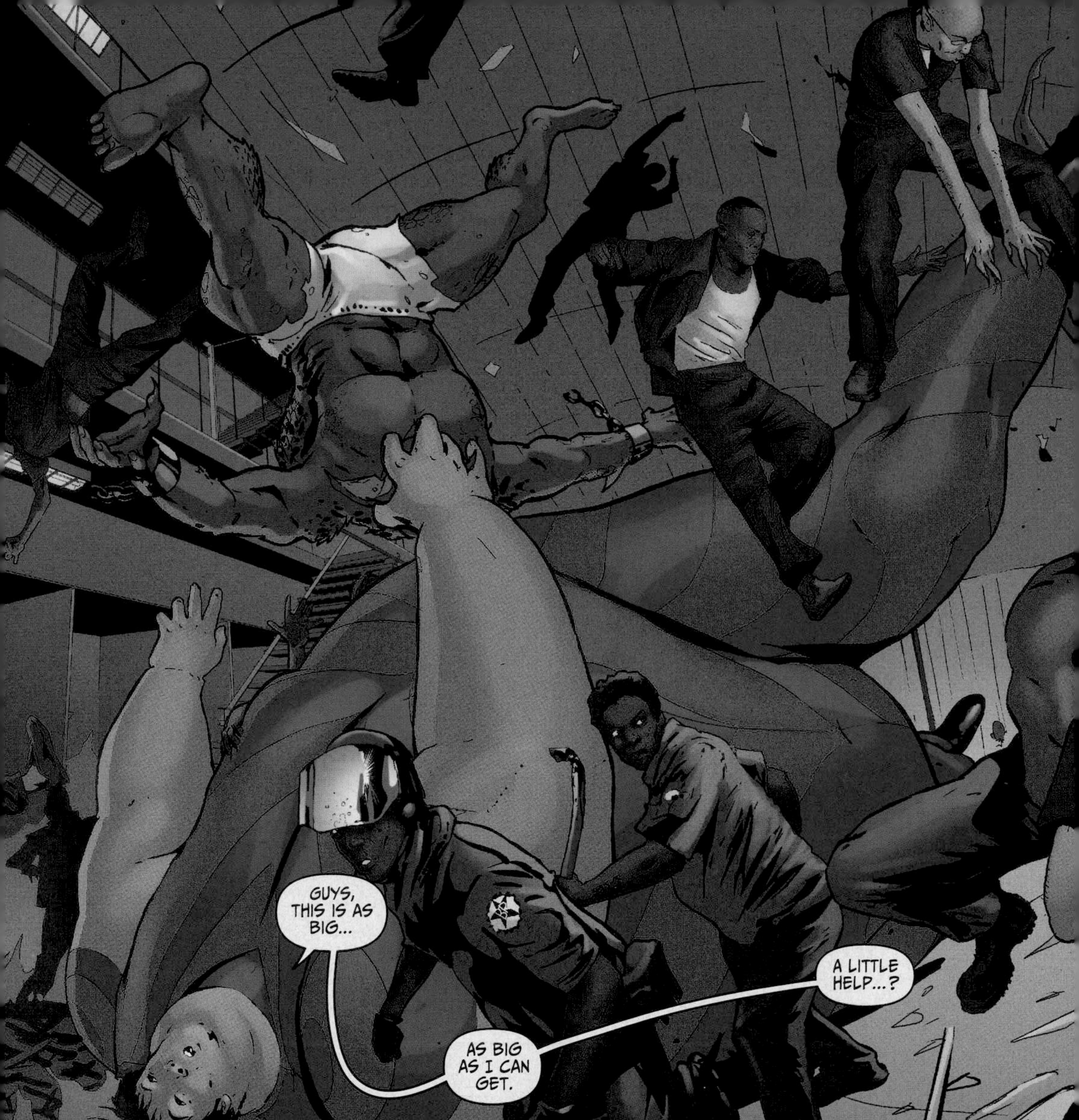
GUYS, THIS IS AS BIG...
AS BIG AS I CAN GET.
A LITTLE HELP...?

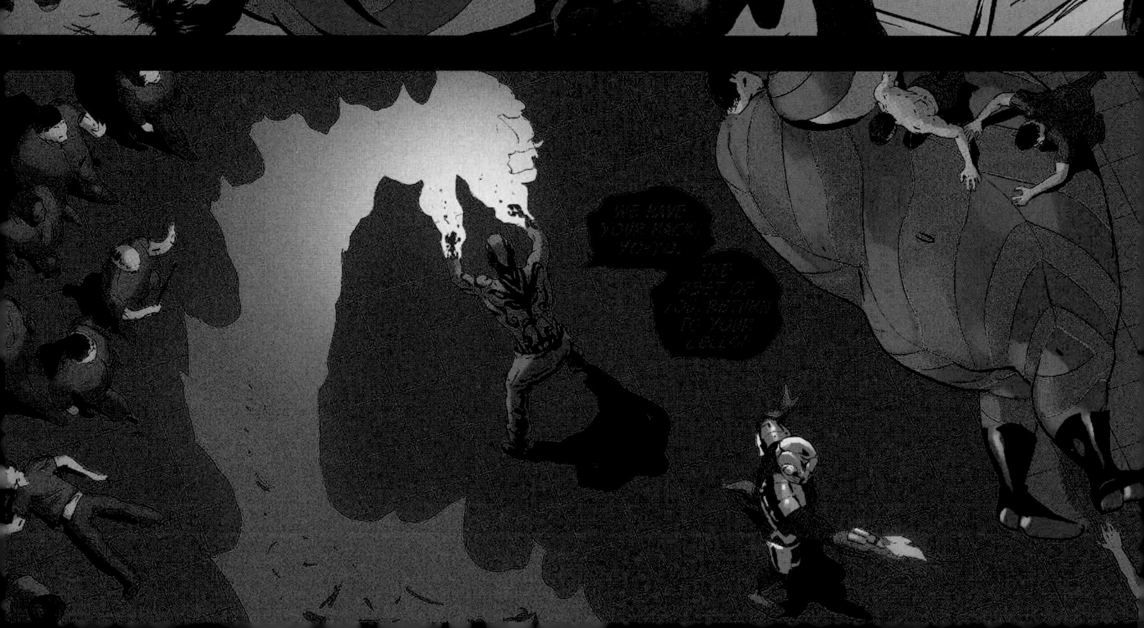
WE HAVE YOUR BACK,

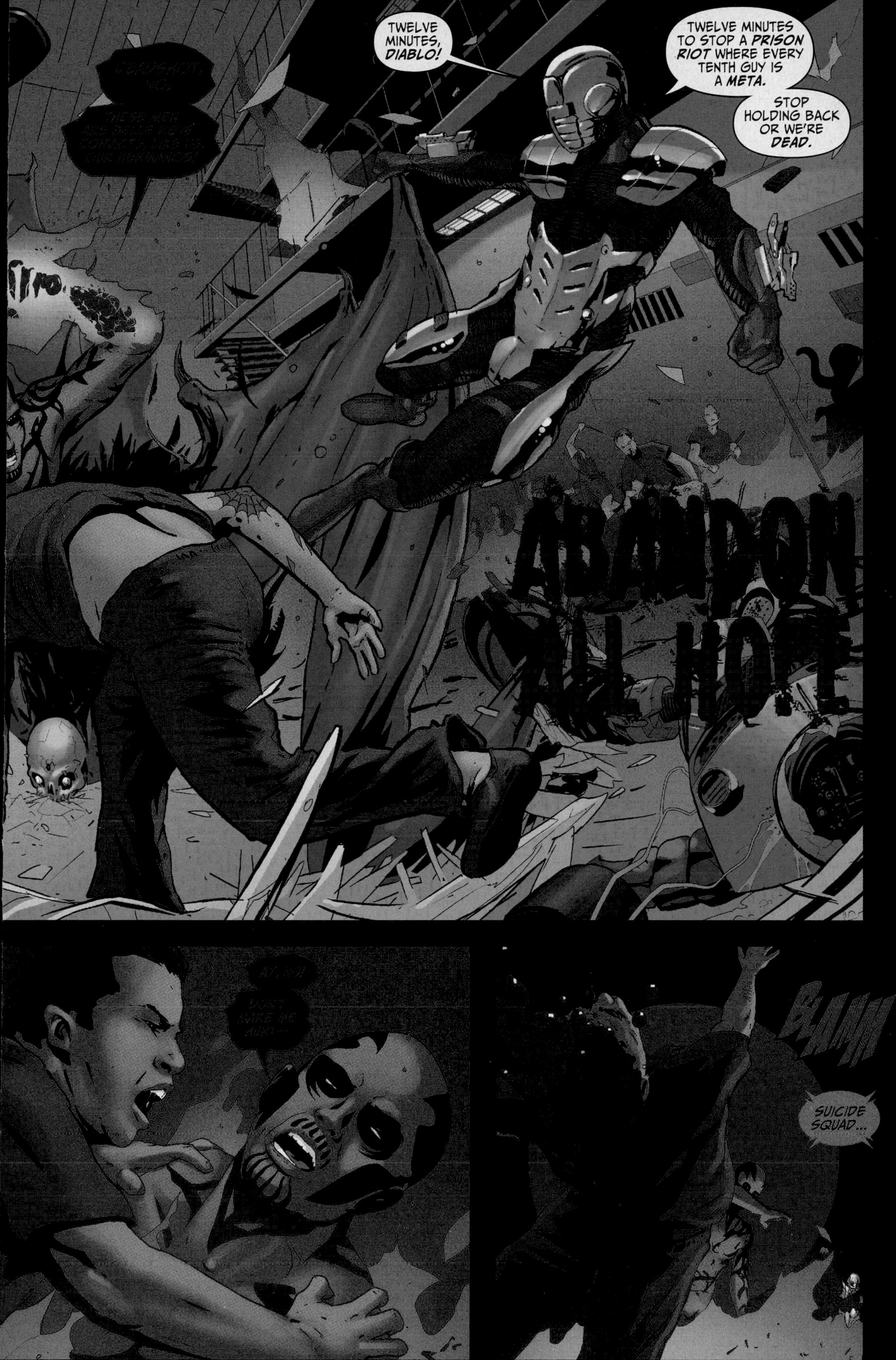
TWELVE MINUTES, DIABLO!
TWELVE MINUTES TO STOP A PRISON RIOT WHERE EVERY TENTH GUY IS A META.
STOP HOLDING BACK OR WE'RE DEAD.
ABANDON
ALL HOPE
BLAMM
SUICIDE SQUAD...

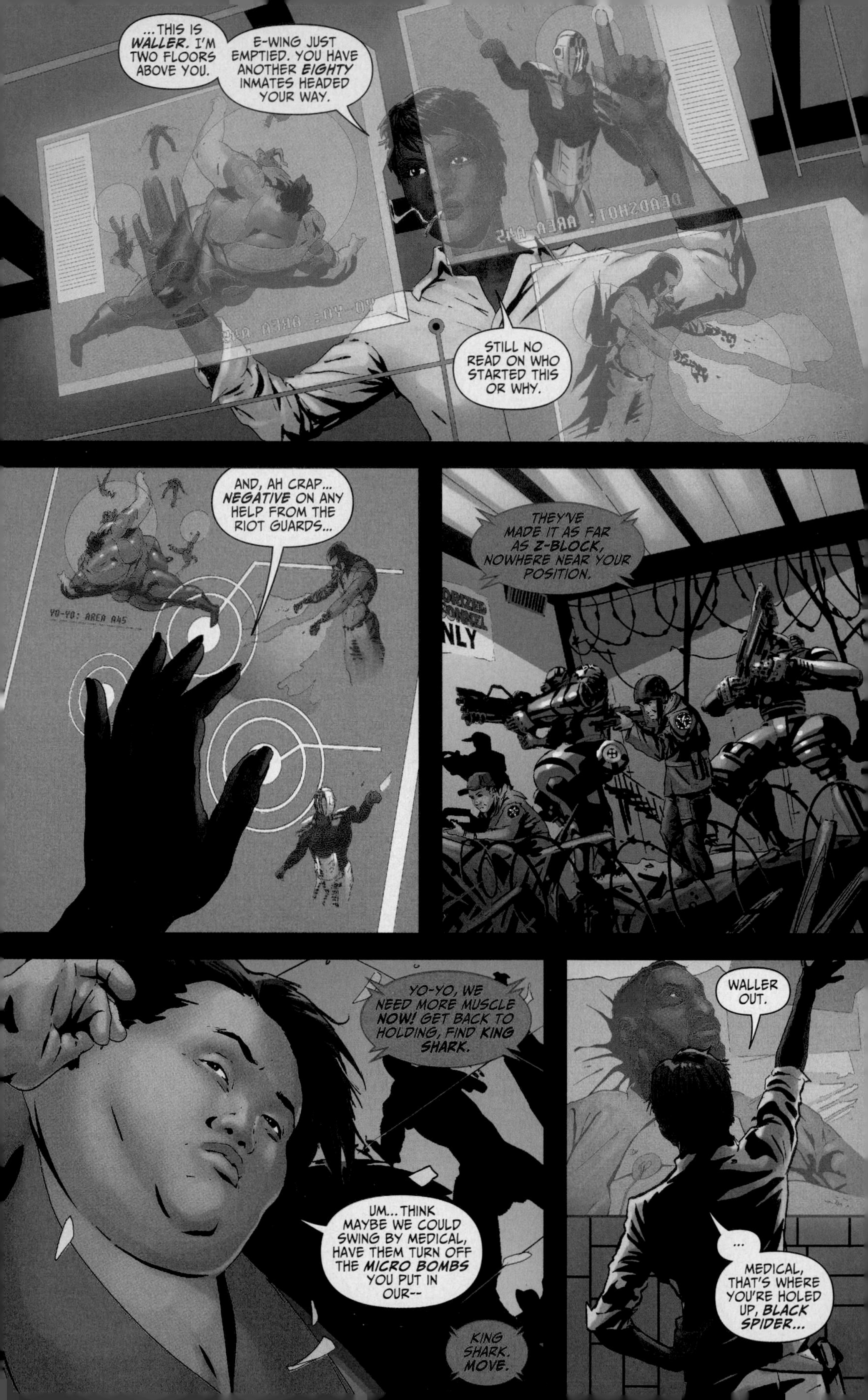
...THIS IS WALLER. I'M TWO FLOORS ABOVE YOU.
E-WING JUST EMPTIED. YOU HAVE ANOTHER EIGHTY INMATES HEADED YOUR WAY.
DEADSHOT: AREA A45
YO-YO: AREA A45
STILL NO READ ON WHO STARTED THIS OR WHY.
AND, AH CRAP... NEGATIVE ON ANY HELP FROM THE RIOT GUARDS...
YO-YO: AREA A45
THEY'VE MADE IT AS FAR AS Z-BLOCK, NOWHERE NEAR YOUR POSITION.
NLY
YO-YO, WE NEED MORE MUSCLE NOW! GET BACK TO HOLDING, FIND KING SHARK.
UM...THINK MAYBE WE COULD SWING BY MEDICAL, HAVE THEM TURN OFF THE MICRO BOMBS YOU PUT IN OUR--
KING SHARK. MOVE.
WALLER OUT.
...
MEDICAL, THAT'S WHERE YOU'RE HOLED UP, BLACK SPIDER...

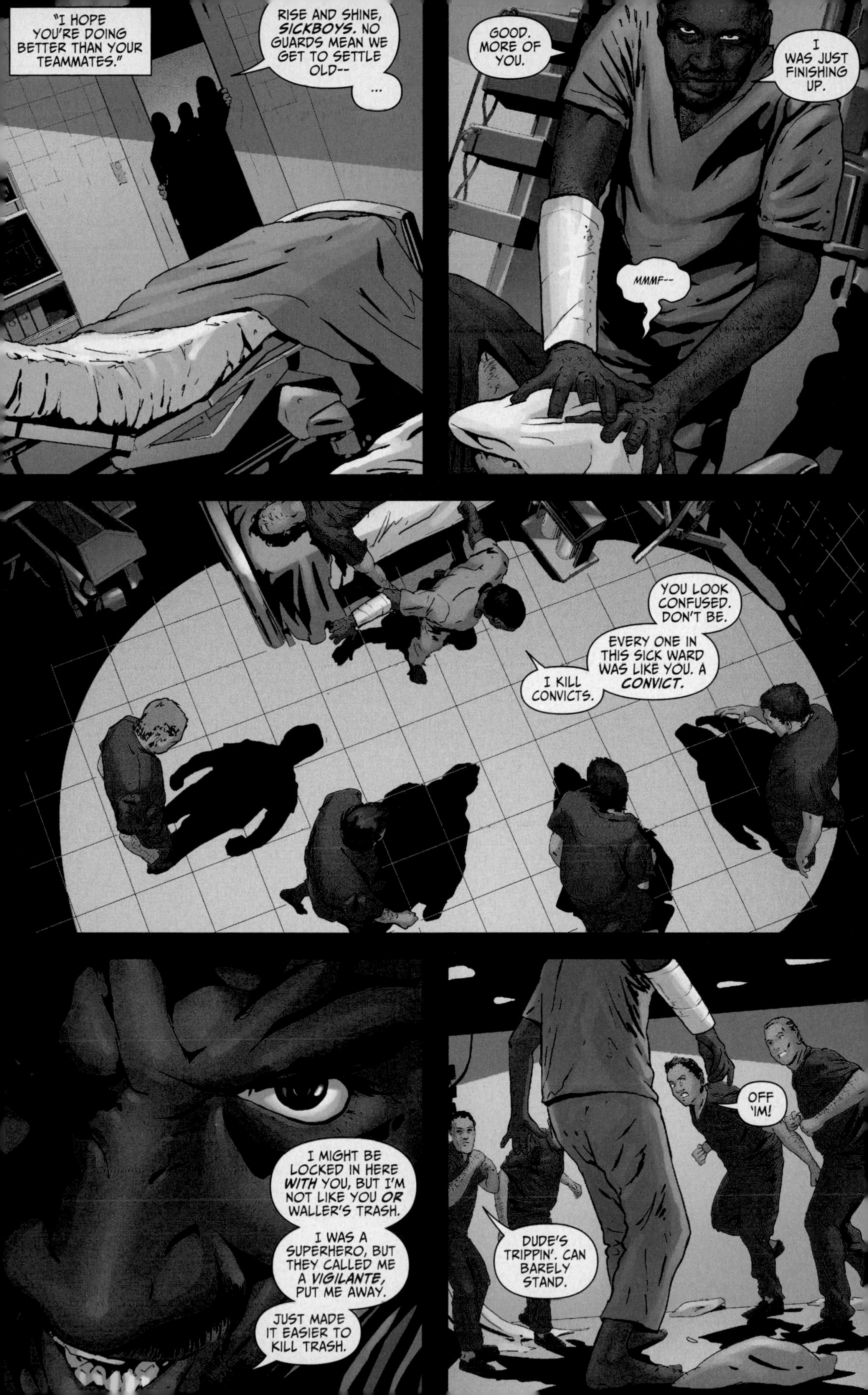
"I HOPE YOU'RE DOING BETTER THAN YOUR TEAMMATES."
RISE AND SHINE, **SICKBOYS.** NO GUARDS MEAN WE GET TO SETTLE OLD--
...
GOOD. MORE OF YOU.
I WAS JUST FINISHING UP.
MMMF--
YOU LOOK CONFUSED. DON'T BE.
EVERY ONE IN THIS SICK WARD WAS LIKE YOU. A **CONVICT.**
I KILL CONVICTS.
I MIGHT BE LOCKED IN HERE **WITH** YOU, BUT I'M NOT LIKE YOU **OR** WALLER'S TRASH.
I WAS A SUPERHERO, BUT THEY CALLED ME A **VIGILANTE,** PUT ME AWAY.
JUST MADE IT EASIER TO KILL TRASH.
OFF 'IM!
DUDE'S TRIPPIN'. CAN BARELY STAND.

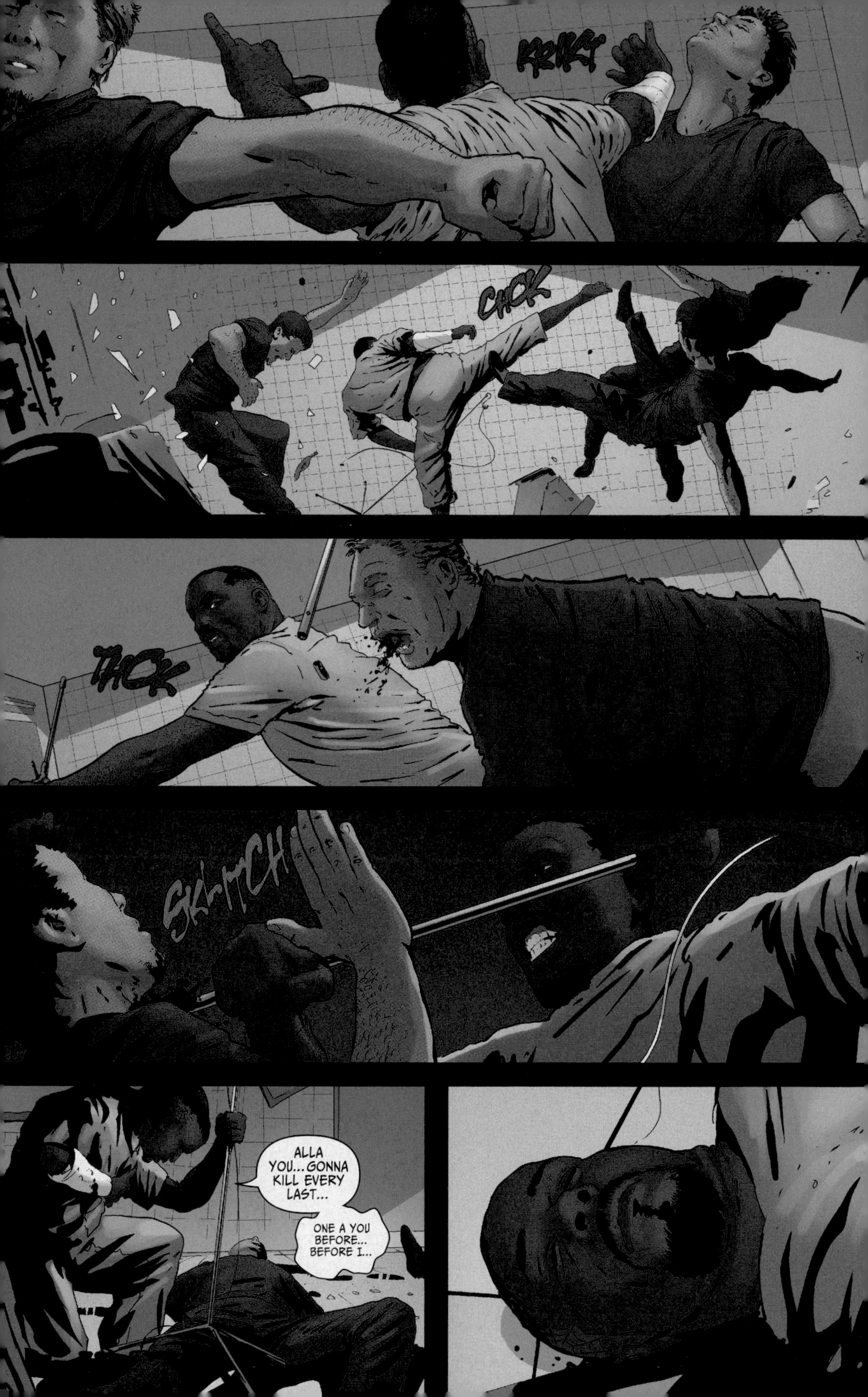
KRAKT
CHOK
THOK
ALLA YOU... GONNA KILL EVERY LAST...
ONE A YOU BEFORE... BEFORE I...

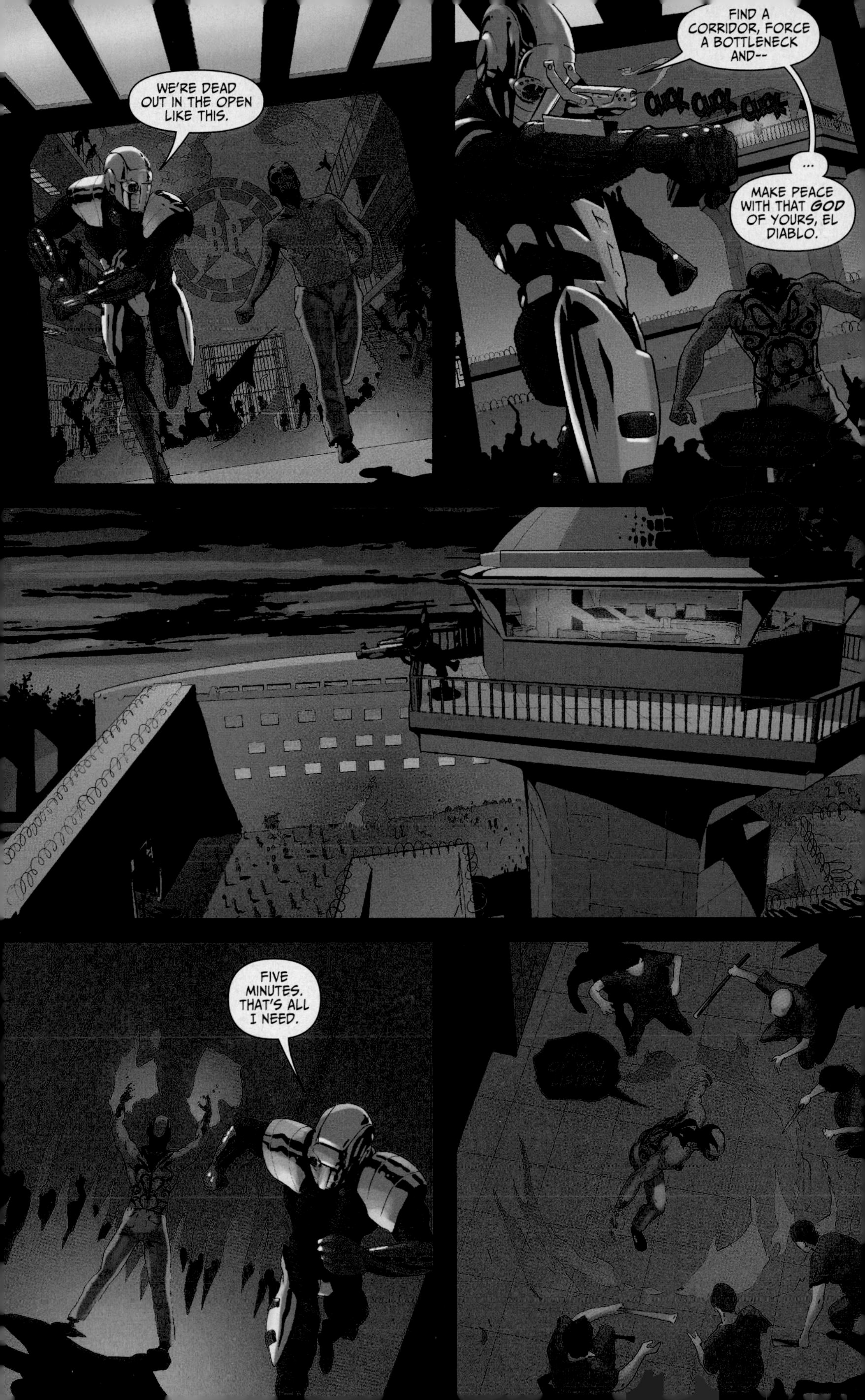
WE'RE DEAD OUT IN THE OPEN LIKE THIS.
FIND A CORRIDOR, FORCE A BOTTLENECK AND--
CLICK CLICK CLICK
...
MAKE PEACE WITH THAT GOD OF YOURS, EL DIABLO.
FIVE MINUTES. THAT'S ALL I NEED.

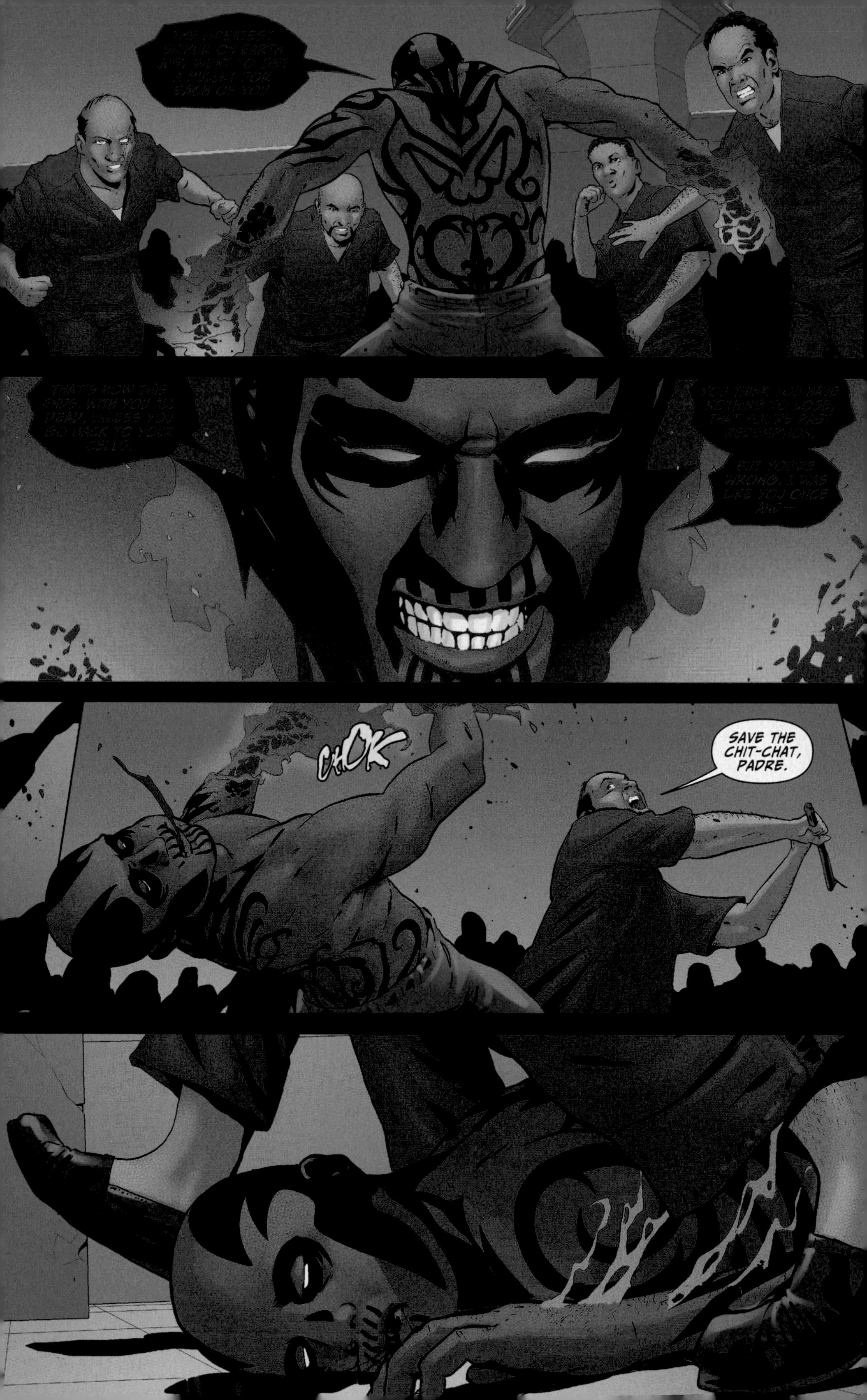
THE GREATEST SNIPER ON EARTH JUST WENT TO GET A BULLET FOR EACH OF YOU.
THAT'S HOW THIS ENDS, WITH YOU ALL DEAD, UNLESS YOU GO BACK TO YOUR CELLS.
YOU THINK YOU HAVE NOTHING TO LOSE, THAT YOU'RE PAST REDEMPTION.
BUT YOU'RE WRONG. I WAS LIKE YOU ONCE AND--
CHOK
SAVE THE CHIT-CHAT, PADRE.

DAMMIT.

I NEED MORE BOOTS ON THE GROUND. WHERE THE HELL IS HARLEY QUINN?

YO-YO, PROGRESS?

SUBJECT IDLE

SUBJECT IDLE

I'M AT THE HOLDING CELL, BUT SOMETHING'S WRONG WITH KING SHARK.

HE'S JUST...SITTING THERE.

KING SHARK...?

HEY BUDDY, IT'S ME, YO-YO.

NOTHING.

I THINK HE'S SICK. HE'S SO STILL HE MIGHT EVEN BE--

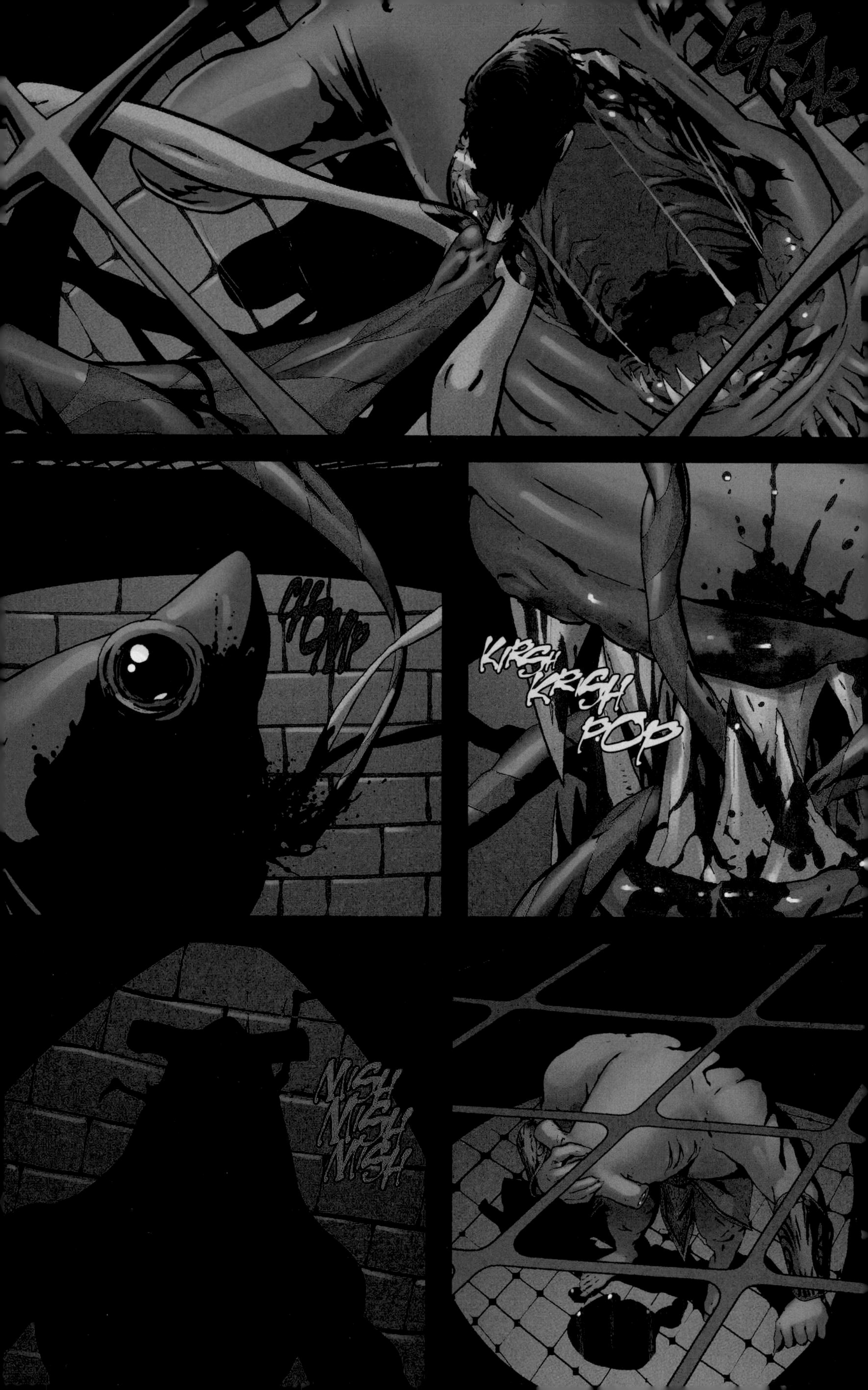
GRAR
CHOMP
KIRSH KRISH POP
NISH NISH NISH

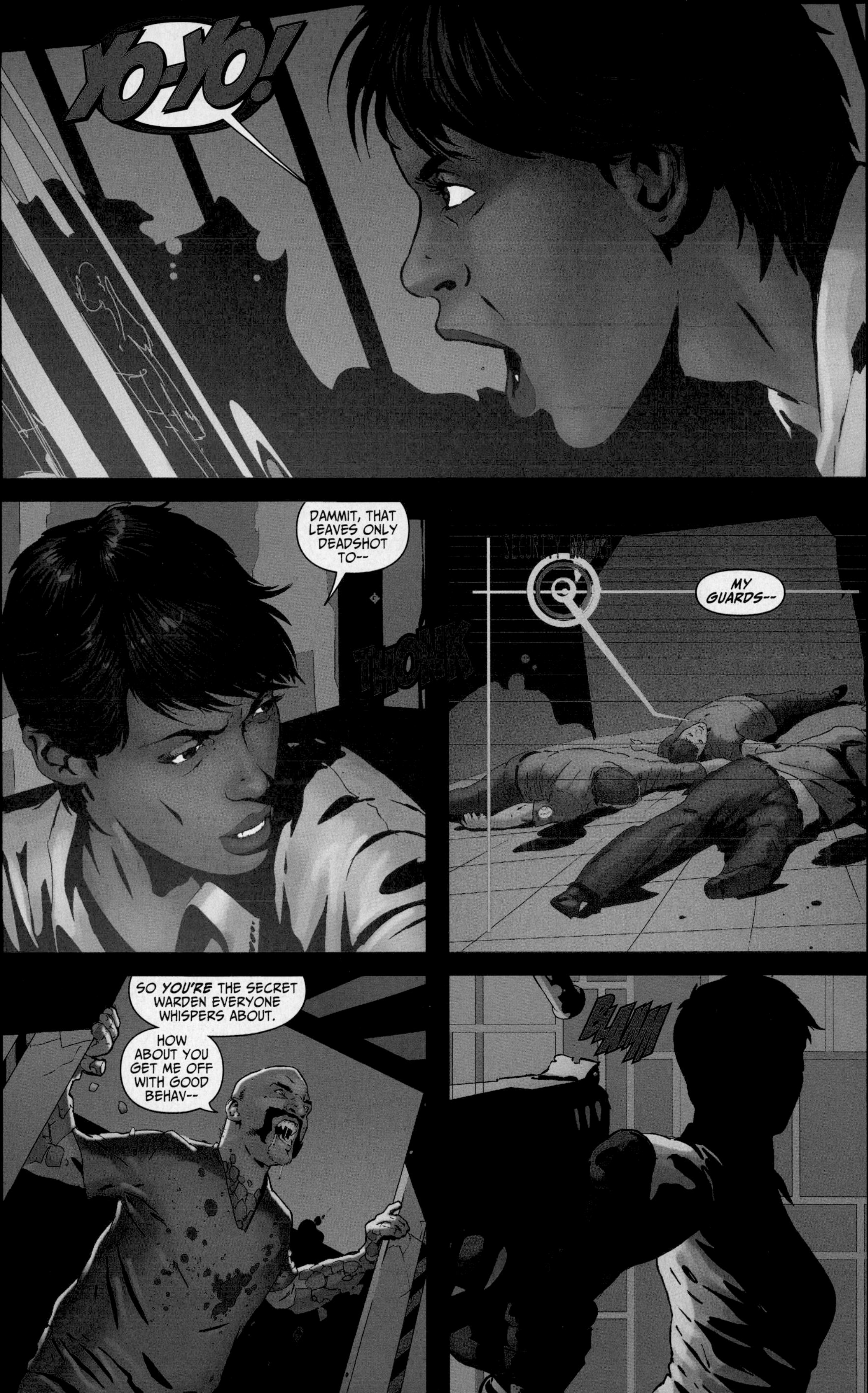
YO-YO!
DAMMIT, THAT LEAVES ONLY DEADSHOT TO--
THONK
MY GUARDS--
SO YOU'RE THE SECRET WARDEN EVERYONE WHISPERS ABOUT.
HOW ABOUT YOU GET ME OFF WITH GOOD BEHAV--
BLAM

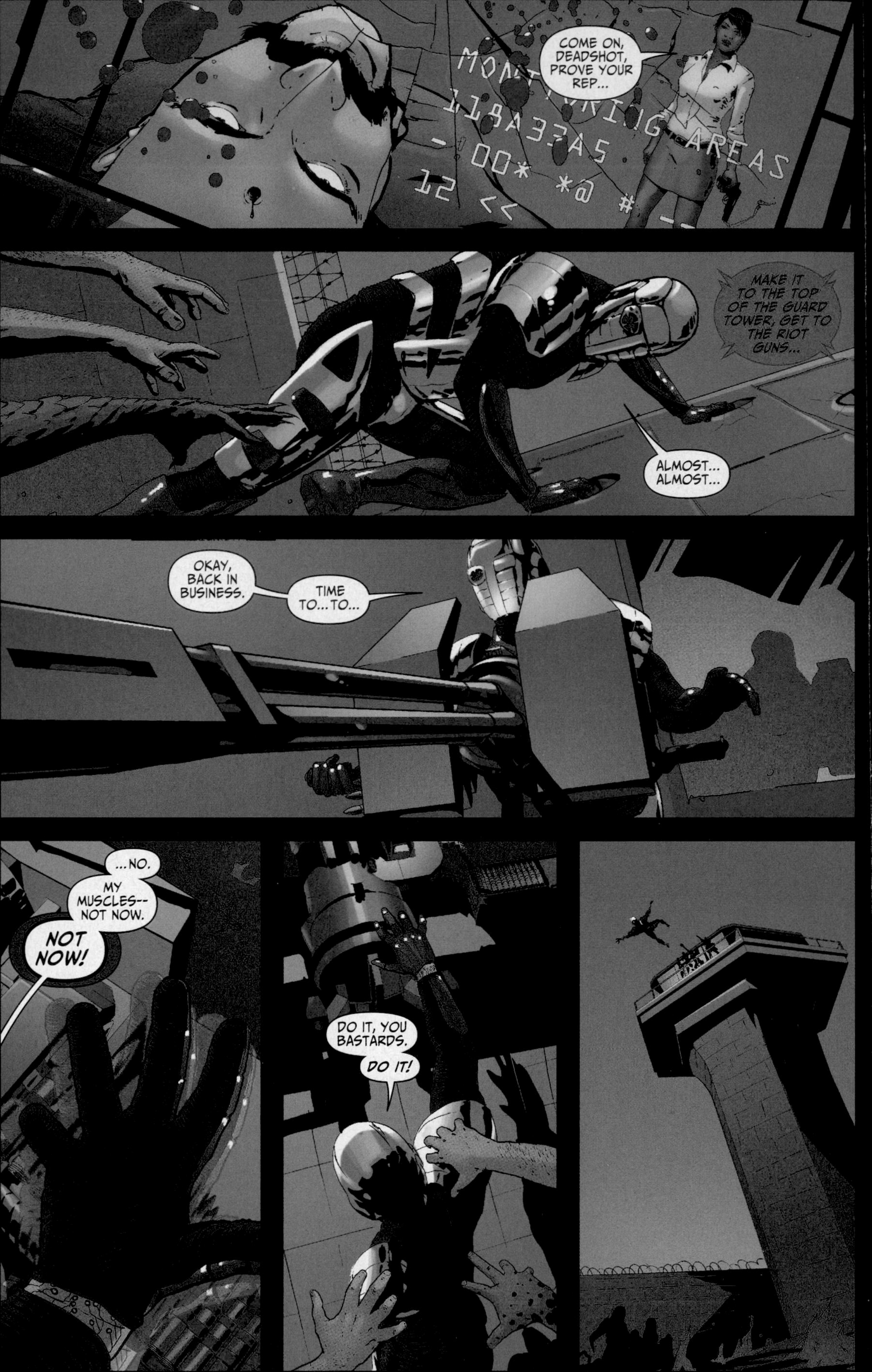

MONITORING AREAS
118A33A5
-00* *@ #
12 <<
COME ON, DEADSHOT, PROVE YOUR REP...
MAKE IT TO THE TOP OF THE GUARD TOWER, GET TO THE RIOT GUNS...
ALMOST... ALMOST...
OKAY, BACK IN BUSINESS.
TIME TO... TO...
...NO.
MY MUSCLES-- NOT NOW.
NOT NOW!
DO IT, YOU BASTARDS.
DO IT!

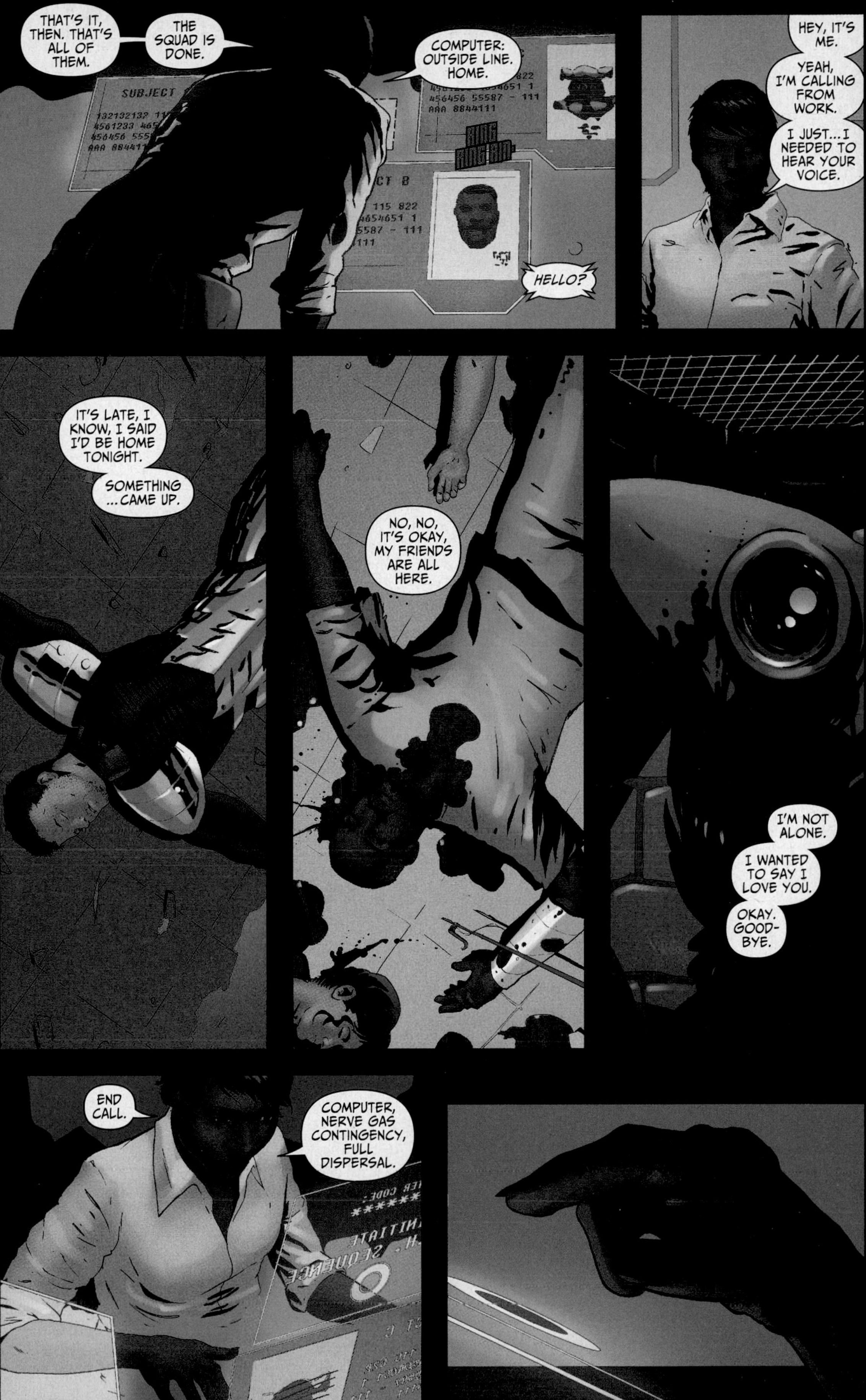
THAT'S IT, THEN. THAT'S ALL OF THEM.
THE SQUAD IS DONE.
COMPUTER: OUTSIDE LINE. HOME.
RING RING RIN-
HELLO?
HEY, IT'S ME.
YEAH, I'M CALLING FROM WORK.
I JUST...I NEEDED TO HEAR YOUR VOICE.
IT'S LATE, I KNOW, I SAID I'D BE HOME TONIGHT.
SOMETHING ...CAME UP.
NO, NO, IT'S OKAY, MY FRIENDS ARE ALL HERE.
I'M NOT ALONE.
I WANTED TO SAY I LOVE YOU.
OKAY. GOOD-BYE.
END CALL.
COMPUTER, NERVE GAS CONTINGENCY, FULL DISPERSAL.

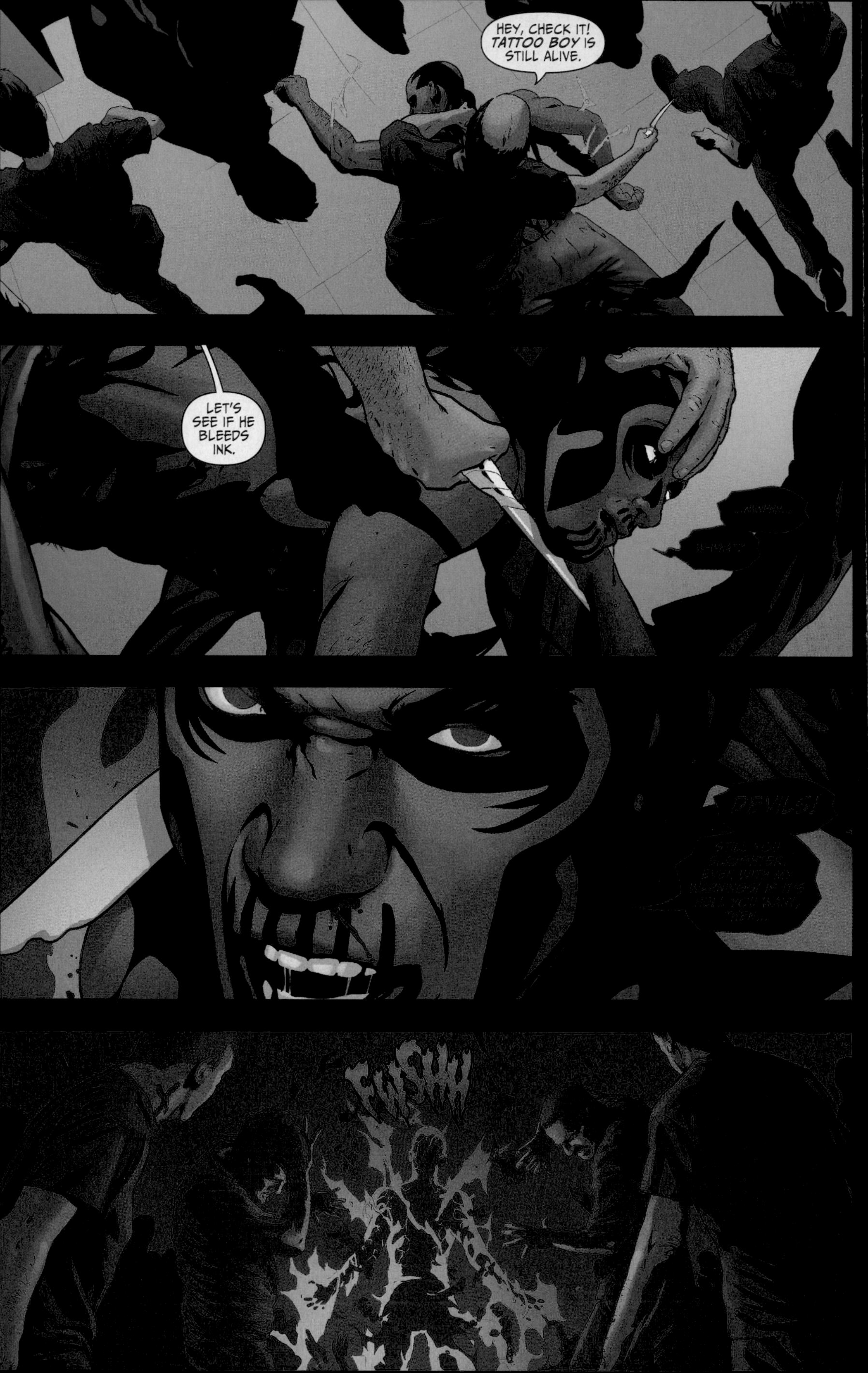
HEY, CHECK IT! *TATTOO BOY* IS STILL ALIVE.
LET'S SEE IF HE BLEEDS INK.
W-WHAT?
DEVILS!

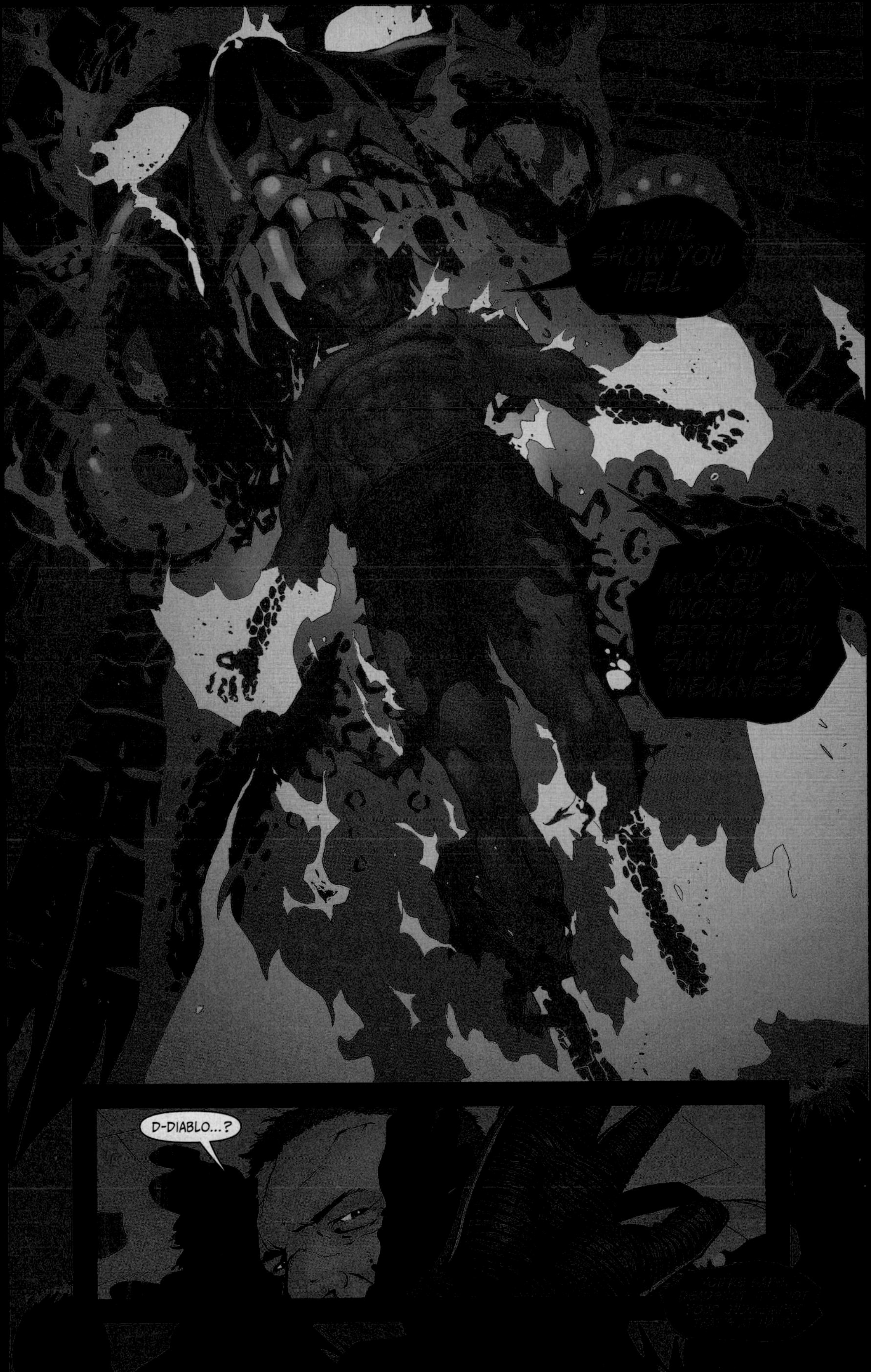
I WILL SHOW YOU HELL.
YOU MOCKED MY WORDS OF REDEMPTION, SAW IT AS A WEAKNESS
D-DIABLO...?

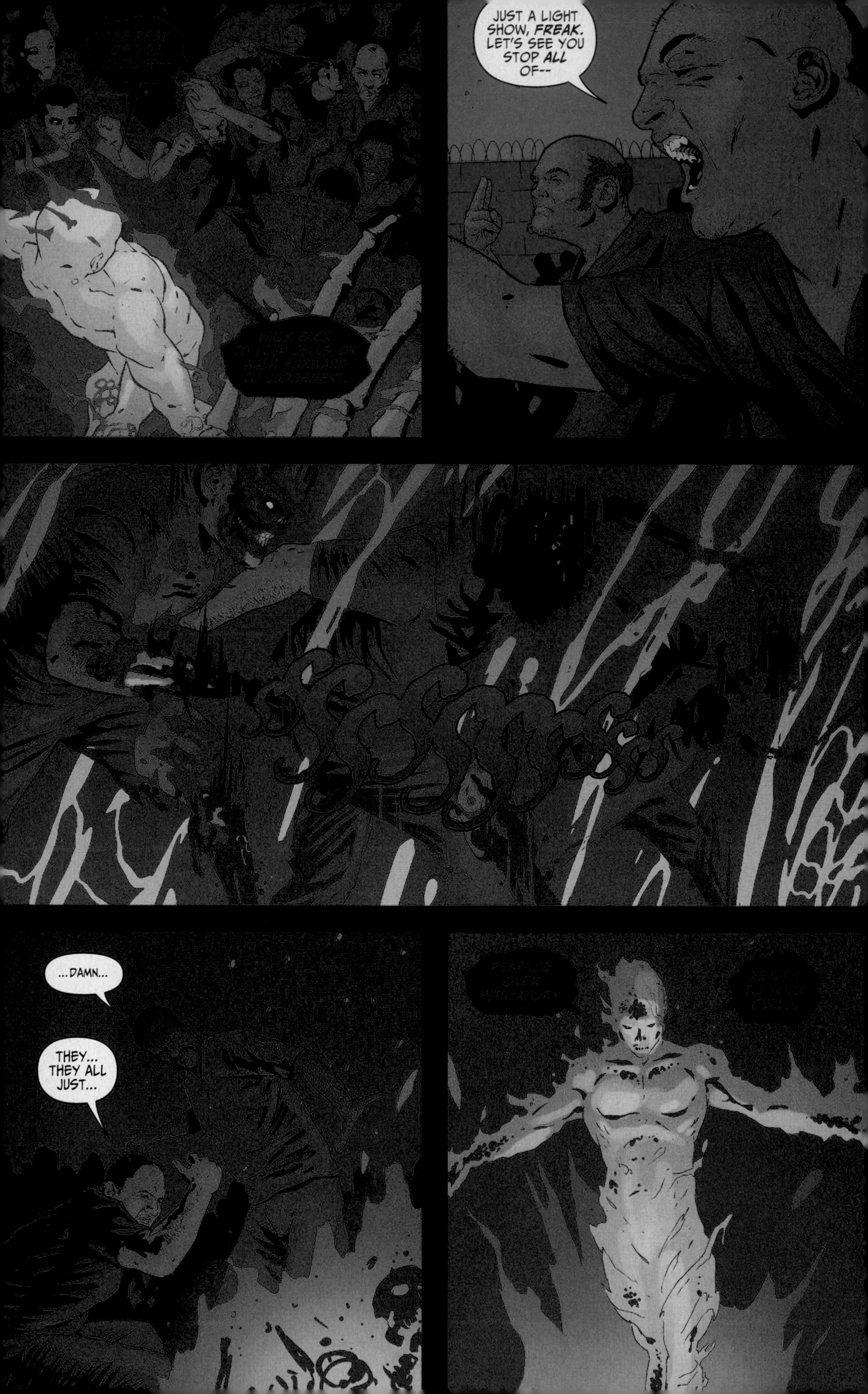
WALK BACK TO YOUR CELLS OR WALK FORWARD TO JUDGMENT.
JUST A LIGHT SHOW, FREAK. LET'S SEE YOU STOP ALL OF--
...DAMN...
THEY... THEY ALL JUST...

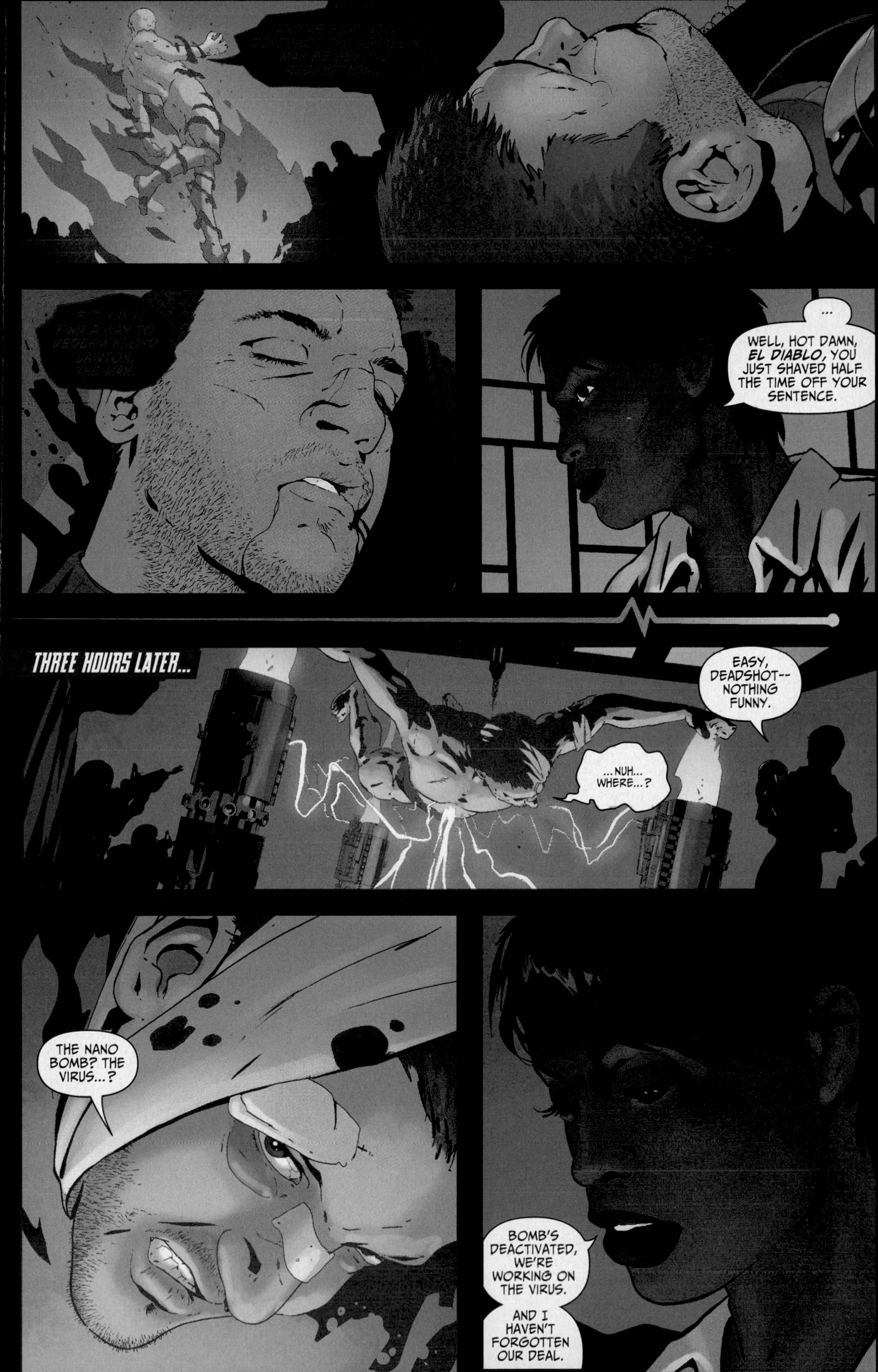
BUT I WILL FIND A WAY TO REDEEM FLOYD LAWTON, THE MAN.
...
WELL, HOT DAMN, EL DIABLO, YOU JUST SHAVED HALF THE TIME OFF YOUR SENTENCE.
THREE HOURS LATER...
EASY, DEADSHOT-- NOTHING FUNNY.
...NUH... WHERE...?
THE NANO BOMB? THE VIRUS...?
BOMB'S DEACTIVATED, WE'RE WORKING ON THE VIRUS.
AND I HAVEN'T FORGOTTEN OUR DEAL.

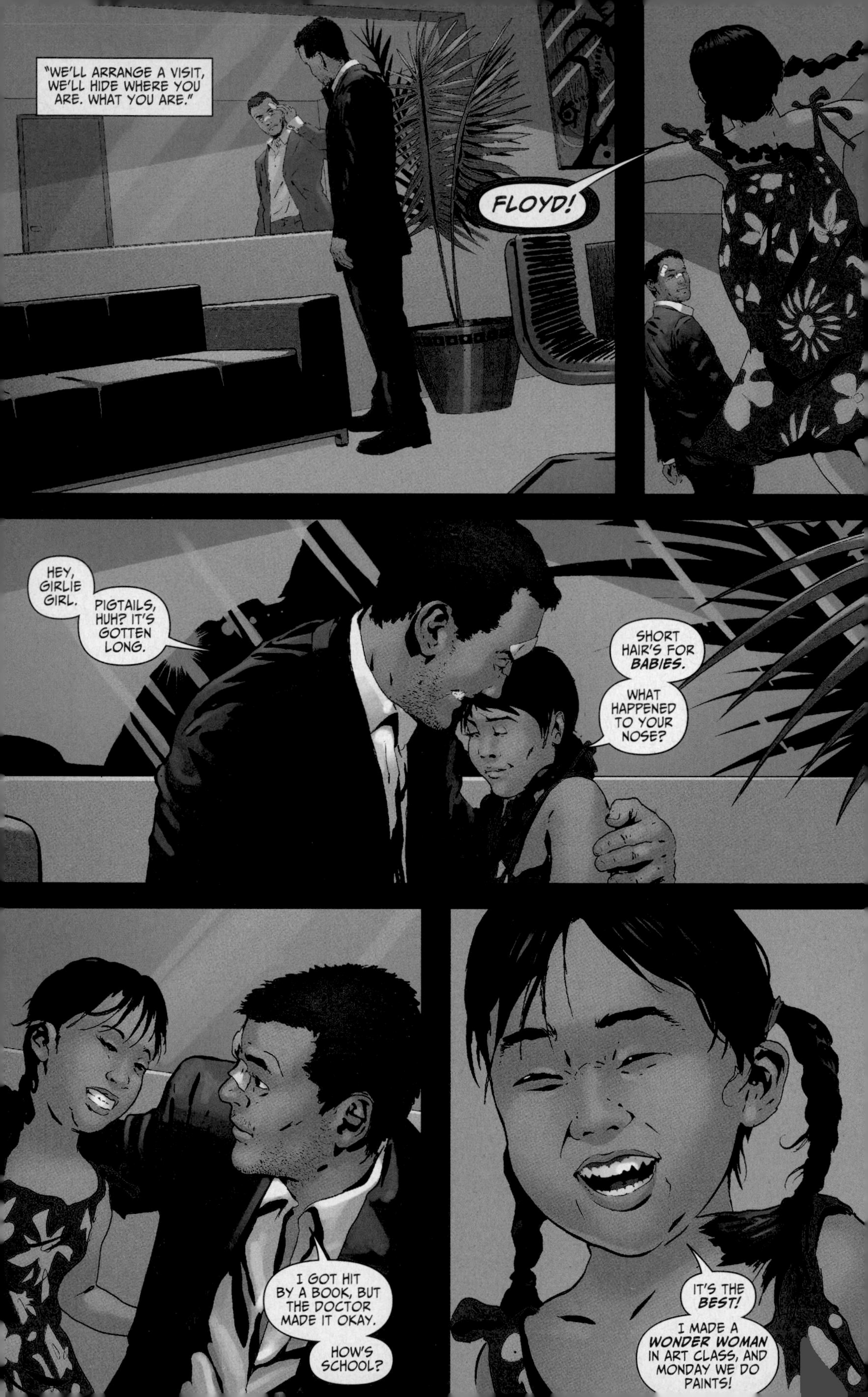
"WE'LL ARRANGE A VISIT, WE'LL HIDE WHERE YOU ARE. WHAT YOU ARE."
FLOYD!
HEY, GIRLIE GIRL.
PIGTAILS, HUH? IT'S GOTTEN LONG.
SHORT HAIR'S FOR *BABIES.*
WHAT HAPPENED TO YOUR NOSE?
I GOT HIT BY A BOOK, BUT THE DOCTOR MADE IT OKAY.
HOW'S SCHOOL?
IT'S THE *BEST!*
I MADE A *WONDER WOMAN* IN ART CLASS, AND MONDAY WE DO PAINTS!

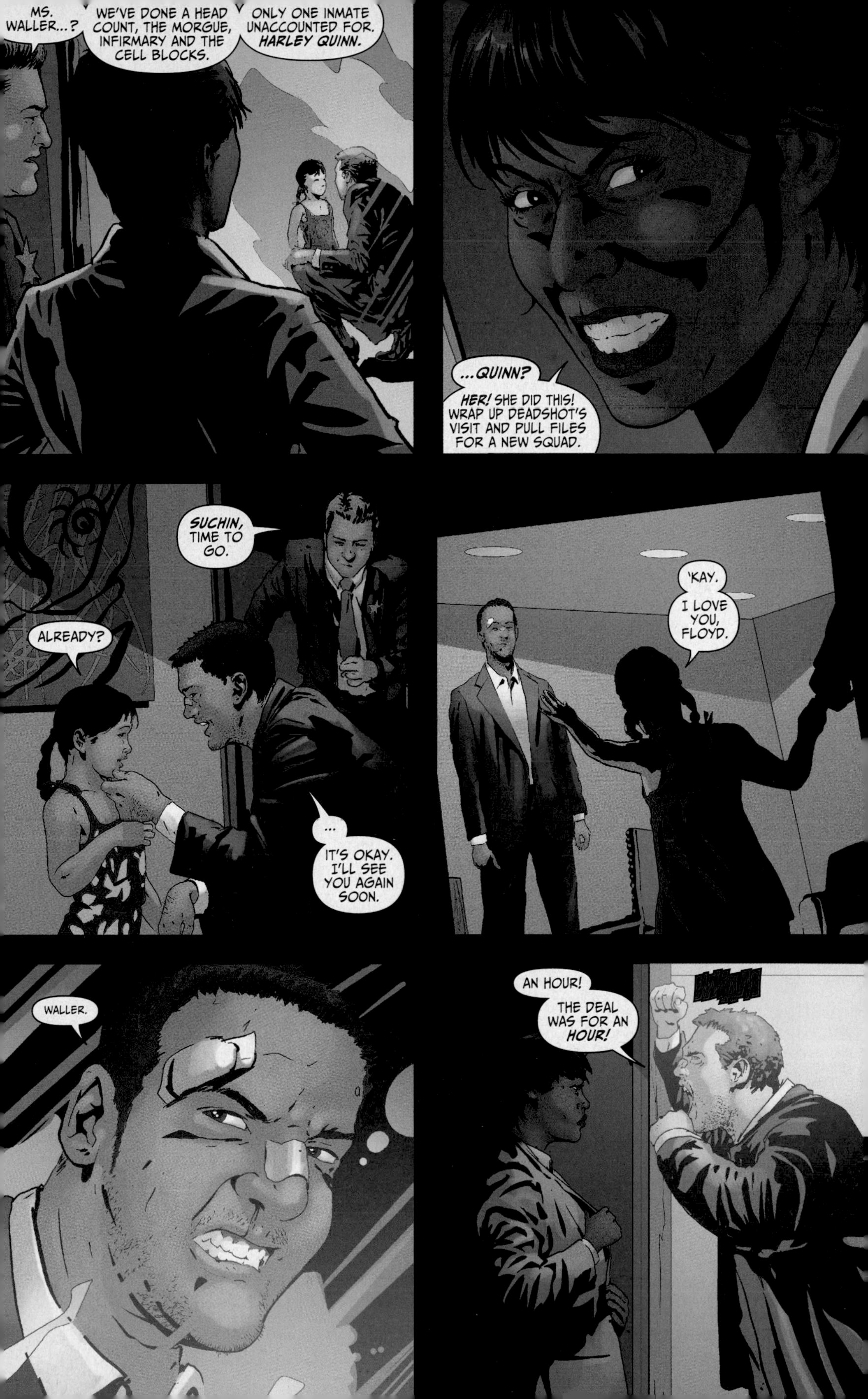
MS. WALLER...?
WE'VE DONE A HEAD COUNT, THE MORGUE, INFIRMARY AND THE CELL BLOCKS.
ONLY ONE INMATE UNACCOUNTED FOR. HARLEY QUINN.
...QUINN?
HER! SHE DID THIS! WRAP UP DEADSHOT'S VISIT AND PULL FILES FOR A NEW SQUAD.
SUCHIN, TIME TO GO.
ALREADY?
... IT'S OKAY. I'LL SEE YOU AGAIN SOON.
'KAY. I LOVE YOU, FLOYD.
WALLER.
AN HOUR!
THE DEAL WAS FOR AN HOUR!

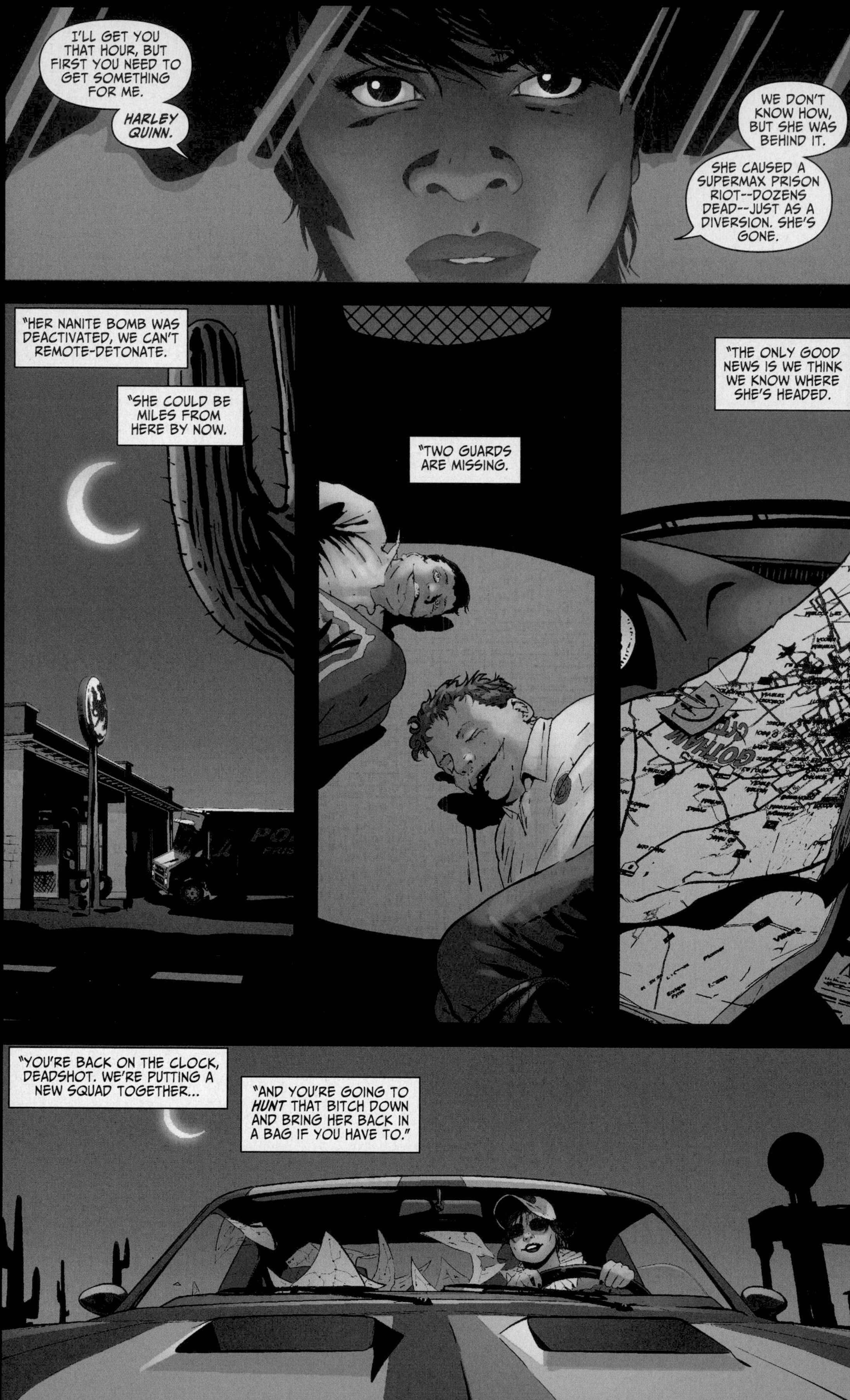

I'LL GET YOU THAT HOUR, BUT FIRST YOU NEED TO GET SOMETHING FOR ME.
HARLEY QUINN.
WE DON'T KNOW HOW, BUT SHE WAS BEHIND IT.
SHE CAUSED A SUPERMAX PRISON RIOT--DOZENS DEAD--JUST AS A DIVERSION. SHE'S GONE.
"HER NANITE BOMB WAS DEACTIVATED, WE CAN'T REMOTE-DETONATE.
"SHE COULD BE MILES FROM HERE BY NOW.
"TWO GUARDS ARE MISSING.
"THE ONLY GOOD NEWS IS WE THINK WE KNOW WHERE SHE'S HEADED.
GOTHAM
"YOU'RE BACK ON THE CLOCK, DEADSHOT. WE'RE PUTTING A NEW SQUAD TOGETHER...
"AND YOU'RE GOING TO HUNT THAT BITCH DOWN AND BRING HER BACK IN A BAG IF YOU HAVE TO."

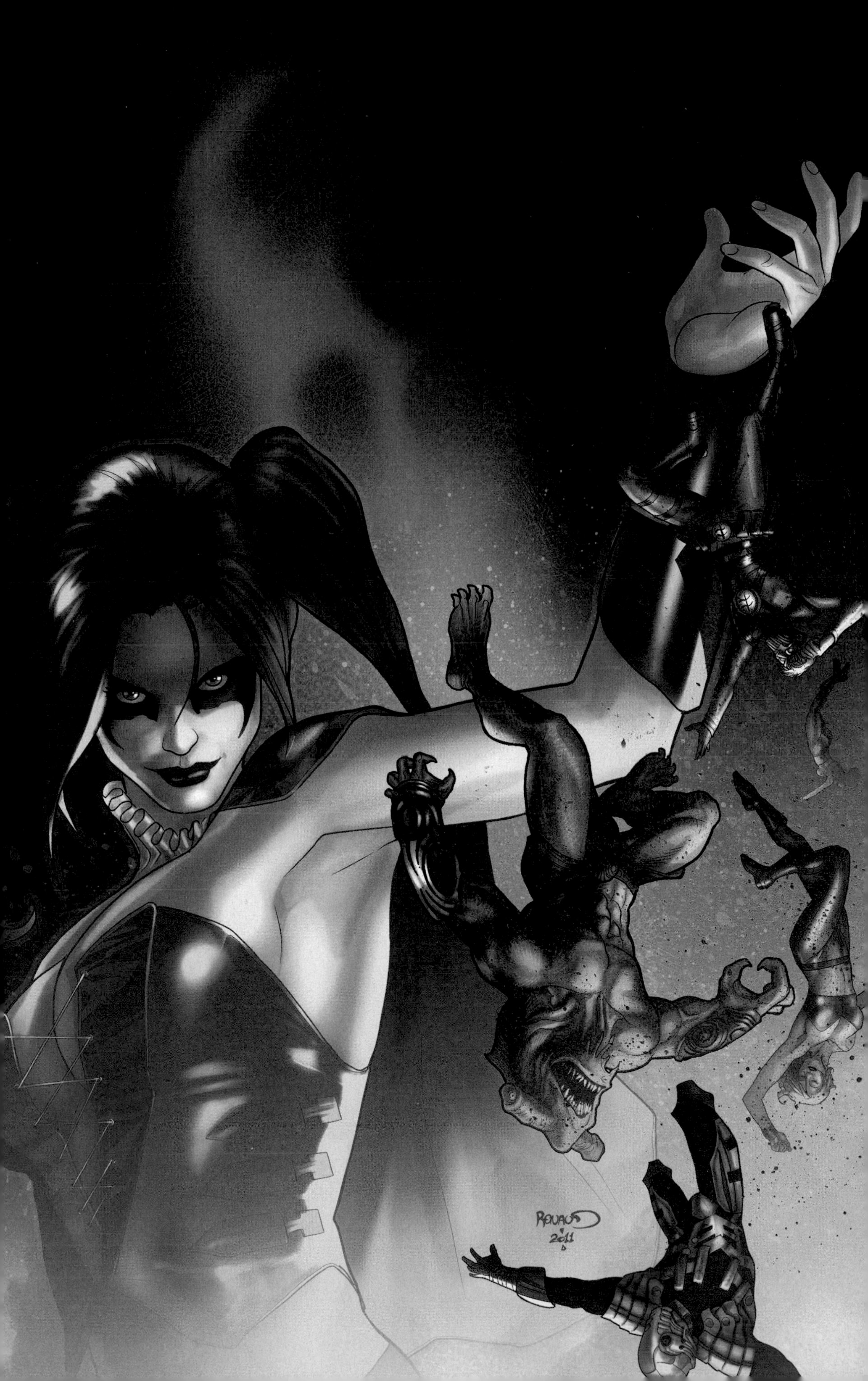
RENAUD
2011

THE HUNT FOR HARLEY QUINN part one

ADAM GLASS
writer

CLAYTON HENRY
penciller

SCOTT HANNA & CLAYTON HENRY
inkers

cover art by PAUL RENAUD

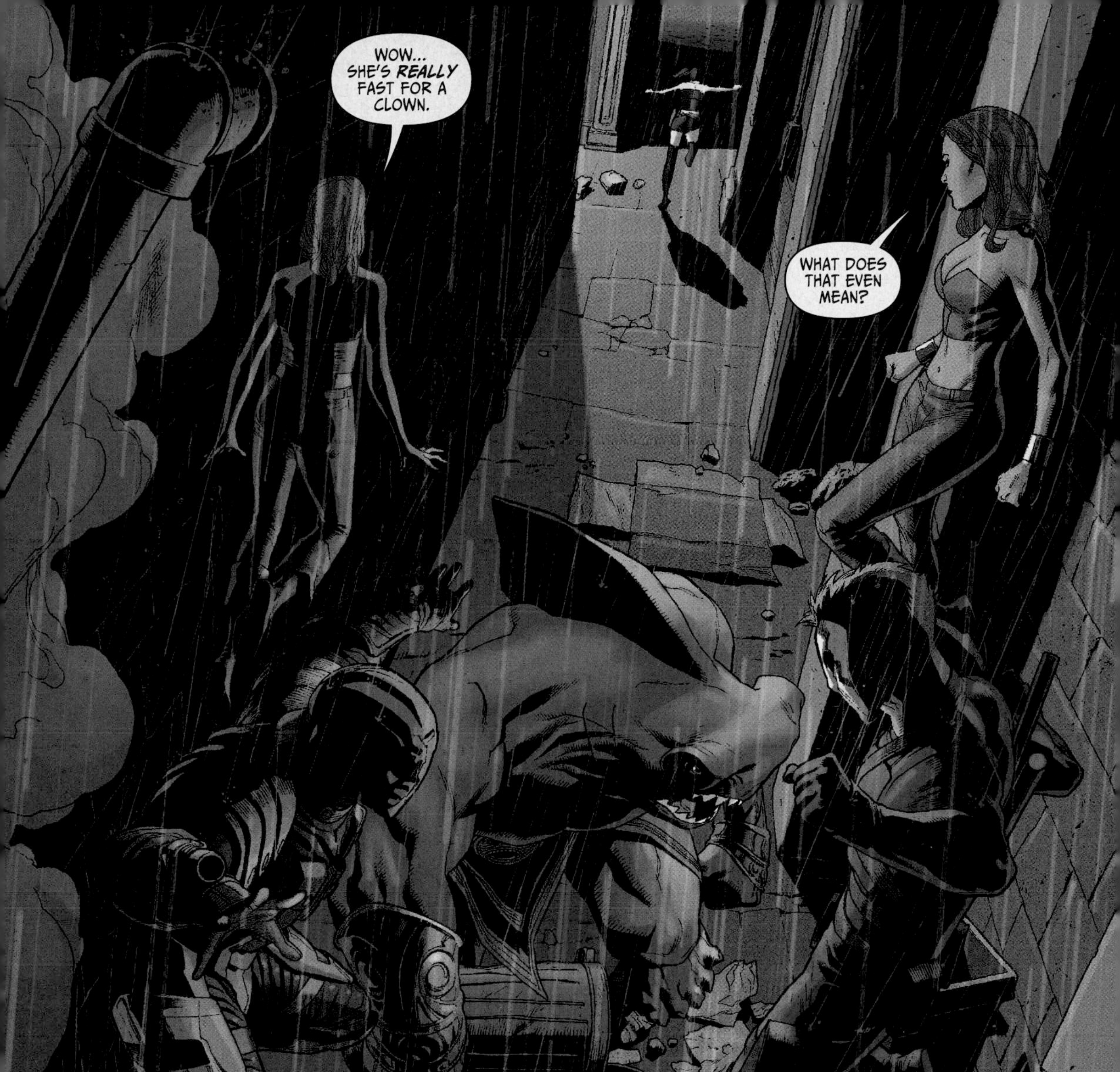
WOW... SHE'S *REALLY* FAST FOR A CLOWN.
WHAT DOES THAT EVEN MEAN?

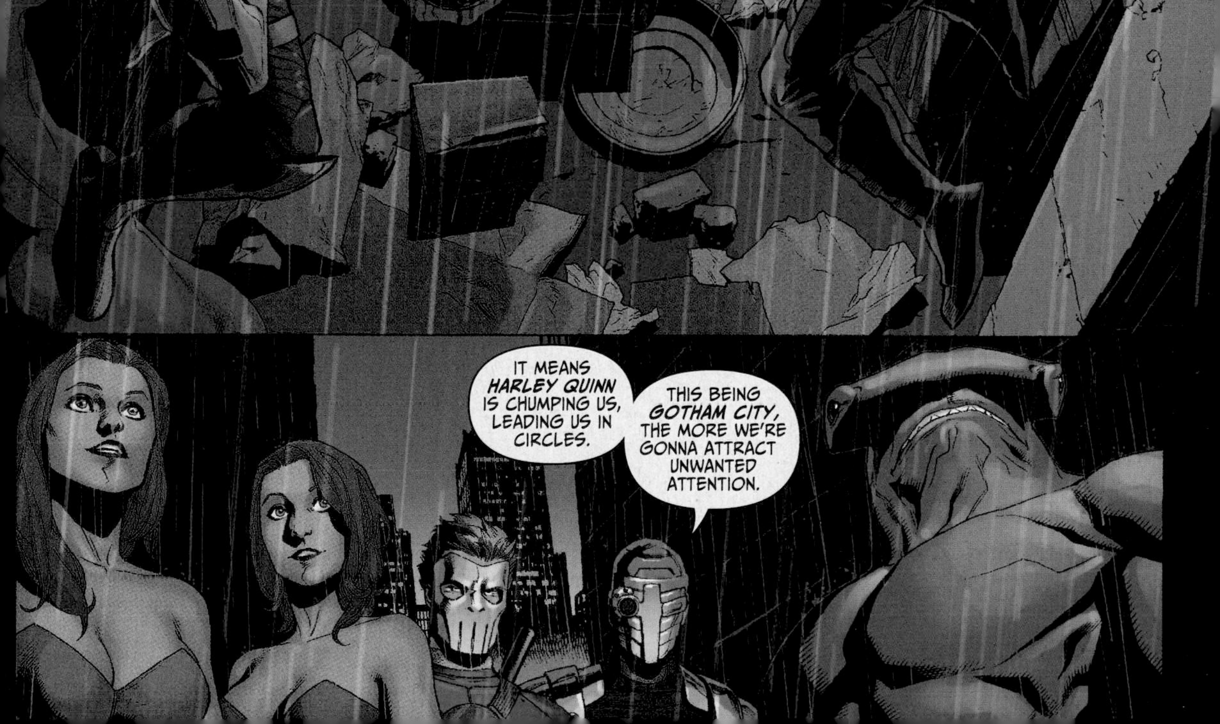
IT MEANS *HARLEY QUINN* IS CHUMPING US, LEADING US IN CIRCLES.
THIS BEING *GOTHAM CITY*, THE MORE WE'RE GONNA ATTRACT UNWANTED ATTENTION.

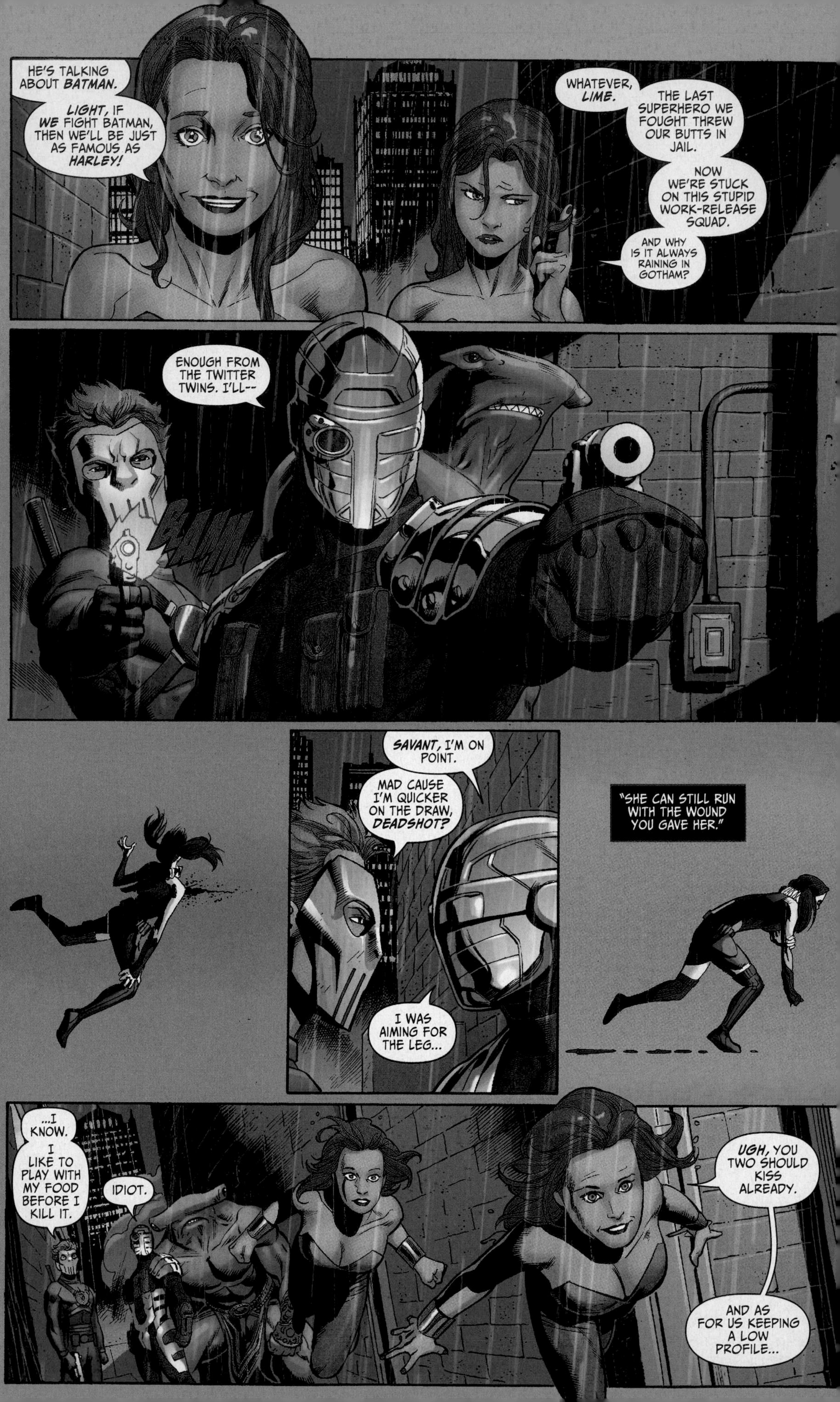
HE'S TALKING ABOUT BATMAN.
LIGHT, IF WE FIGHT BATMAN, THEN WE'LL BE JUST AS FAMOUS AS HARLEY!
WHATEVER, LIME.
THE LAST SUPERHERO WE FOUGHT THREW OUR BUTTS IN JAIL.
NOW WE'RE STUCK ON THIS STUPID WORK-RELEASE SQUAD.
AND WHY IS IT ALWAYS RAINING IN GOTHAM?
ENOUGH FROM THE TWITTER TWINS. I'LL--
BLAM
SAVANT, I'M ON POINT.
MAD CAUSE I'M QUICKER ON THE DRAW, DEADSHOT?
I WAS AIMING FOR THE LEG...
"SHE CAN STILL RUN WITH THE WOUND YOU GAVE HER."
...I KNOW.
I LIKE TO PLAY WITH MY FOOD BEFORE I KILL IT.
IDIOT.
UGH, YOU TWO SHOULD KISS ALREADY.
AND AS FOR US KEEPING A LOW PROFILE...

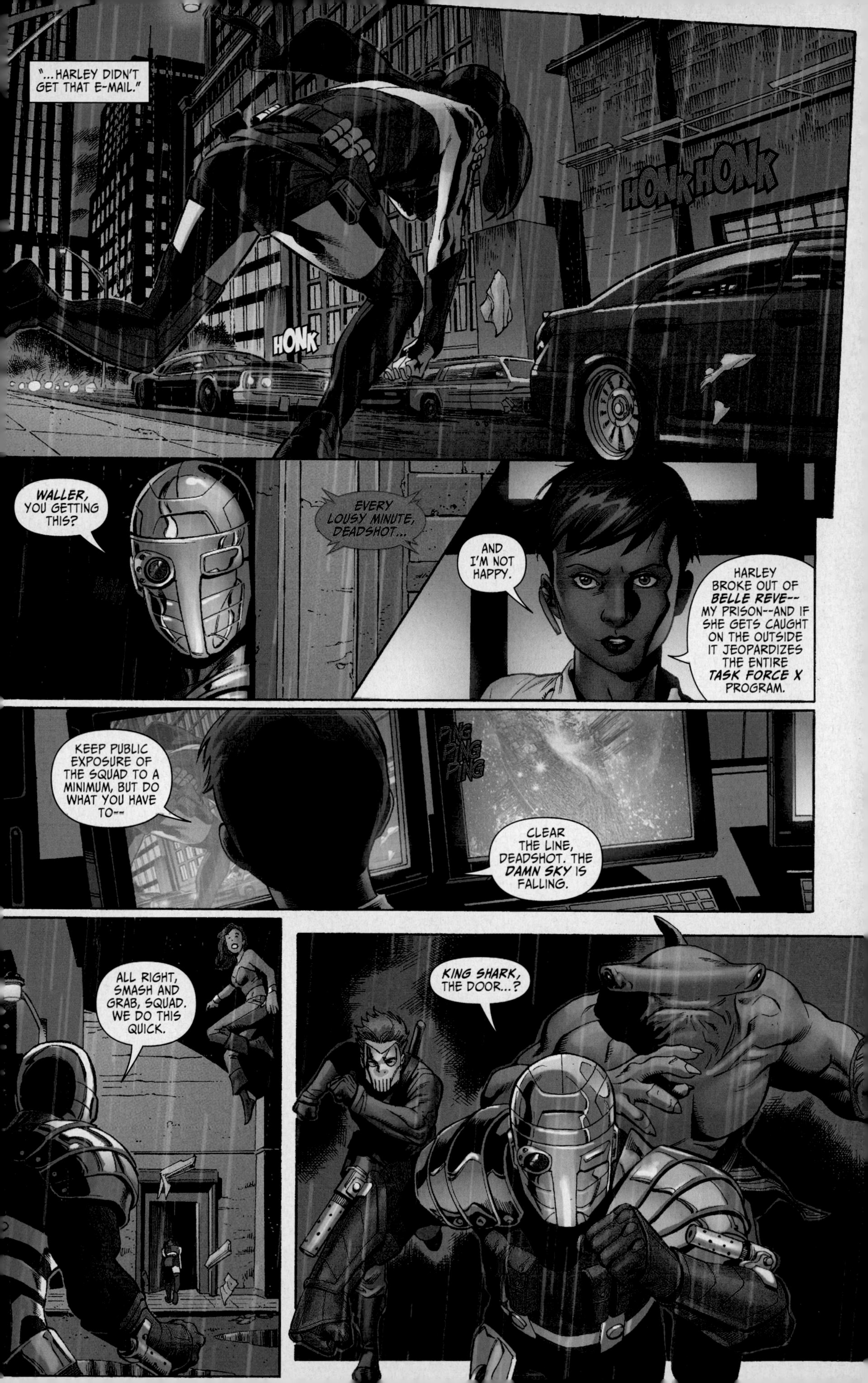
"...HARLEY DIDN'T GET THAT E-MAIL."
HONK HONK
HONK
WALLER, YOU GETTING THIS?
EVERY LOUSY MINUTE, DEADSHOT...
AND I'M NOT HAPPY.
HARLEY BROKE OUT OF BELLE REVE-- MY PRISON--AND IF SHE GETS CAUGHT ON THE OUTSIDE IT JEOPARDIZES THE ENTIRE TASK FORCE X PROGRAM.
KEEP PUBLIC EXPOSURE OF THE SQUAD TO A MINIMUM, BUT DO WHAT YOU HAVE TO--
PING PING PING
CLEAR THE LINE, DEADSHOT. THE DAMN SKY IS FALLING.
ALL RIGHT, SMASH AND GRAB, SQUAD. WE DO THIS QUICK.
KING SHARK, THE DOOR...?

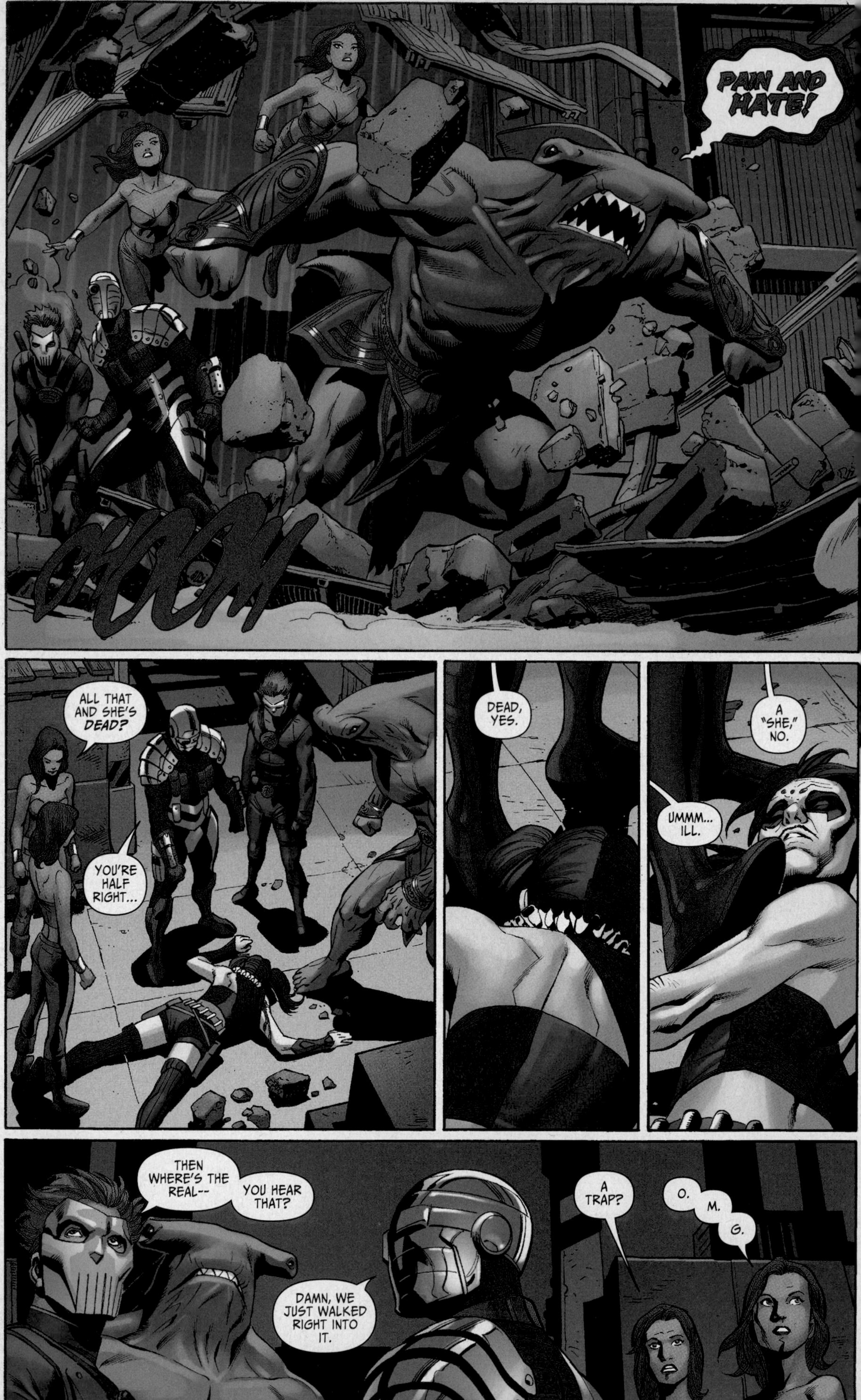
PAIN AND HATE!
CHOOM
ALL THAT AND SHE'S DEAD?
YOU'RE HALF RIGHT...
DEAD, YES.
A "SHE," NO.
UMMM... ILL.
THEN WHERE'S THE REAL--
YOU HEAR THAT?
DAMN, WE JUST WALKED RIGHT INTO IT.
A TRAP?
O.
M.
G.

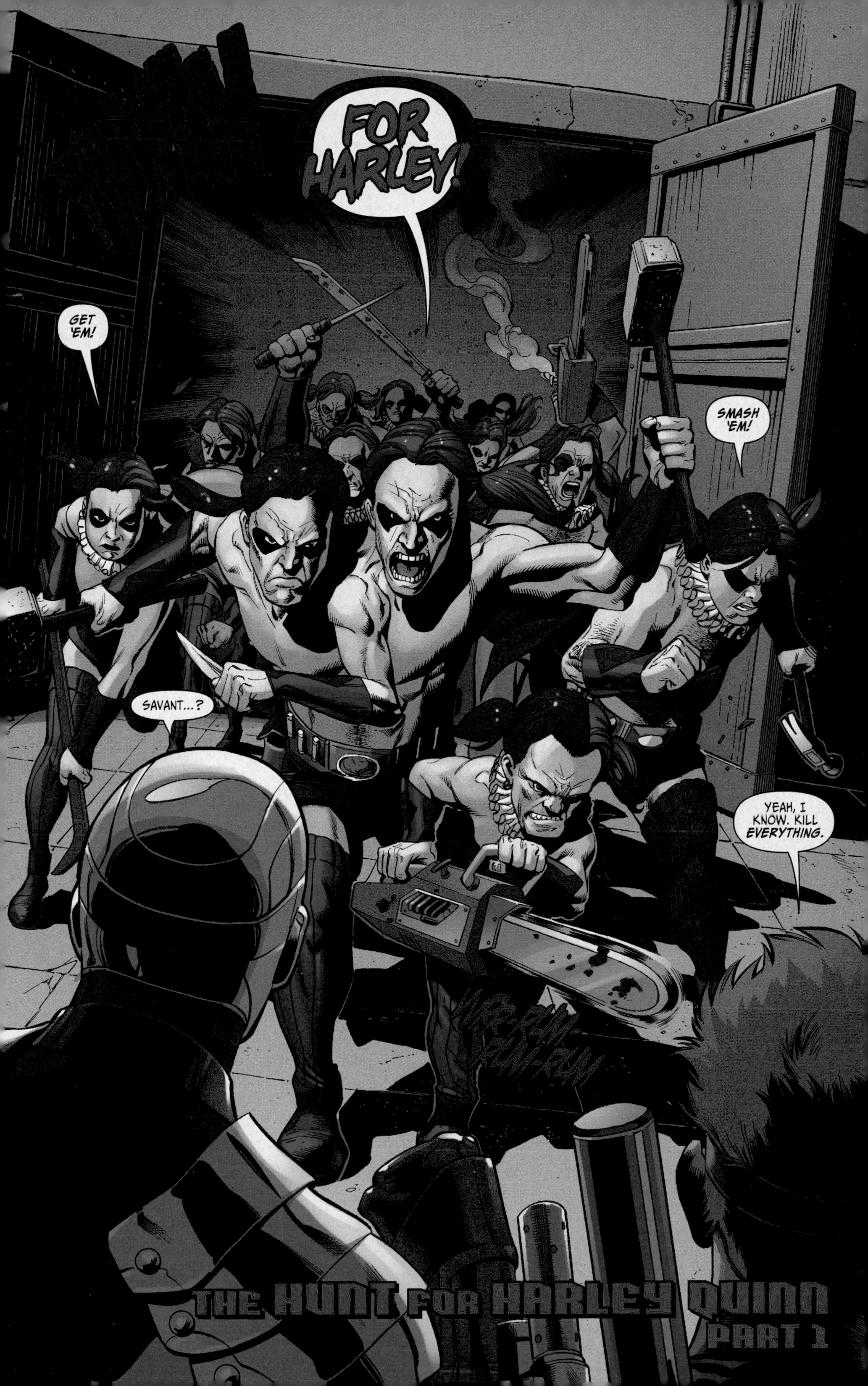
FOR HARLEY!
GET 'EM!
SMASH 'EM!
SAVANT...?
YEAH, I KNOW. KILL EVERYTHING.
THE HUNT FOR HARLEY QUINN
PART 1

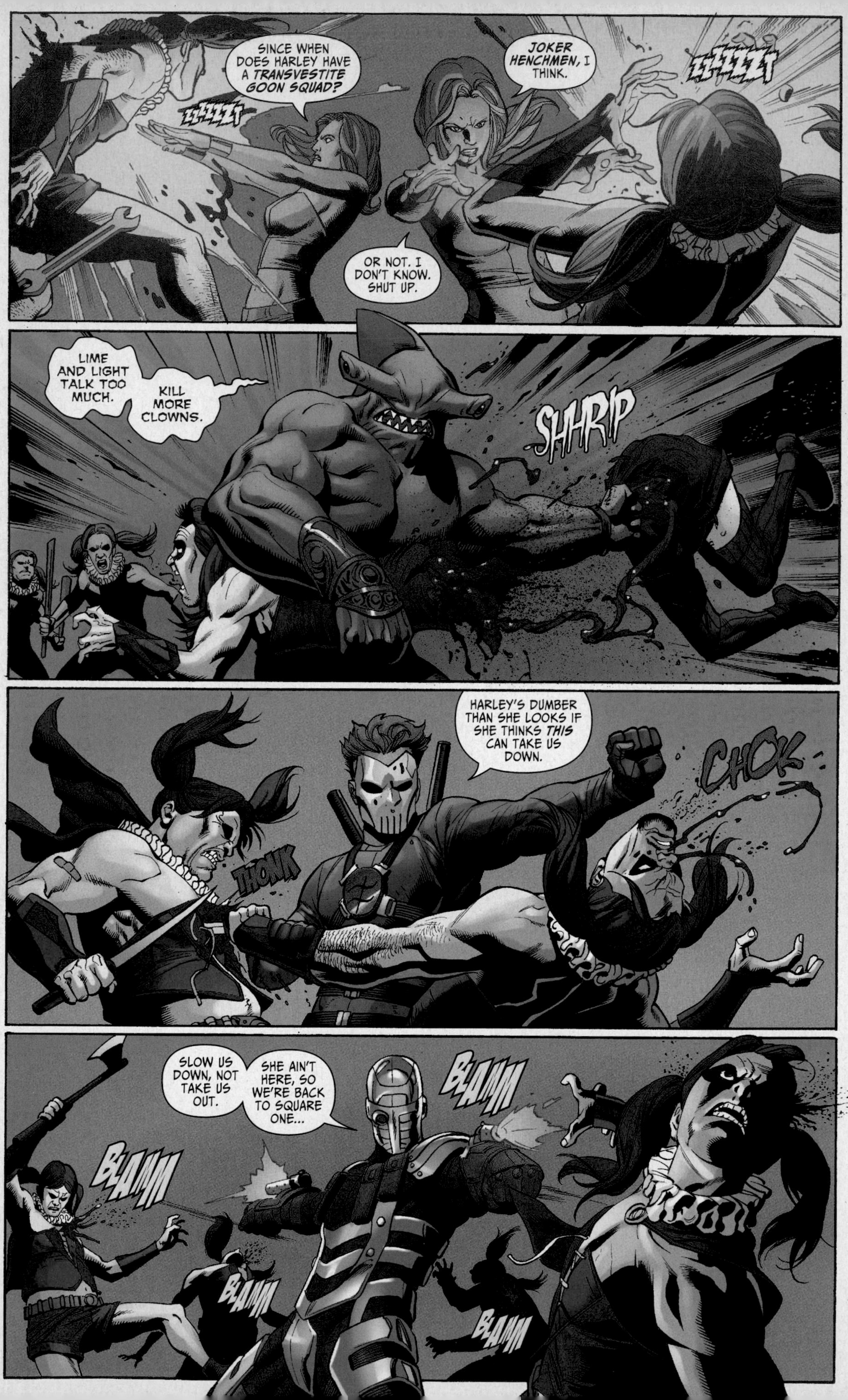

SINCE WHEN DOES HARLEY HAVE A TRANSVESTITE GOON SQUAD?
JOKER HENCHMEN, I THINK.
ZZZZZZT
ZZZZZZT
OR NOT. I DON'T KNOW. SHUT UP.
LIME AND LIGHT TALK TOO MUCH.
KILL MORE CLOWNS.
SHHRIP
HARLEY'S DUMBER THAN SHE LOOKS IF SHE THINKS THIS CAN TAKE US DOWN.
CHOK
THONK
SLOW US DOWN, NOT TAKE US OUT.
SHE AIN'T HERE, SO WE'RE BACK TO SQUARE ONE...
BLAMM
BLAMM
BLAMM
BLAMM

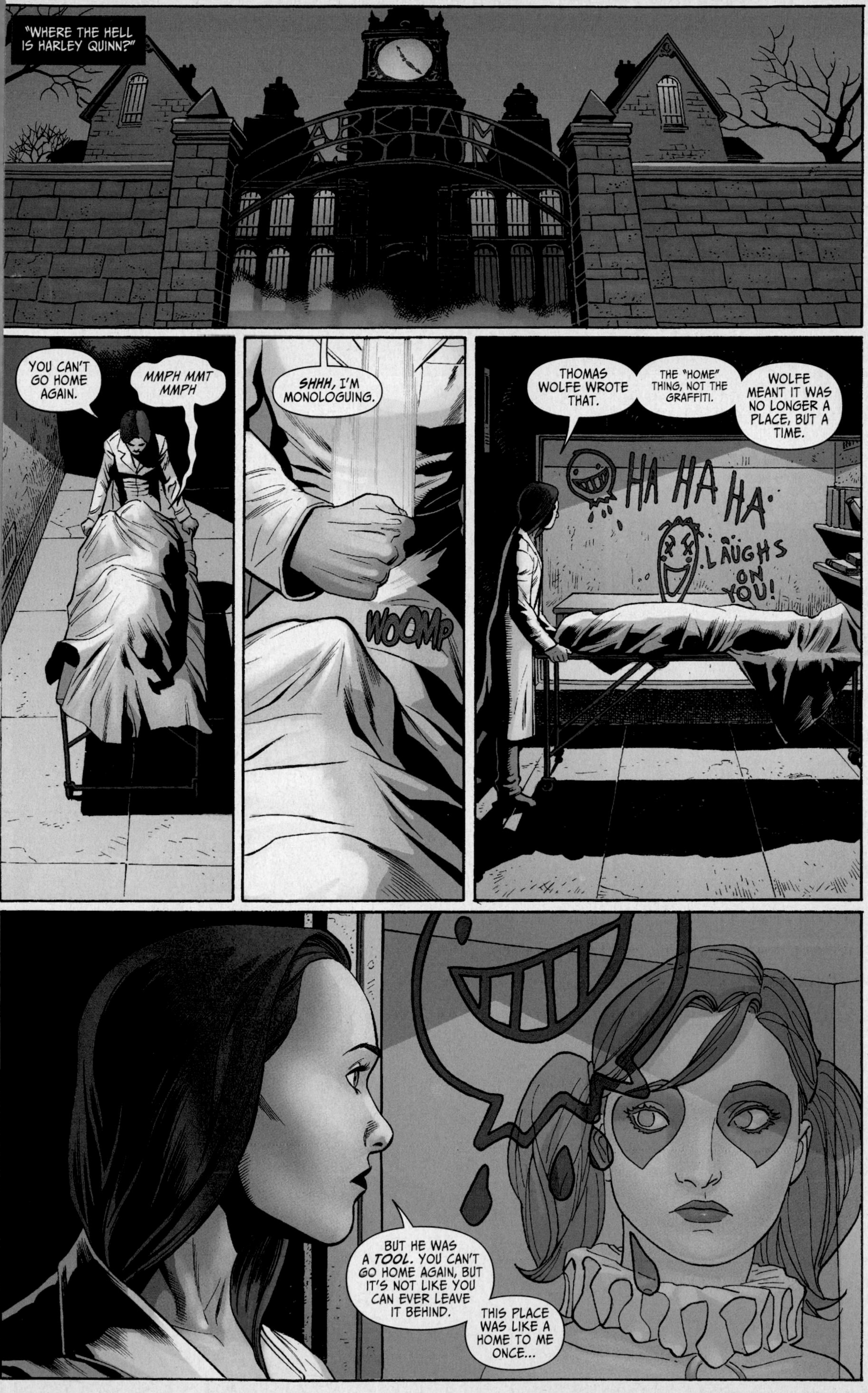
"WHERE THE HELL IS HARLEY QUINN?"
ARKHAM ASYLUM
YOU CAN'T GO HOME AGAIN.
MMPH MMT MMPH
SHHH, I'M MONOLOGUING.
WOOMP
THOMAS WOLFE WROTE THAT.
THE "HOME" THING, NOT THE GRAFFITI.
WOLFE MEANT IT WAS NO LONGER A PLACE, BUT A TIME.
HA HA HA
LAUGHS ON YOU!
BUT HE WAS A TOOL. YOU CAN'T GO HOME AGAIN, BUT IT'S NOT LIKE YOU CAN EVER LEAVE IT BEHIND.
THIS PLACE WAS LIKE A HOME TO ME ONCE...

LET ME GUESS... LOCAL GIRL DONE GOOD. NATIONAL HONOR SOCIETY, SCHOLARSHIPS, *ETCETERA, ETCETERA.*

BUT SOMETHING'S *MISSING.* SOMETHING THAT DRIVES YOU. SOMETHING YOU WANT BUT CAN'T HAVE.

PSYCH 101. WE ALL HAVE SOMETHING WE WANT, BUT CAN'T HAVE.

SO, TOMORROW LET'S START WITH WHAT THAT IS FOR *YOU.*

AND ONE MORE THING...

IF YOU THINK OF STABBING ME WITH WHATEVER'S IN YOUR POCKET, YOU BETTER HOPE YOU DON'T MISS...

BECAUSE IF YOU *DO,* I WILL KICK YOUR NUTS UP THROUGH YOUR MOUTH AND SHOW YOU HOW WE DO IT IN CANARSIE.

NOT EXACTLY FIREWORKS.

BUT THERE WAS A *SPARK.*

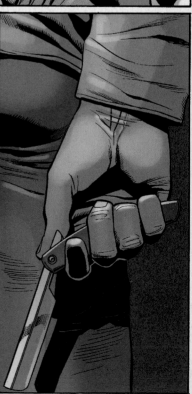

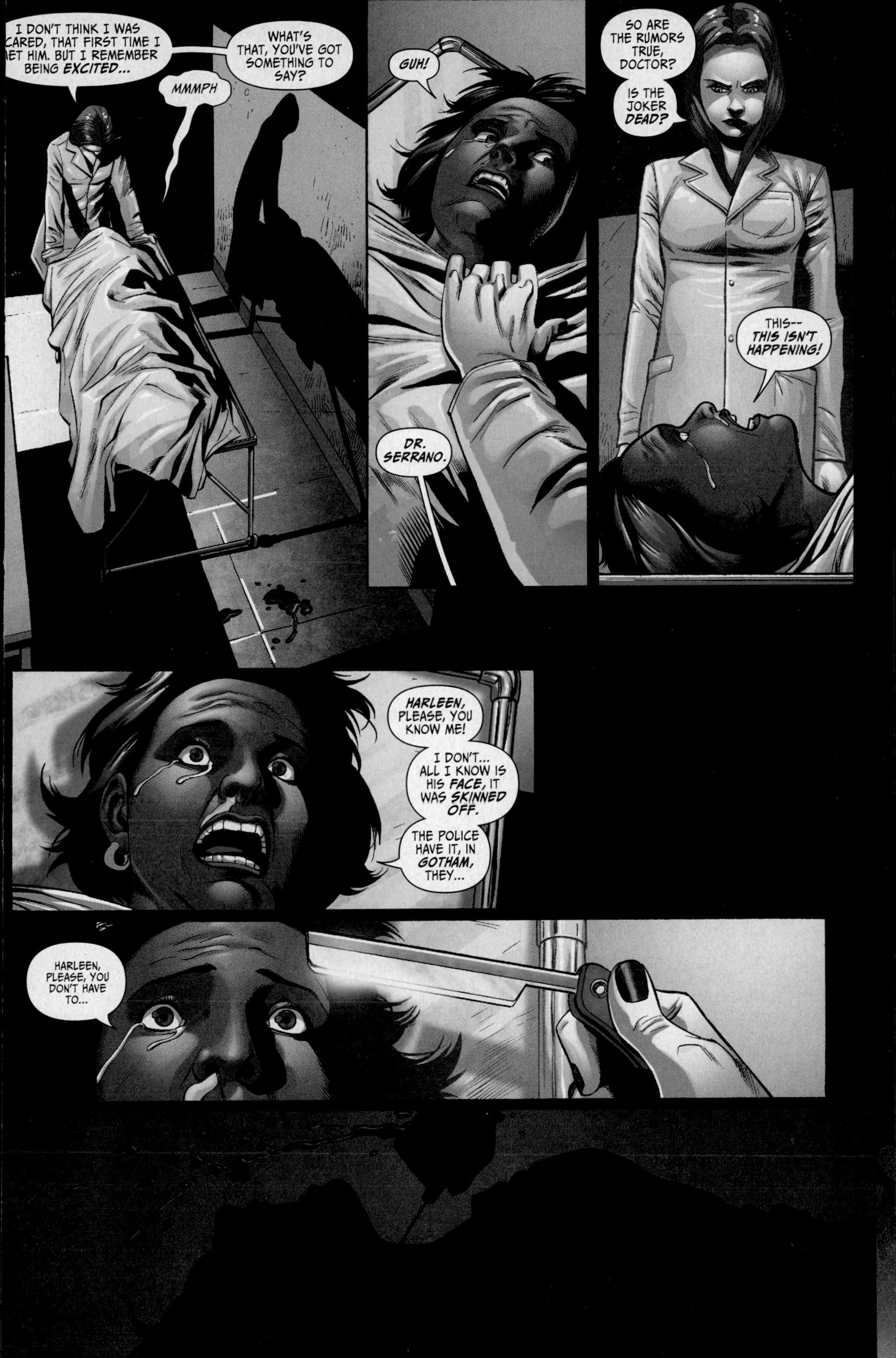
I DON'T THINK I WAS
CARED, THAT FIRST TIME I
MET HIM. BUT I REMEMBER
BEING EXCITED...
WHAT'S THAT, YOU'VE GOT SOMETHING TO SAY?
MMMPH
GUH!
DR. SERRANO.
SO ARE THE RUMORS TRUE, DOCTOR?
IS THE JOKER DEAD?
THIS-- THIS ISN'T HAPPENING!
HARLEEN, PLEASE, YOU KNOW ME!
I DON'T... ALL I KNOW IS HIS FACE, IT WAS SKINNED OFF.
THE POLICE HAVE IT, IN GOTHAM, THEY...
HARLEEN, PLEASE, YOU DON'T HAVE TO...

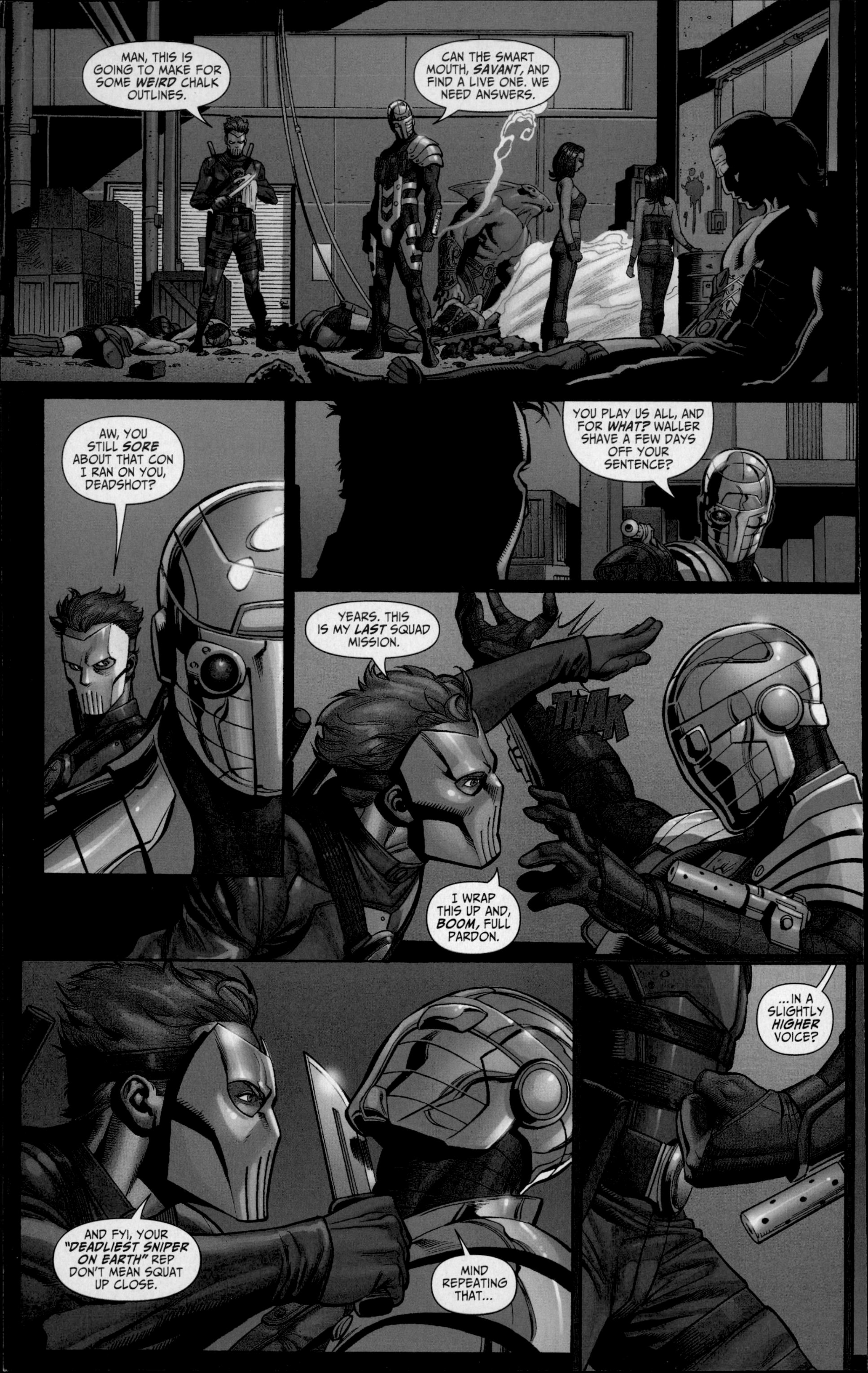
MAN, THIS IS GOING TO MAKE FOR SOME *WEIRD* CHALK OUTLINES.
CAN THE SMART MOUTH, *SAVANT*, AND FIND A LIVE ONE. WE NEED ANSWERS.
AW, YOU STILL *SORE* ABOUT THAT CON I RAN ON YOU, DEADSHOT?
YOU PLAY US ALL, AND FOR *WHAT?* WALLER SHAVE A FEW DAYS OFF YOUR SENTENCE?
YEARS. THIS IS MY *LAST* SQUAD MISSION.
THAK
I WRAP THIS UP AND, *BOOM*, FULL PARDON.
AND FYI, YOUR *"DEADLIEST SNIPER ON EARTH"* REP DON'T MEAN SQUAT UP CLOSE.
MIND REPEATING THAT...
...IN A SLIGHTLY *HIGHER* VOICE?

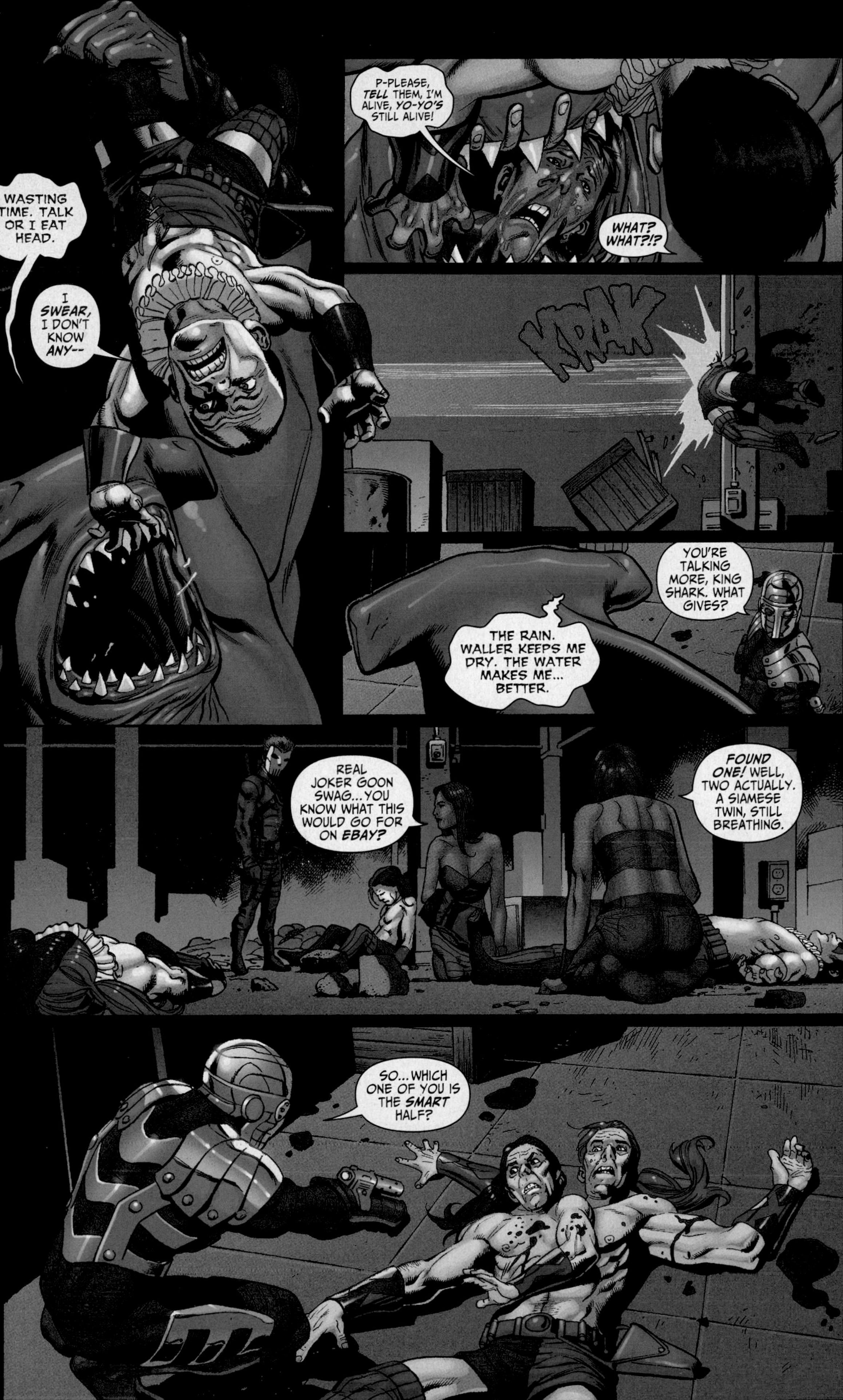
WASTING TIME. TALK OR I EAT HEAD.
I SWEAR, I DON'T KNOW ANY--
P-PLEASE, TELL THEM, I'M ALIVE, YO-YO'S STILL ALIVE!
WHAT? WHAT?!?
KRAK
YOU'RE TALKING MORE, KING SHARK. WHAT GIVES?
THE RAIN. WALLER KEEPS ME DRY. THE WATER MAKES ME... BETTER.
REAL JOKER GOON SWAG... YOU KNOW WHAT THIS WOULD GO FOR ON EBAY?
FOUND ONE! WELL, TWO ACTUALLY. A SIAMESE TWIN, STILL BREATHING.
SO... WHICH ONE OF YOU IS THE SMART HALF?

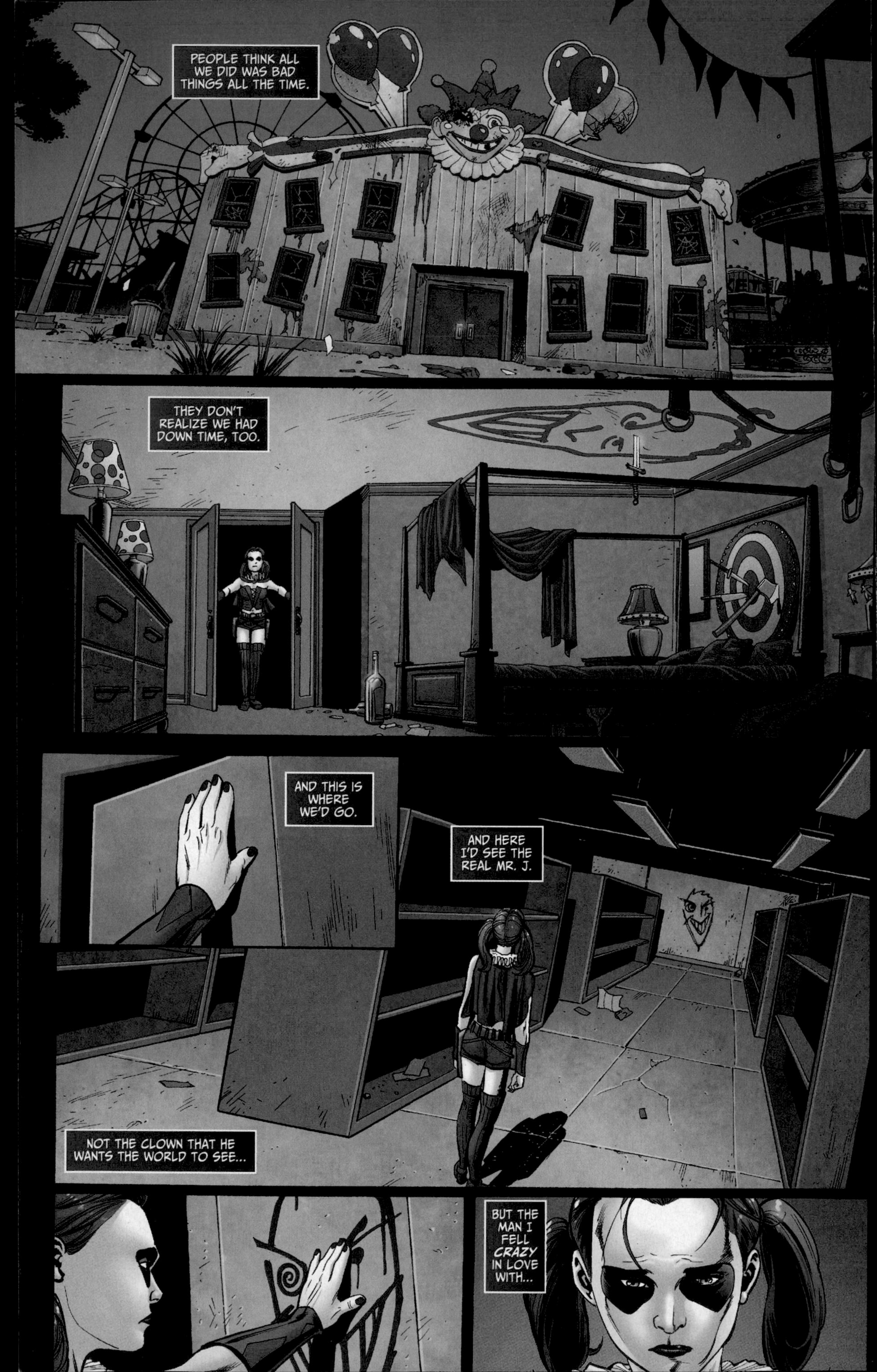
PEOPLE THINK ALL WE DID WAS BAD THINGS ALL THE TIME.
THEY DON'T REALIZE WE HAD DOWN TIME, TOO.
AND THIS IS WHERE WE'D GO.
AND HERE I'D SEE THE REAL MR. J.
NOT THE CLOWN THAT HE WANTS THE WORLD TO SEE...
BUT THE MAN I FELL CRAZY IN LOVE WITH...

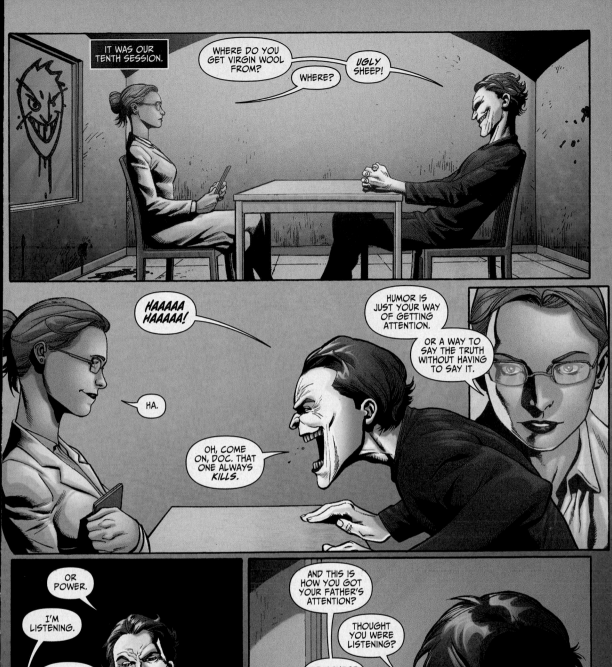

IT WAS OUR TENTH SESSION.

WHERE DO YOU GET VIRGIN WOOL FROM?

WHERE?

UGLY SHEEP!

HAAAAA HAAAAA!

HUMOR IS JUST YOUR WAY OF GETTING ATTENTION.

OR A WAY TO SAY THE TRUTH WITHOUT HAVING TO SAY IT.

HA.

OH, COME ON, DOC. THAT ONE ALWAYS KILLS.

OR POWER.

I'M LISTENING.

MAKE 'EM LAUGH, YOU HAVE A PIECE OF THEM.

AND THIS IS HOW YOU GOT YOUR FATHER'S ATTENTION?

THOUGHT YOU WERE LISTENING?

OF COURSE, I'M SORRY. GO ON.

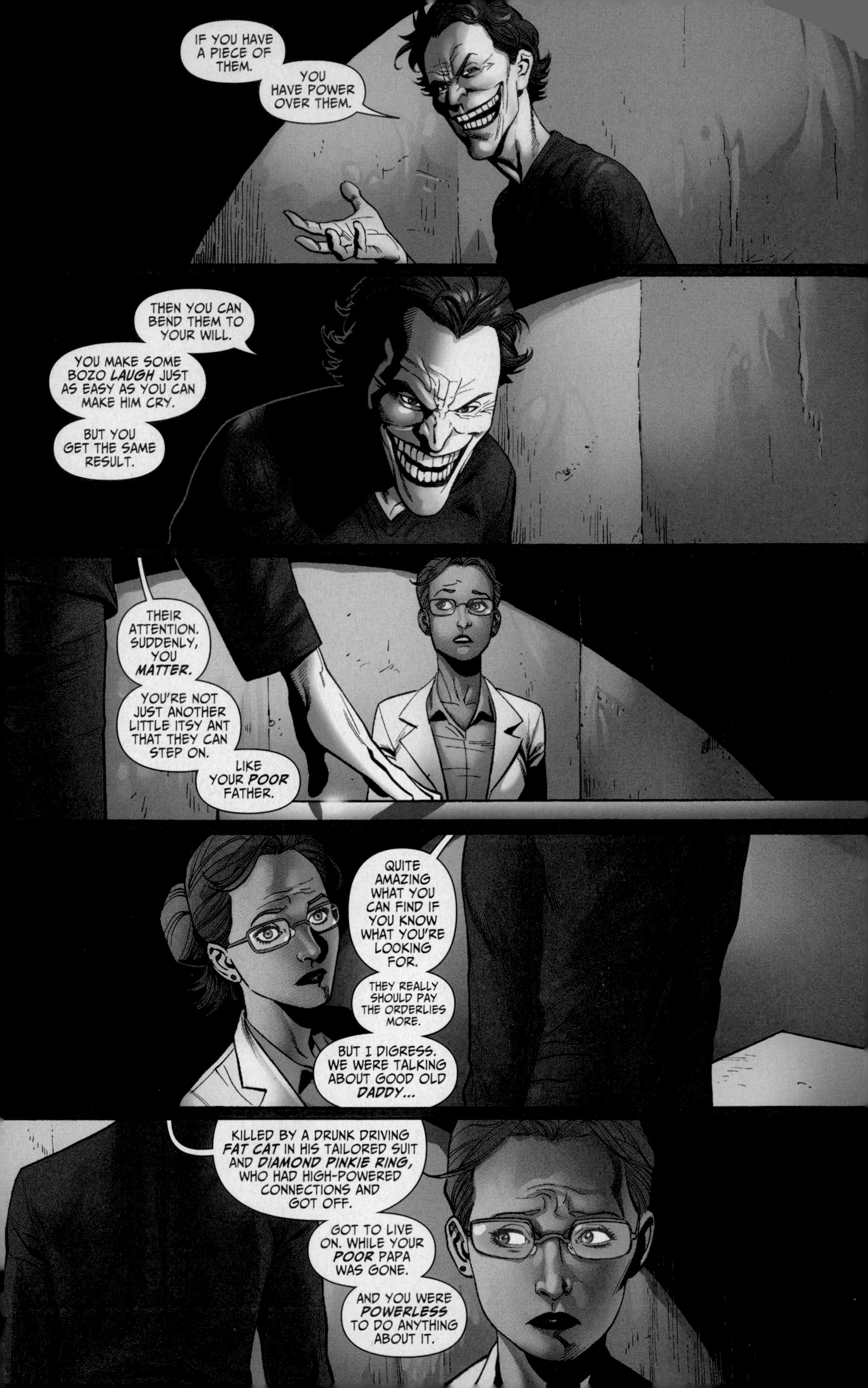
IF YOU HAVE A PIECE OF THEM.
YOU HAVE POWER OVER THEM.
THEN YOU CAN BEND THEM TO YOUR WILL.
YOU MAKE SOME BOZO LAUGH JUST AS EASY AS YOU CAN MAKE HIM CRY.
BUT YOU GET THE SAME RESULT.
THEIR ATTENTION. SUDDENLY, YOU MATTER.
YOU'RE NOT JUST ANOTHER LITTLE ITSY ANT THAT THEY CAN STEP ON.
LIKE YOUR POOR FATHER.
QUITE AMAZING WHAT YOU CAN FIND IF YOU KNOW WHAT YOU'RE LOOKING FOR.
THEY REALLY SHOULD PAY THE ORDERLIES MORE.
BUT I DIGRESS. WE WERE TALKING ABOUT GOOD OLD DADDY...
KILLED BY A DRUNK DRIVING FAT CAT IN HIS TAILORED SUIT AND DIAMOND PINKIE RING, WHO HAD HIGH-POWERED CONNECTIONS AND GOT OFF.
GOT TO LIVE ON. WHILE YOUR POOR PAPA WAS GONE.
AND YOU WERE POWERLESS TO DO ANYTHING ABOUT IT.

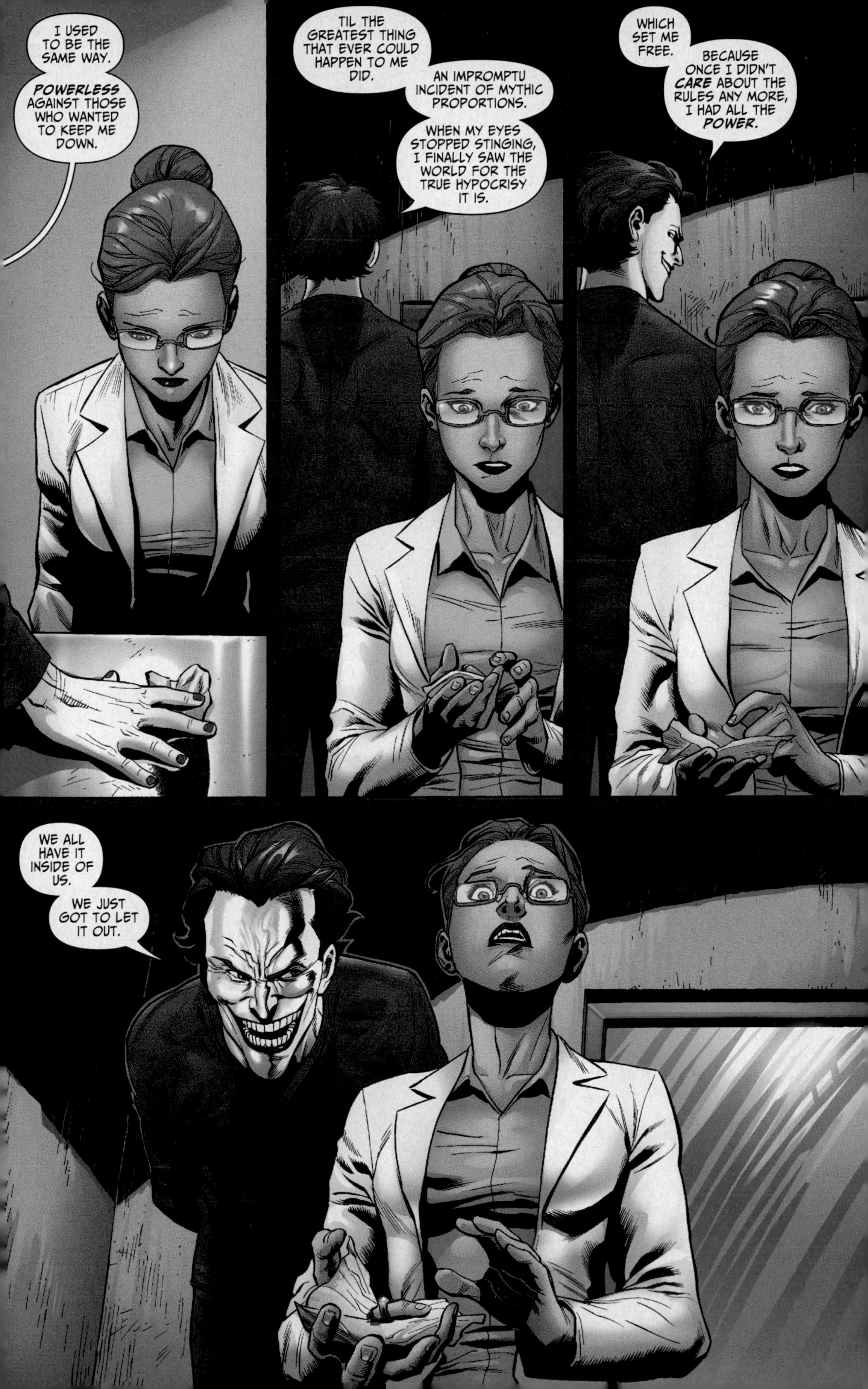
I USED TO BE THE SAME WAY.
POWERLESS AGAINST THOSE WHO WANTED TO KEEP ME DOWN.
TIL THE GREATEST THING THAT EVER COULD HAPPEN TO ME DID.
AN IMPROMPTU INCIDENT OF MYTHIC PROPORTIONS.
WHEN MY EYES STOPPED STINGING, I FINALLY SAW THE WORLD FOR THE TRUE HYPOCRISY IT IS.
WHICH SET ME FREE.
BECAUSE ONCE I DIDN'T *CARE* ABOUT THE RULES ANY MORE, I HAD ALL THE *POWER*.
WE ALL HAVE IT INSIDE OF US.
WE JUST GOT TO LET IT OUT.

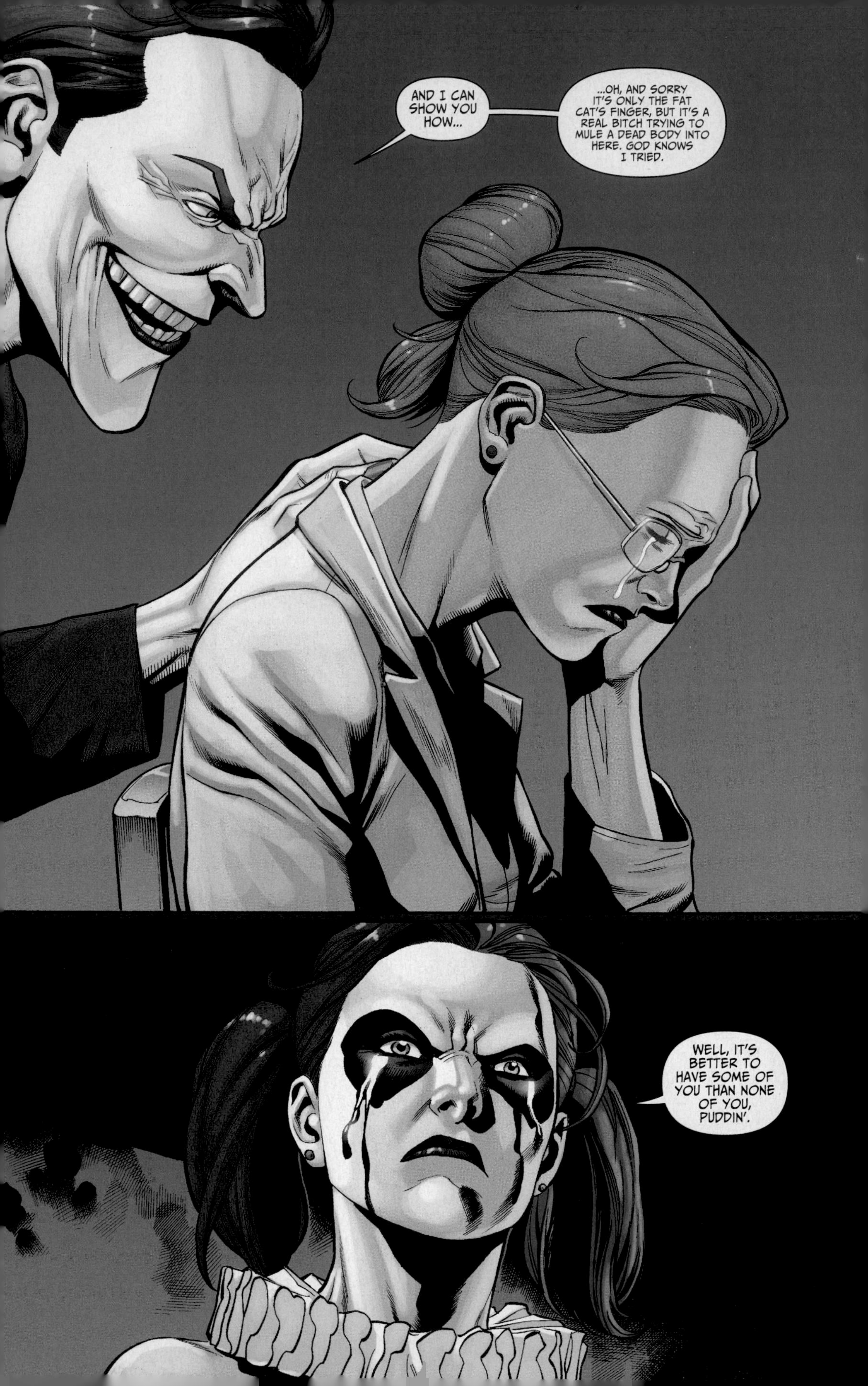
AND I CAN SHOW YOU HOW...
...OH, AND SORRY IT'S ONLY THE FAT CAT'S FINGER, BUT IT'S A REAL BITCH TRYING TO MULE A DEAD BODY INTO HERE. GOD KNOWS I TRIED.
WELL, IT'S BETTER TO HAVE SOME OF YOU THAN NONE OF YOU, PUDDIN'.

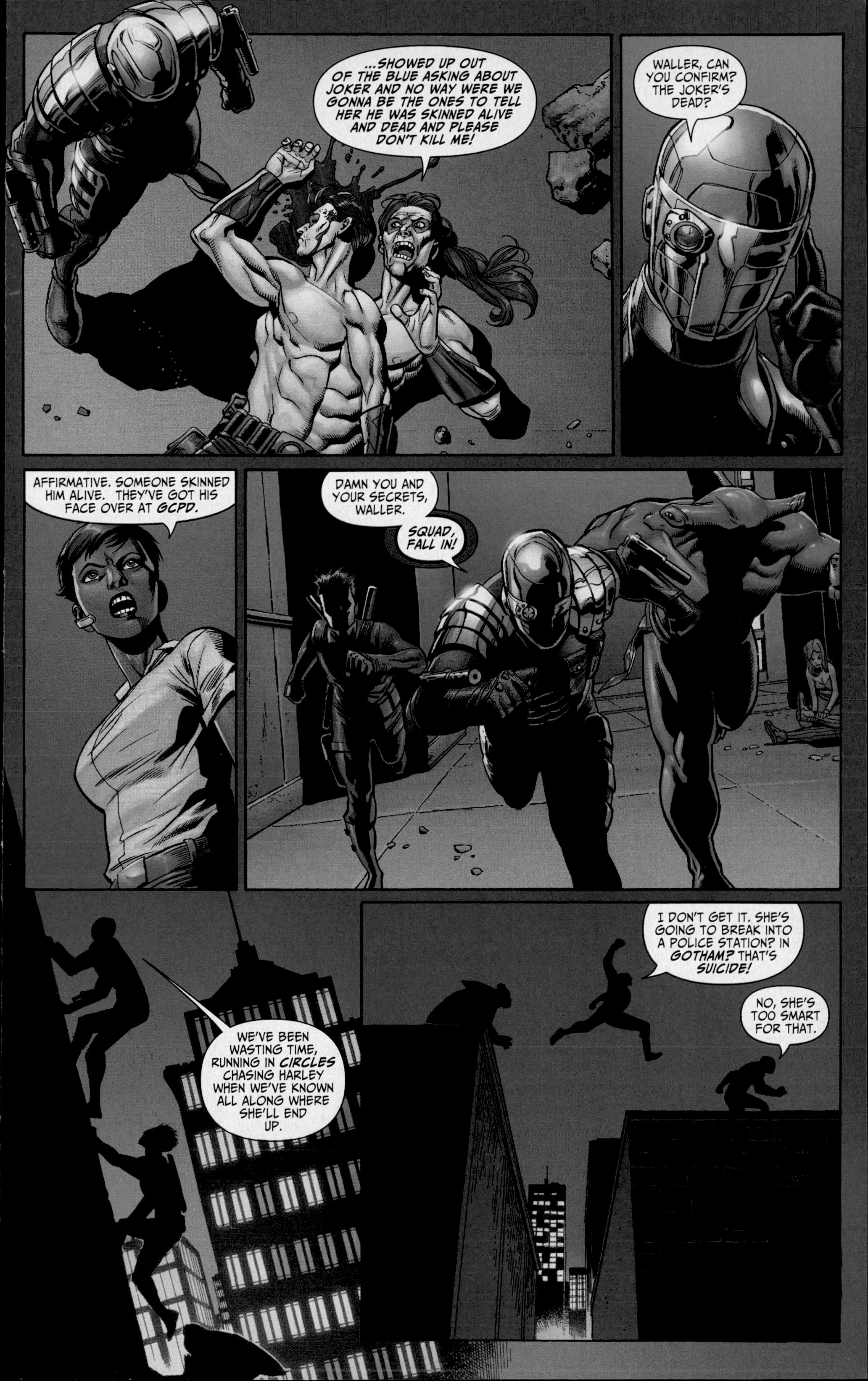
...SHOWED UP OUT OF THE BLUE ASKING ABOUT JOKER AND NO WAY WERE WE GONNA BE THE ONES TO TELL HER HE WAS SKINNED ALIVE AND DEAD AND PLEASE DON'T KILL ME!
WALLER, CAN YOU CONFIRM? THE JOKER'S DEAD?
AFFIRMATIVE. SOMEONE SKINNED HIM ALIVE. THEY'VE GOT HIS FACE OVER AT GCPD.
DAMN YOU AND YOUR SECRETS, WALLER.
SQUAD, FALL IN!
WE'VE BEEN WASTING TIME, RUNNING IN CIRCLES CHASING HARLEY WHEN WE'VE KNOWN ALL ALONG WHERE SHE'LL END UP.
I DON'T GET IT. SHE'S GOING TO BREAK INTO A POLICE STATION? IN GOTHAM? THAT'S SUICIDE!
NO, SHE'S TOO SMART FOR THAT.

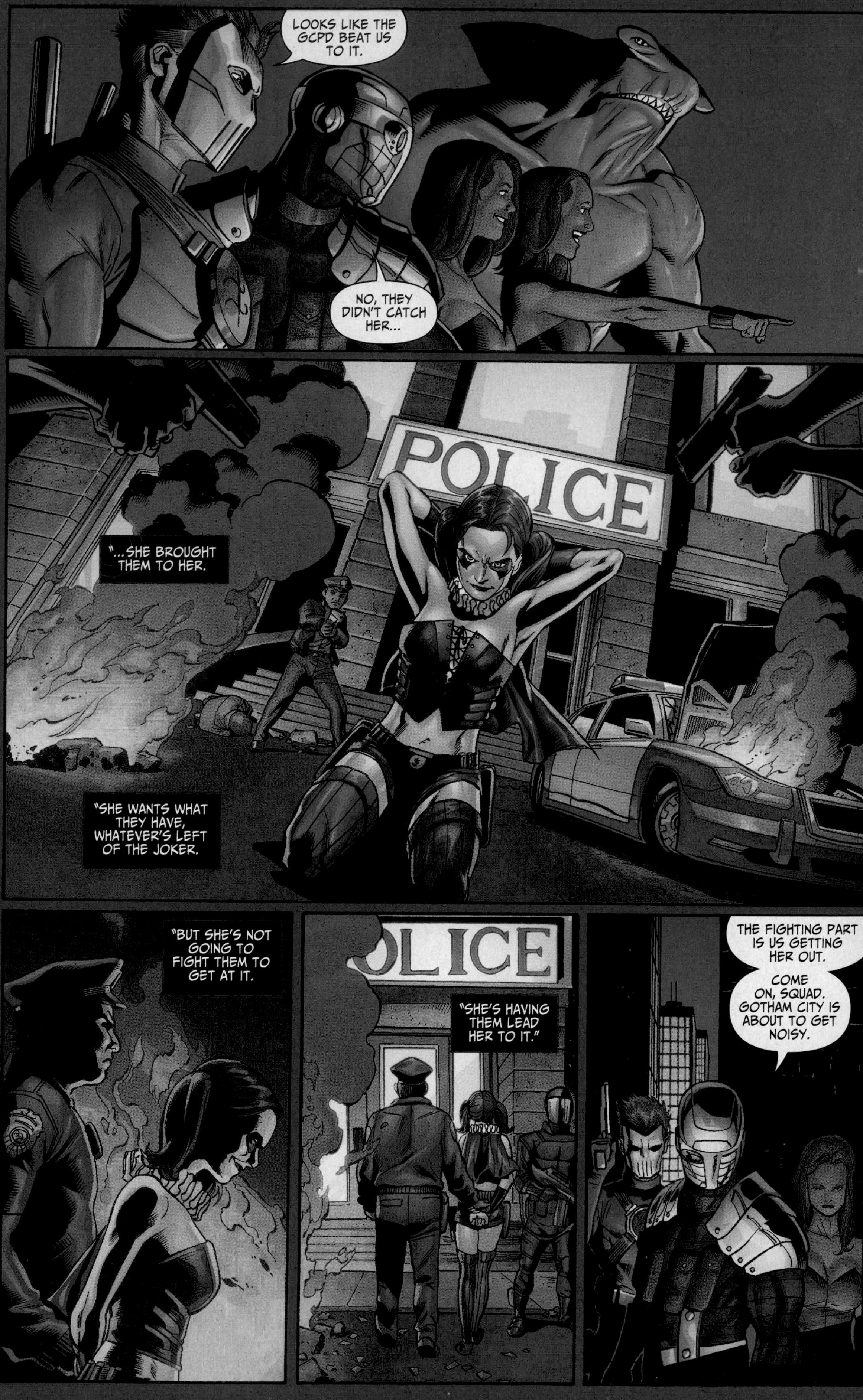
LOOKS LIKE THE GCPD BEAT US TO IT.
NO, THEY DIDN'T CATCH HER...
POLICE
"...SHE BROUGHT THEM TO HER.
"SHE WANTS WHAT THEY HAVE, WHATEVER'S LEFT OF THE JOKER.
"BUT SHE'S NOT GOING TO FIGHT THEM TO GET AT IT.
OLICE
"SHE'S HAVING THEM LEAD HER TO IT."
THE FIGHTING PART IS US GETTING HER OUT.
COME ON, SQUAD. GOTHAM CITY IS ABOUT TO GET NOISY.

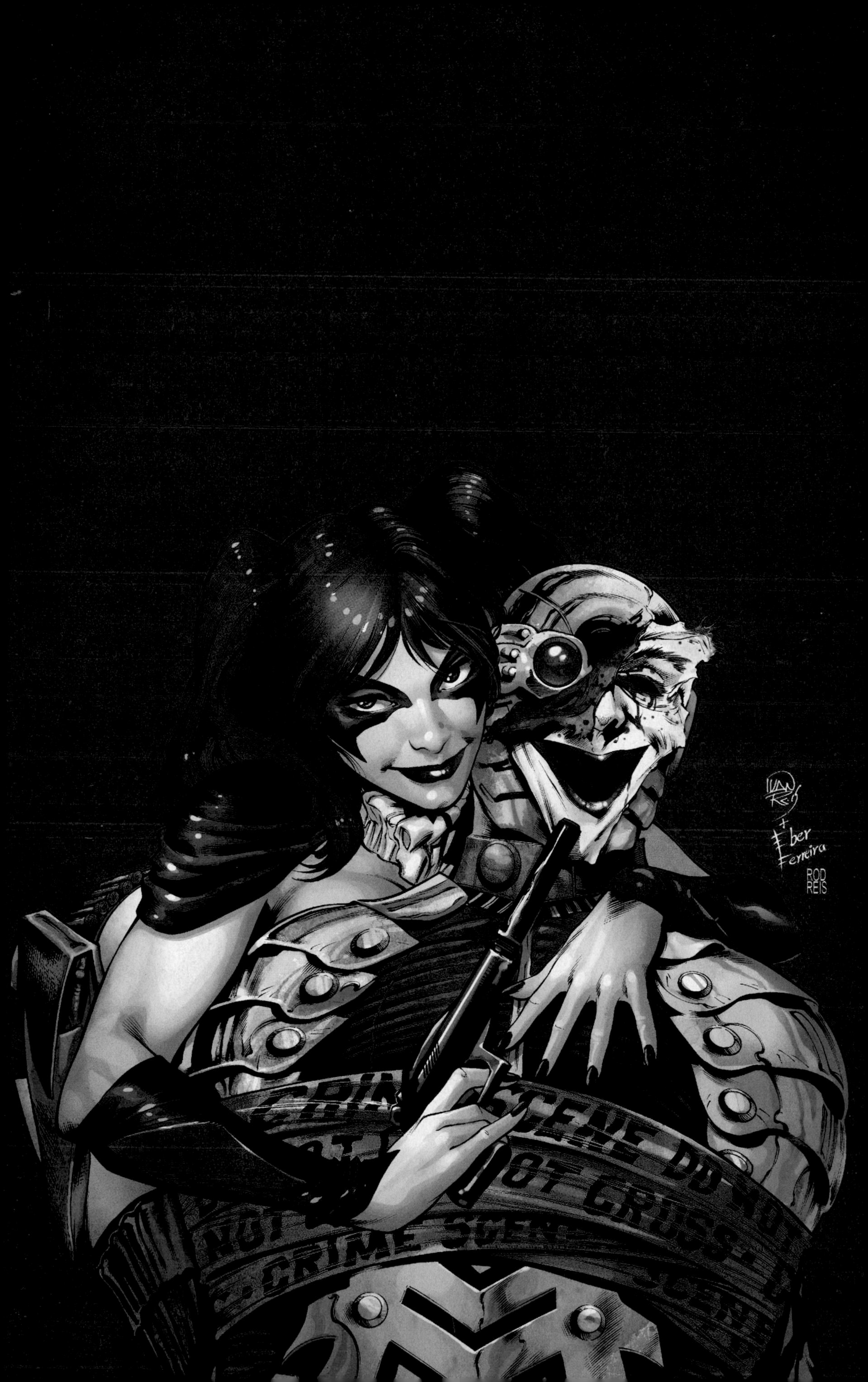
Eber
Ferreira
ROD
REIS

THE HUNT FOR HARLEY QUINN part two

ADAM GLASS
writer

CLAYTON HENRY & IG GUARA
pencillers

SCOTT HANNA
inker

cover art by IVAN REIS, EBER FERREIRA & ROD REIS

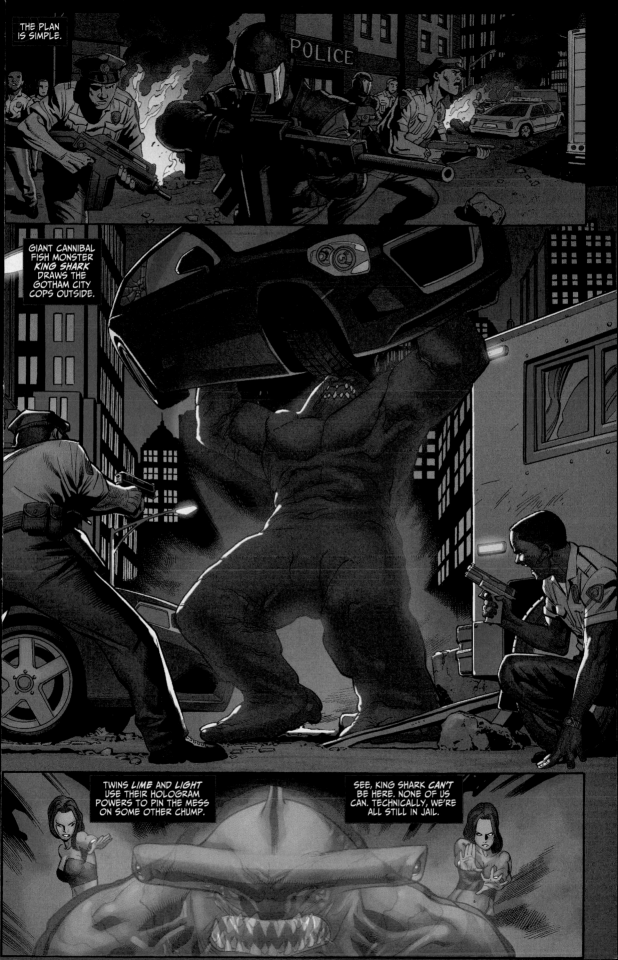

THE PLAN IS SIMPLE.

GIANT CANNIBAL FISH MONSTER *KING SHARK* DRAWS THE GOTHAM CITY COPS OUTSIDE.

TWINS *LIME* AND *LIGHT* USE THEIR HOLOGRAM POWERS TO PIN THE MESS ON SOME OTHER CHUMP.

SEE, KING SHARK *CAN'T* BE HERE. NONE OF US CAN. TECHNICALLY, WE'RE ALL STILL IN JAIL.

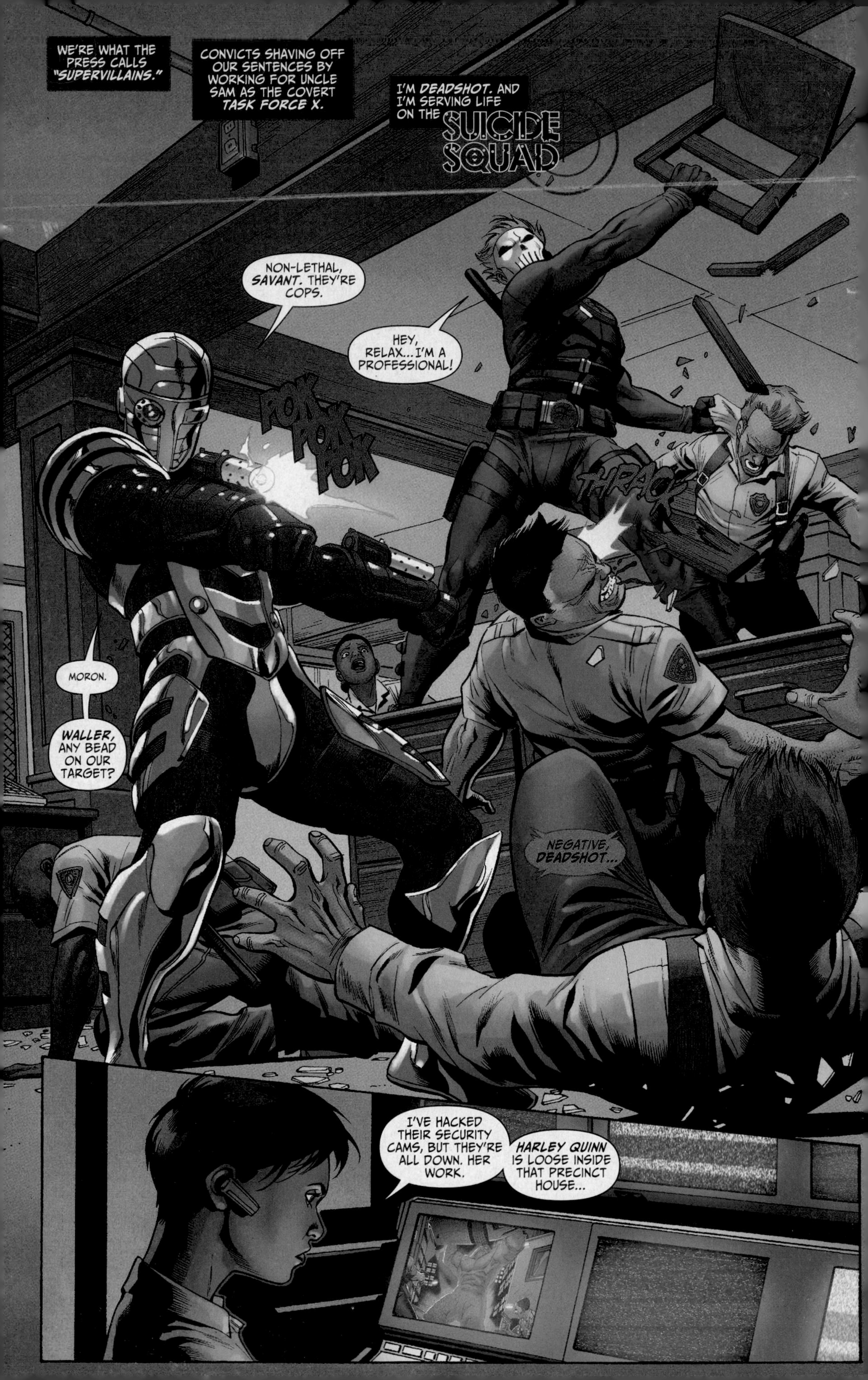
WE'RE WHAT THE PRESS CALLS "SUPERVILLAINS."
CONVICTS SHAVING OFF OUR SENTENCES BY WORKING FOR UNCLE SAM AS THE COVERT TASK FORCE X.
I'M DEADSHOT. AND I'M SERVING LIFE ON THE
SUICIDE SQUAD
NON-LETHAL, SAVANT. THEY'RE COPS.
HEY, RELAX... I'M A PROFESSIONAL!
POK POK POK
THRACK
MORON.
WALLER, ANY BEAD ON OUR TARGET?
NEGATIVE, DEADSHOT...
I'VE HACKED THEIR SECURITY CAMS, BUT THEY'RE ALL DOWN. HER WORK.
HARLEY QUINN IS LOOSE INSIDE THAT PRECINCT HOUSE...

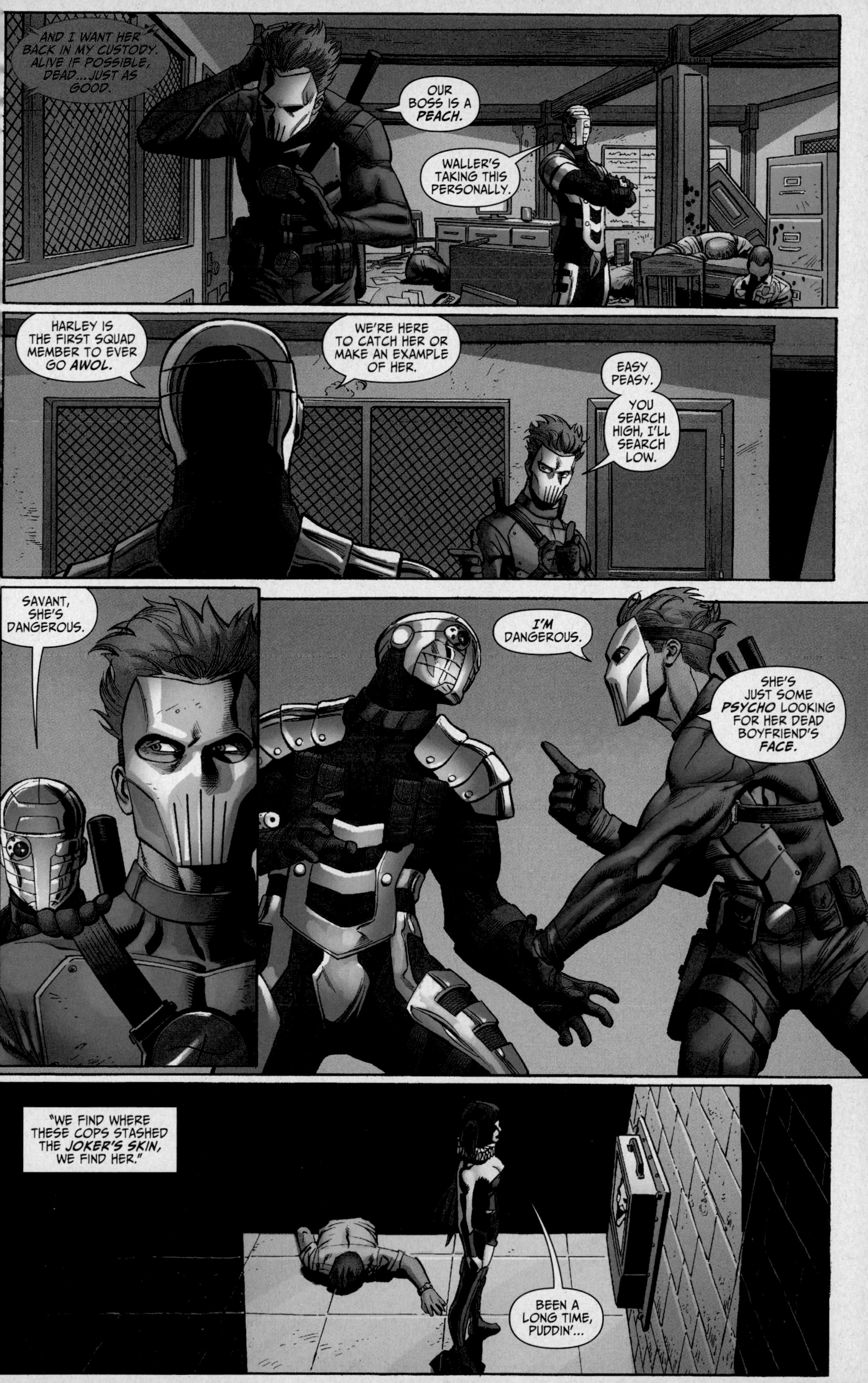
AND I WANT HER BACK IN MY CUSTODY. ALIVE IF POSSIBLE, DEAD... JUST AS GOOD.
OUR BOSS IS A PEACH.
WALLER'S TAKING THIS PERSONALLY.
HARLEY IS THE FIRST SQUAD MEMBER TO EVER GO AWOL.
WE'RE HERE TO CATCH HER OR MAKE AN EXAMPLE OF HER.
EASY PEASY.
YOU SEARCH HIGH, I'LL SEARCH LOW.
SAVANT, SHE'S DANGEROUS.
I'M DANGEROUS.
SHE'S JUST SOME PSYCHO LOOKING FOR HER DEAD BOYFRIEND'S FACE.
"WE FIND WHERE THESE COPS STASHED THE JOKER'S SKIN, WE FIND HER."
BEEN A LONG TIME, PUDDIN'...

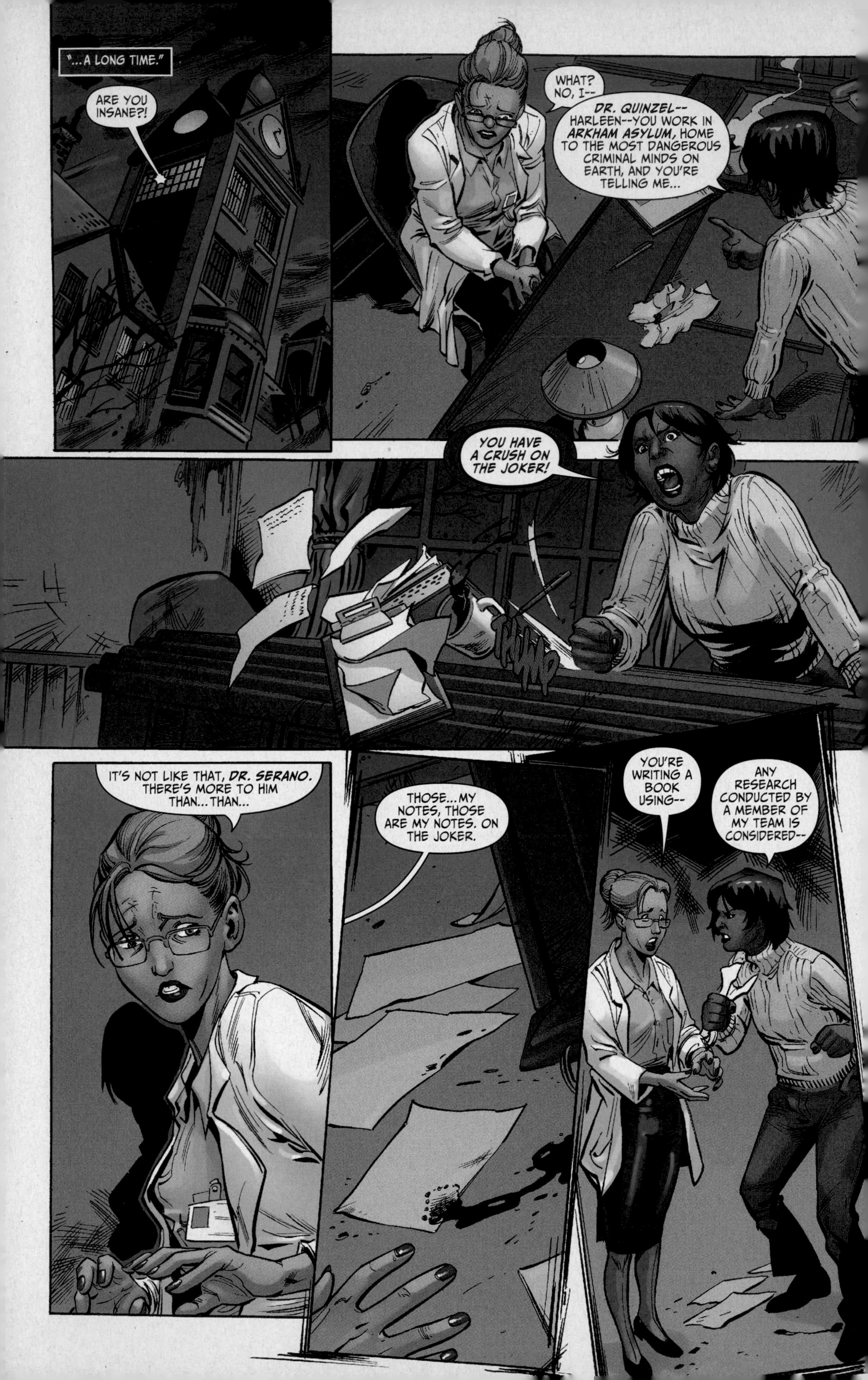
"...A LONG TIME."
ARE YOU INSANE?!
WHAT? NO, I--
DR. QUINZEL-- HARLEEN--YOU WORK IN ARKHAM ASYLUM, HOME TO THE MOST DANGEROUS CRIMINAL MINDS ON EARTH, AND YOU'RE TELLING ME...
YOU HAVE A CRUSH ON THE JOKER!
THUMP
IT'S NOT LIKE THAT, DR. SERANO. THERE'S MORE TO HIM THAN...THAN...
THOSE...MY NOTES, THOSE ARE MY NOTES. ON THE JOKER.
YOU'RE WRITING A BOOK USING--
ANY RESEARCH CONDUCTED BY A MEMBER OF MY TEAM IS CONSIDERED--

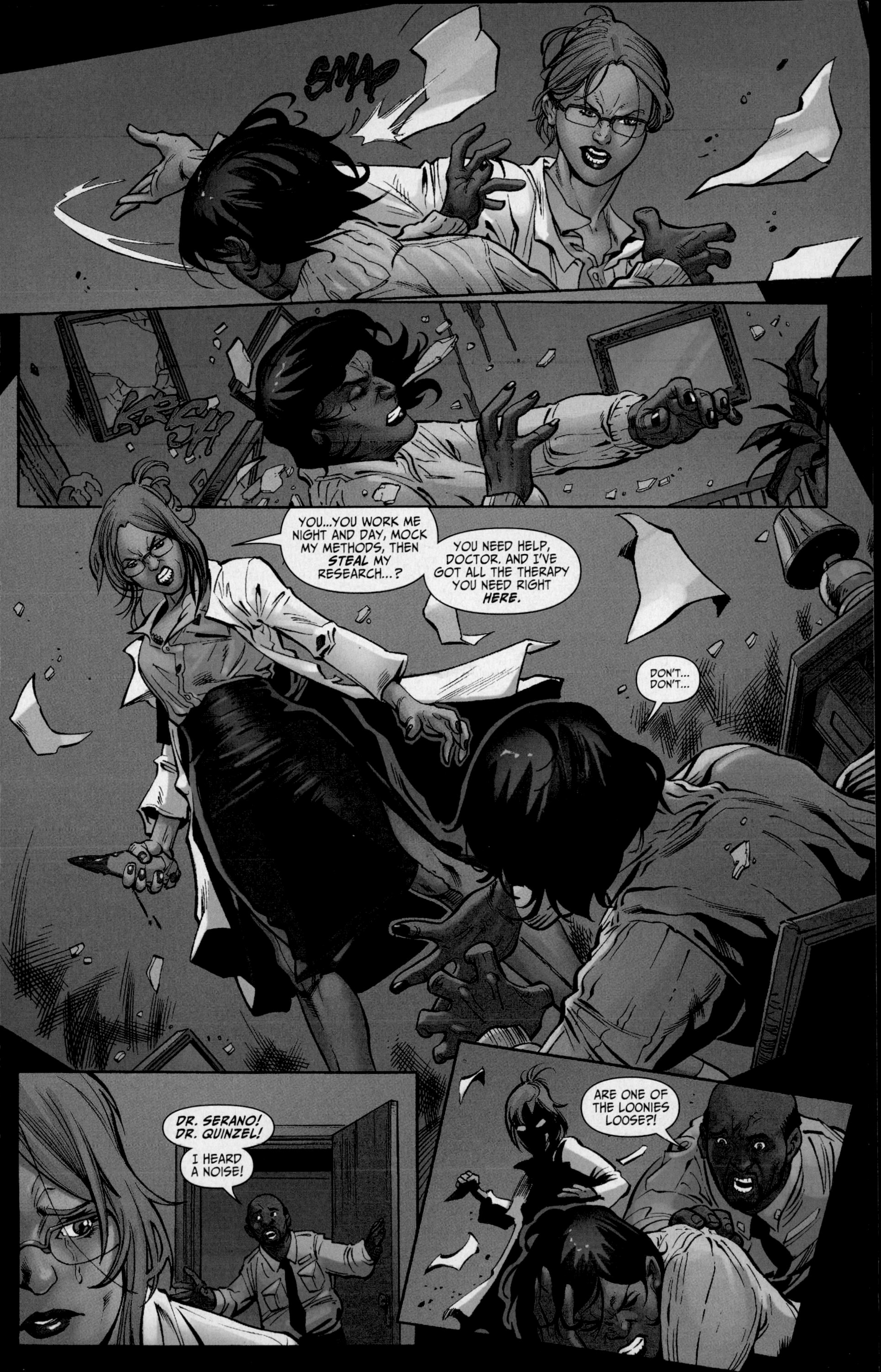

SMAP
KRSH
YOU...YOU WORK ME NIGHT AND DAY, MOCK MY METHODS, THEN STEAL MY RESEARCH...?
YOU NEED HELP, DOCTOR. AND I'VE GOT ALL THE THERAPY YOU NEED RIGHT HERE.
DON'T... DON'T...
DR. SERANO! DR. QUINZEL!
I HEARD A NOISE!
ARE ONE OF THE LOONIES LOOSE?!

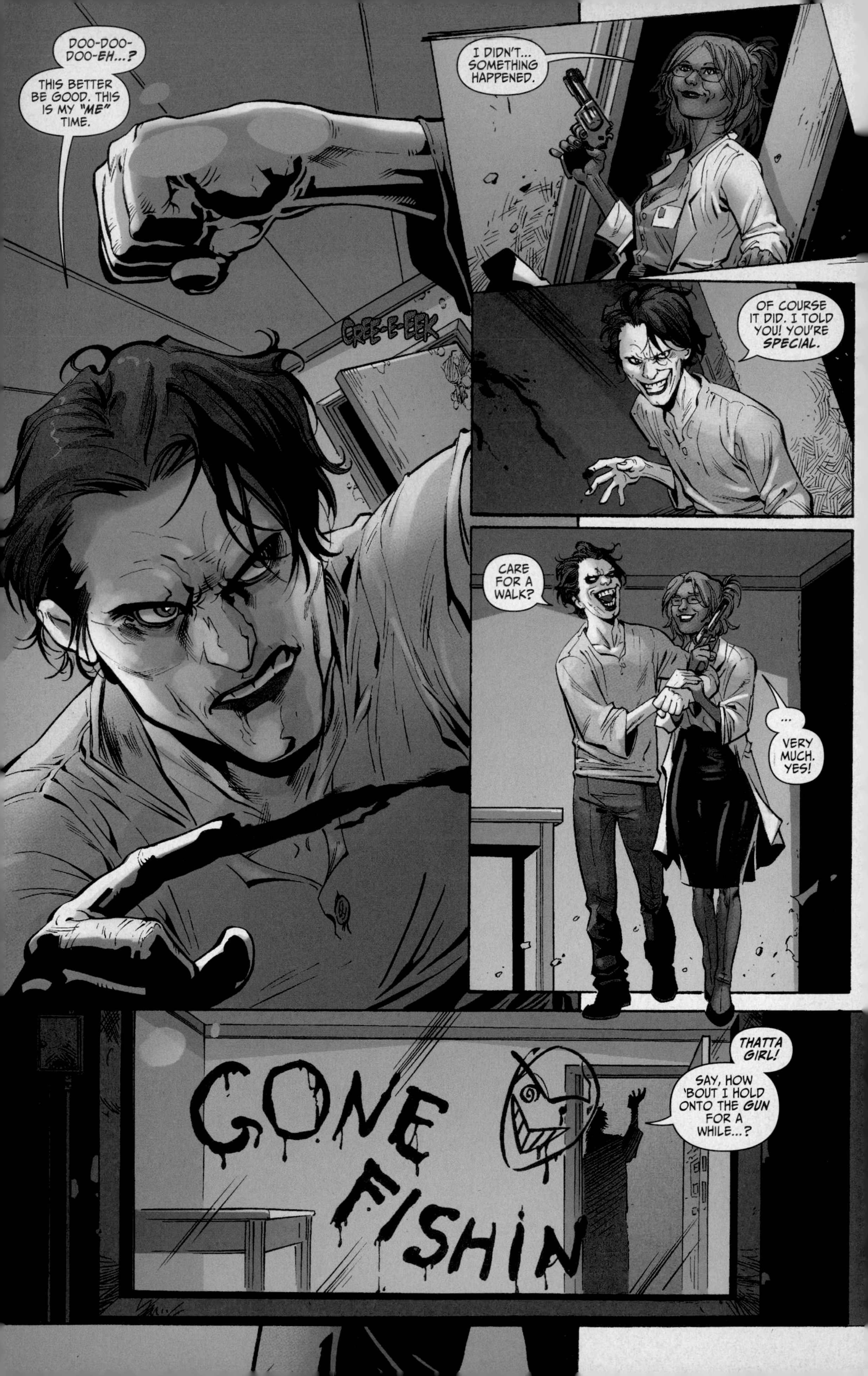
DOO-DOO-DOO-EH...?
THIS BETTER BE GOOD. THIS IS MY "ME" TIME.
I DIDN'T... SOMETHING HAPPENED.
CREE-E-EEK
OF COURSE IT DID. I TOLD YOU! YOU'RE SPECIAL.
CARE FOR A WALK?
... VERY MUCH. YES!
GONE FISHIN
THATTA GIRL!
SAY, HOW 'BOUT I HOLD ONTO THE GUN FOR A WHILE...?

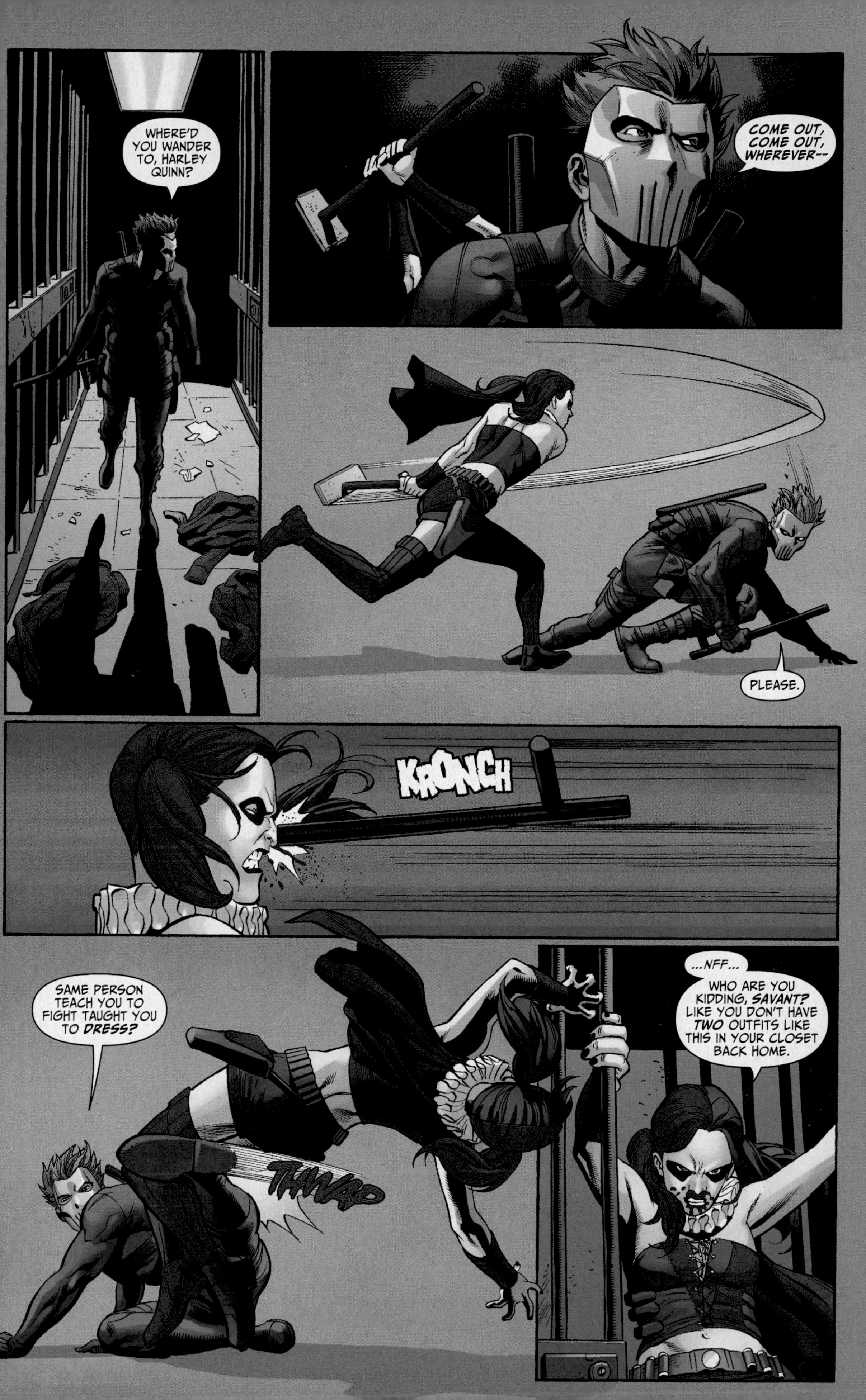
WHERE'D YOU WANDER TO, HARLEY QUINN?
COME OUT, COME OUT, WHEREVER--
PLEASE.
KRONCH
SAME PERSON TEACH YOU TO FIGHT TAUGHT YOU TO DRESS?
THWAP
...NFF...
WHO ARE YOU KIDDING, SAVANT? LIKE YOU DON'T HAVE TWO OUTFITS LIKE THIS IN YOUR CLOSET BACK HOME.

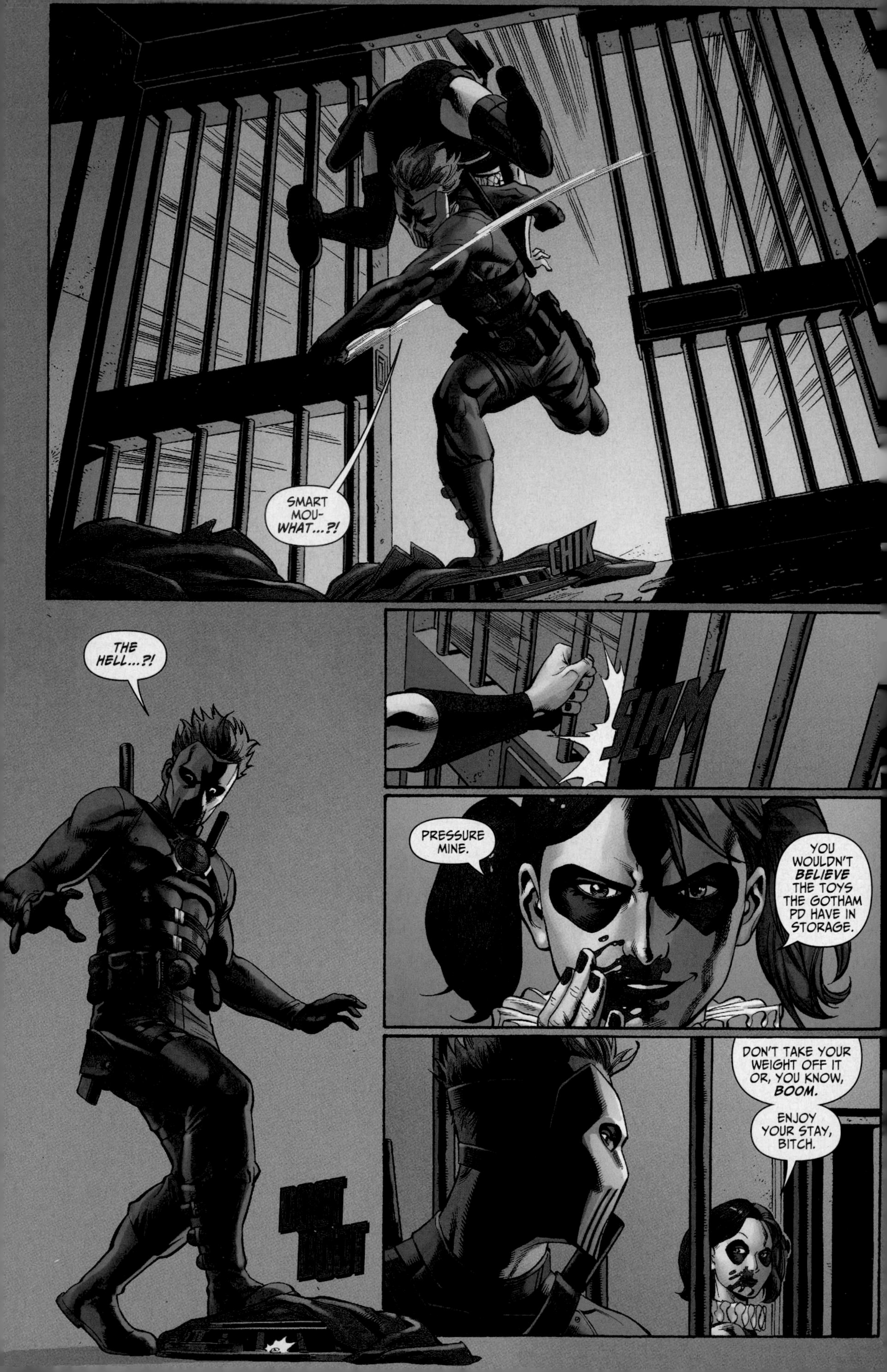
SMART MOU- WHAT...?!
CHIK
THE HELL...?!
SLAM
PRESSURE MINE.
YOU WOULDN'T **BELIEVE** THE TOYS THE GOTHAM PD HAVE IN STORAGE.
DON'T TAKE YOUR WEIGHT OFF IT OR, YOU KNOW, **BOOM.**
ENJOY YOUR STAY, BITCH.

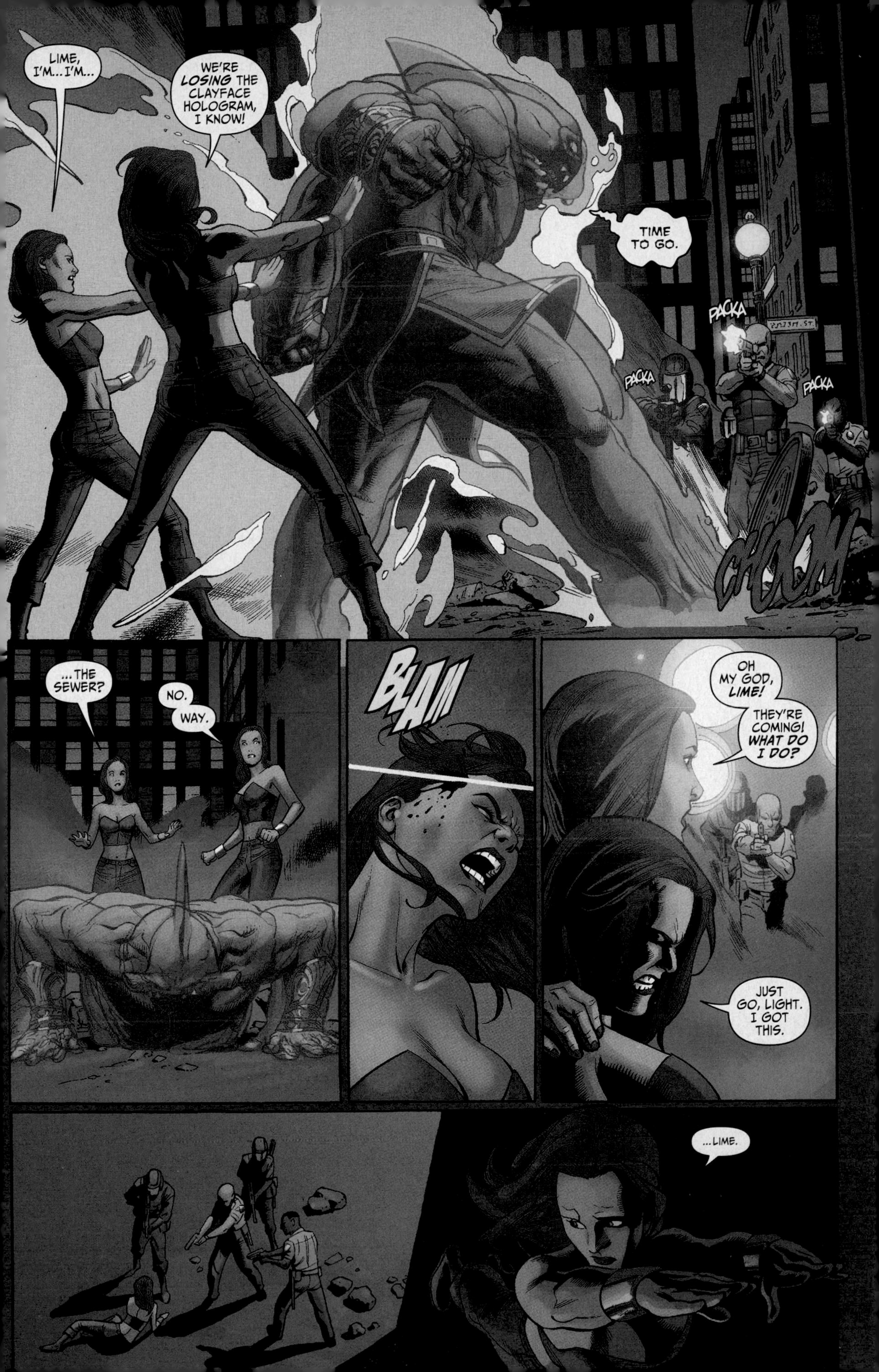
LIME, I'M...I'M...
WE'RE LOSING THE CLAYFACE HOLOGRAM, I KNOW!
TIME TO GO.
PACKA
PACKA
PACKA
CHOOM
...THE SEWER?
NO. WAY.
BLAM
OH MY GOD, LIME!
THEY'RE COMING! WHAT DO I DO?
JUST GO, LIGHT. I GOT THIS.
...LIME.

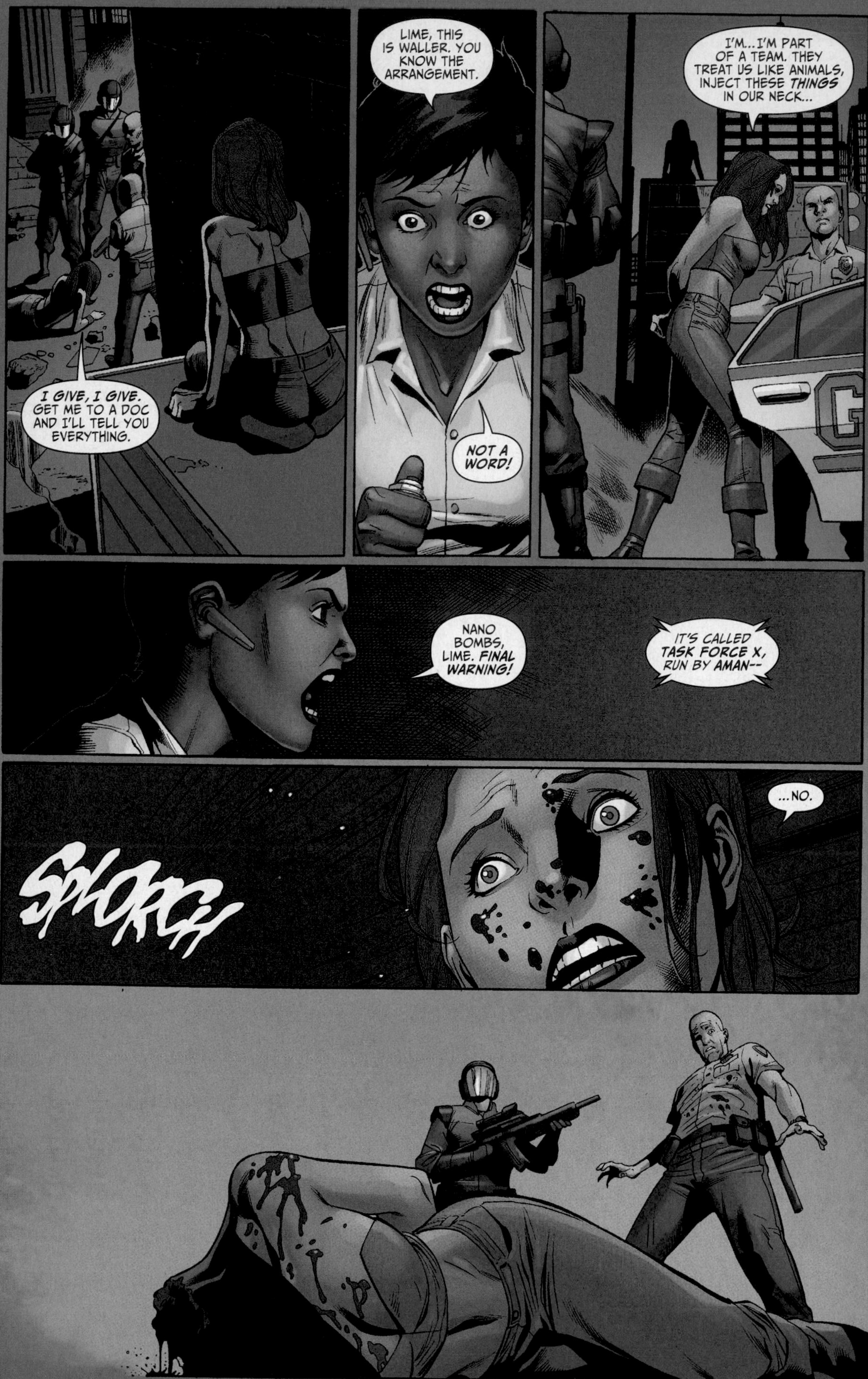
I GIVE, I GIVE. GET ME TO A DOC AND I'LL TELL YOU EVERYTHING.
LIME, THIS IS WALLER. YOU KNOW THE ARRANGEMENT.
NOT A WORD!
I'M...I'M PART OF A TEAM. THEY TREAT US LIKE ANIMALS, INJECT THESE THINGS IN OUR NECK...
NANO BOMBS, LIME. FINAL WARNING!
IT'S CALLED TASK FORCE X, RUN BY AMAN--
...NO.
SPLORCH

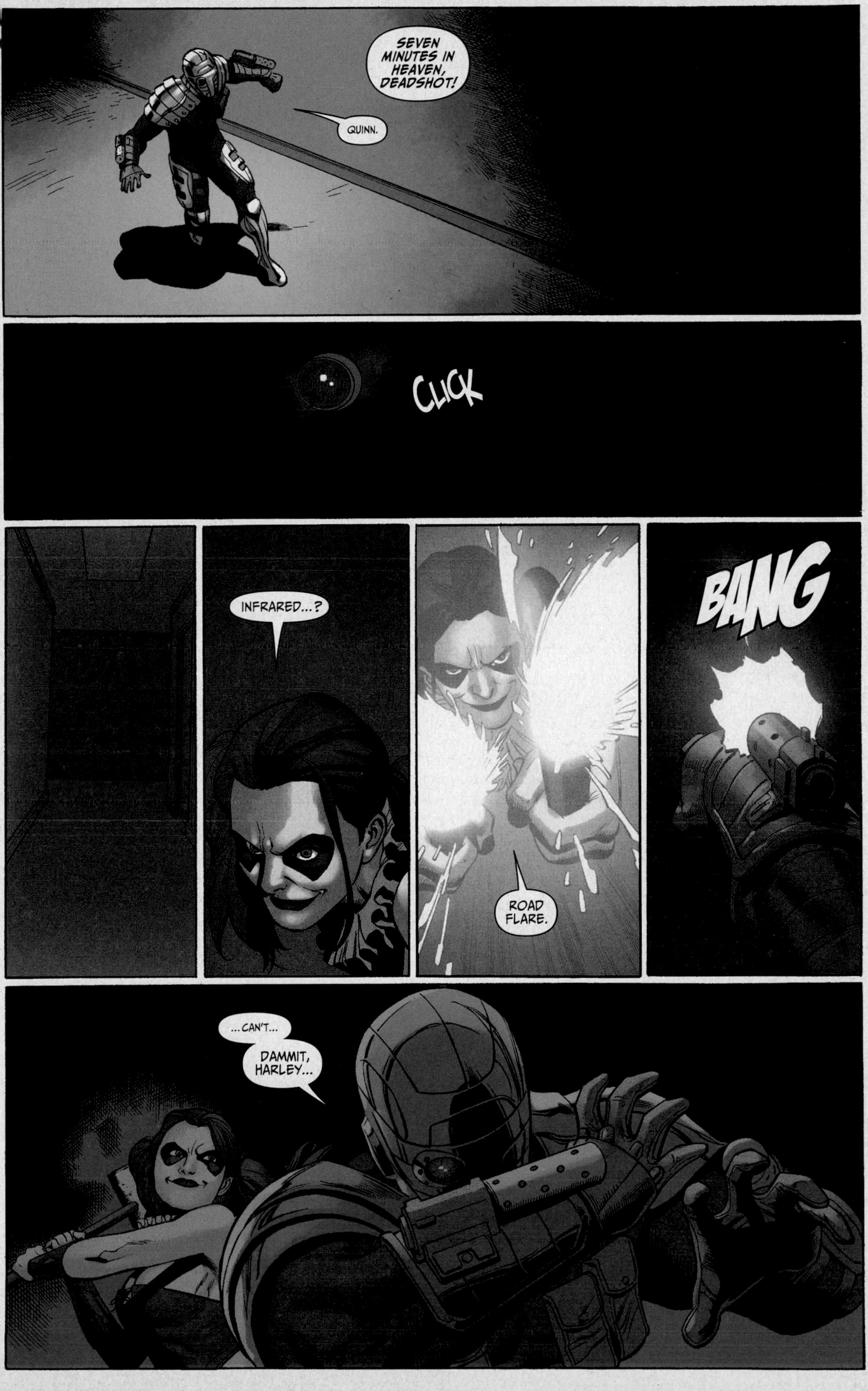
SEVEN MINUTES IN HEAVEN, DEADSHOT!
QUINN.
CLICK
INFRARED...?
ROAD FLARE.
BANG
...CAN'T...
DAMMIT, HARLEY...

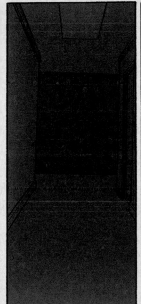

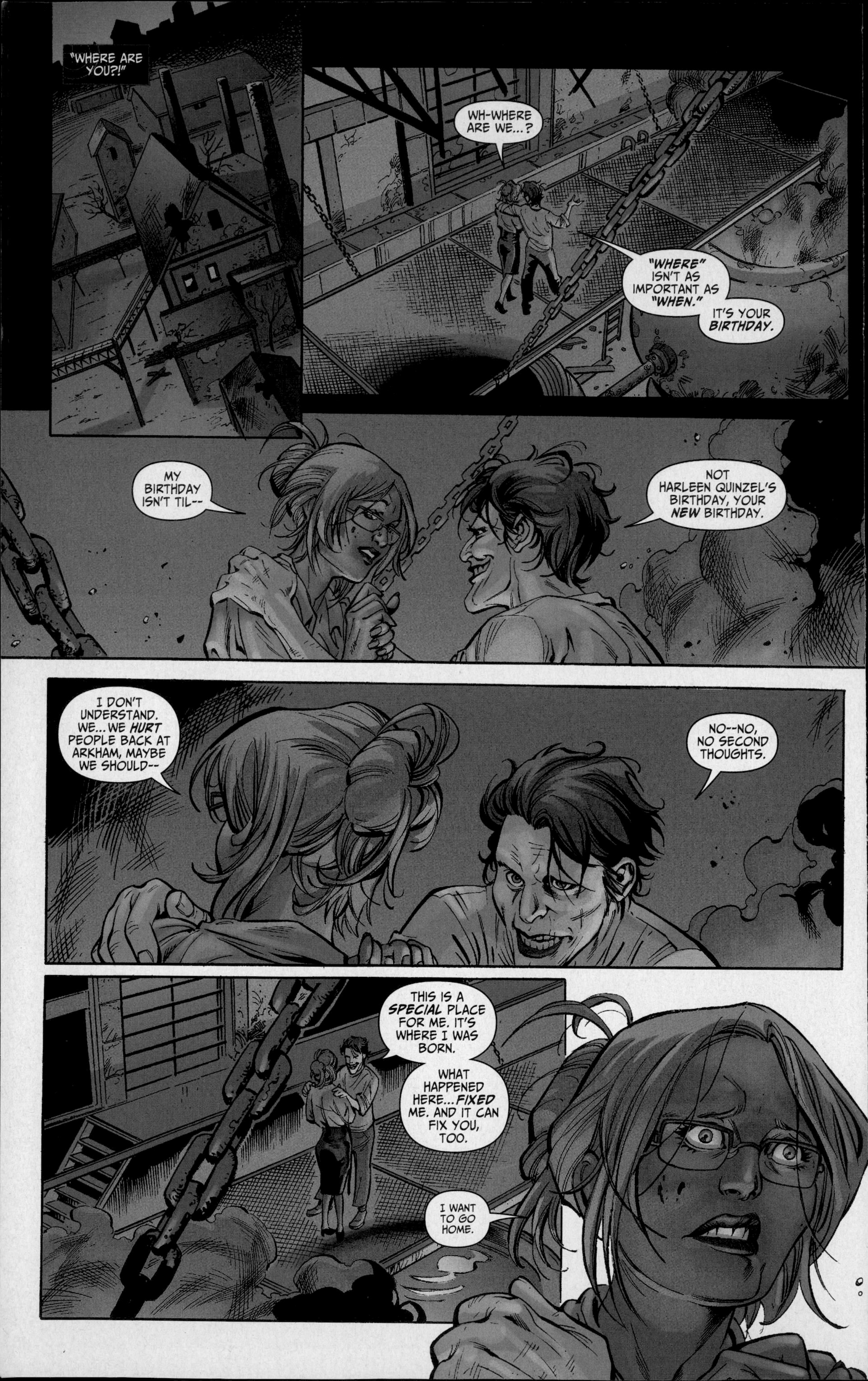
"WHERE ARE YOU?!"
WH-WHERE ARE WE...?
"WHERE" ISN'T AS IMPORTANT AS "WHEN."
IT'S YOUR BIRTHDAY.
MY BIRTHDAY ISN'T TIL--
NOT HARLEEN QUINZEL'S BIRTHDAY, YOUR NEW BIRTHDAY.
I DON'T UNDERSTAND. WE...WE HURT PEOPLE BACK AT ARKHAM, MAYBE WE SHOULD--
NO--NO, NO SECOND THOUGHTS.
THIS IS A SPECIAL PLACE FOR ME. IT'S WHERE I WAS BORN.
WHAT HAPPENED HERE...FIXED ME. AND IT CAN FIX YOU, TOO.
I WANT TO GO HOME.

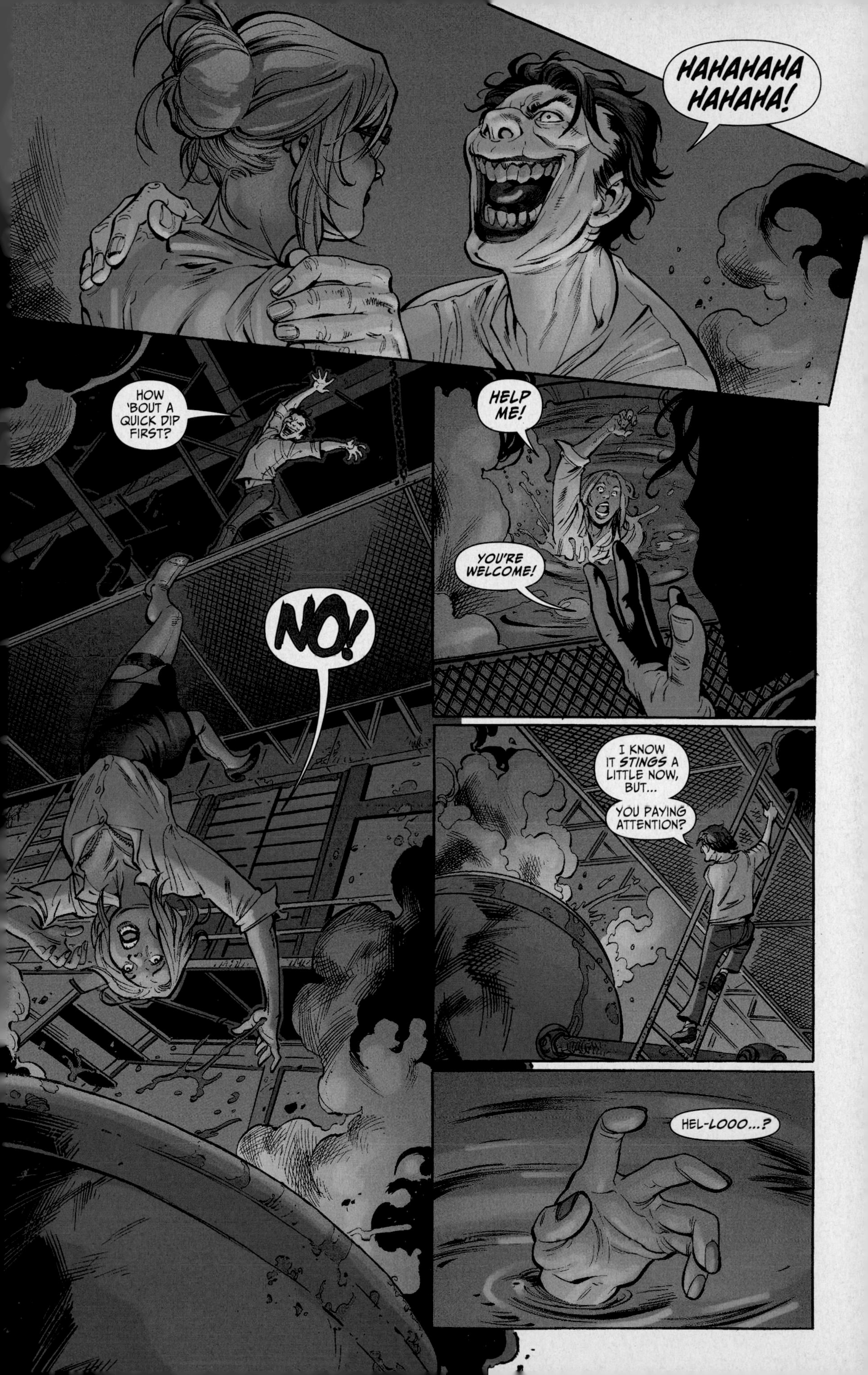
HAHAHAHA
HAHAHA!
HOW 'BOUT A QUICK DIP FIRST?
NO!
HELP ME!
YOU'RE WELCOME!
I KNOW IT STINGS A LITTLE NOW, BUT...
YOU PAYING ATTENTION?
HEL-LOOO...?

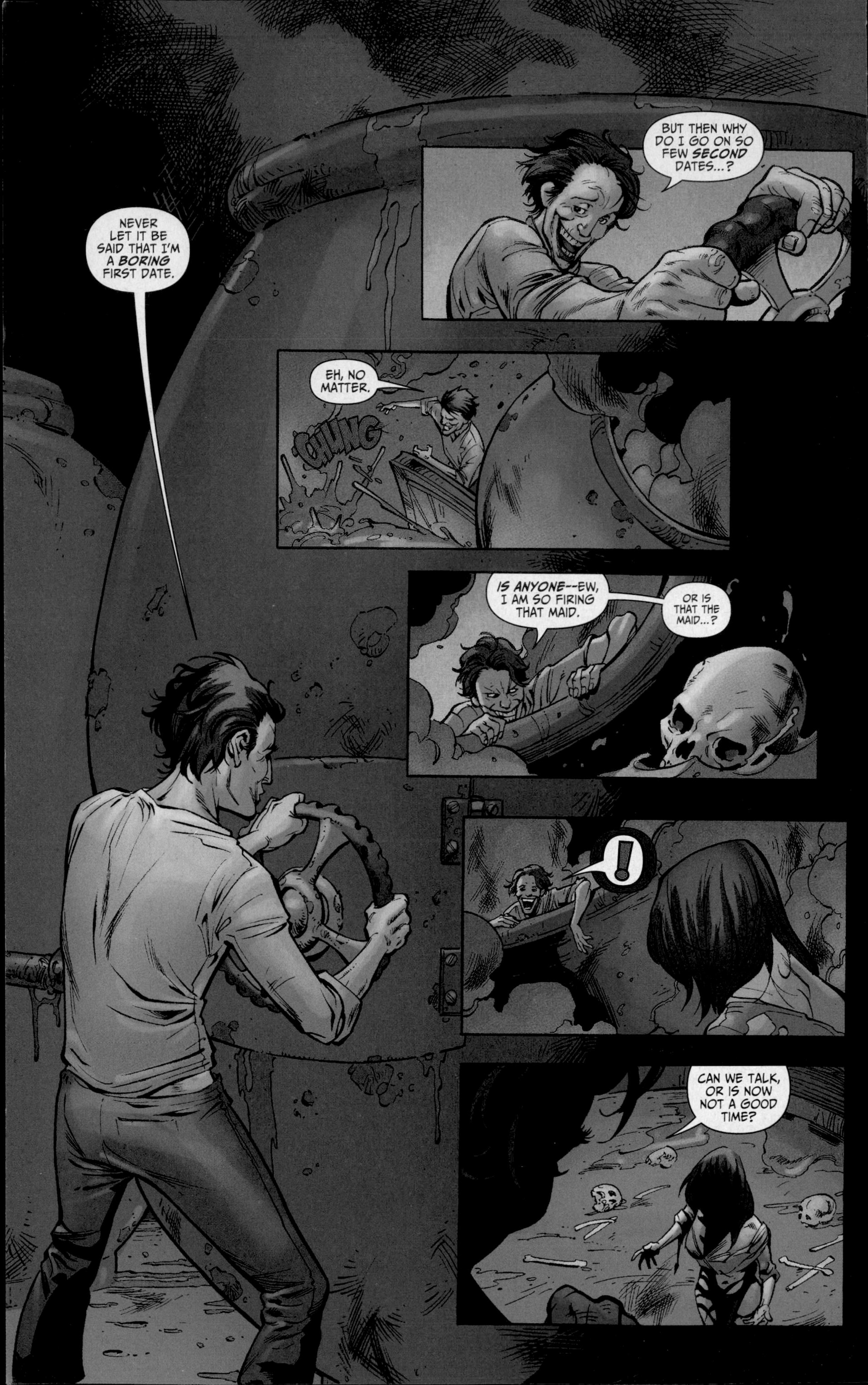

NEVER LET IT BE SAID THAT I'M A BORING FIRST DATE.
BUT THEN WHY DO I GO ON SO FEW SECOND DATES...?
EH, NO MATTER.
CHUNG
IS ANYONE--EW, I AM SO FIRING THAT MAID.
OR IS THAT THE MAID...?
!
CAN WE TALK, OR IS NOW NOT A GOOD TIME?

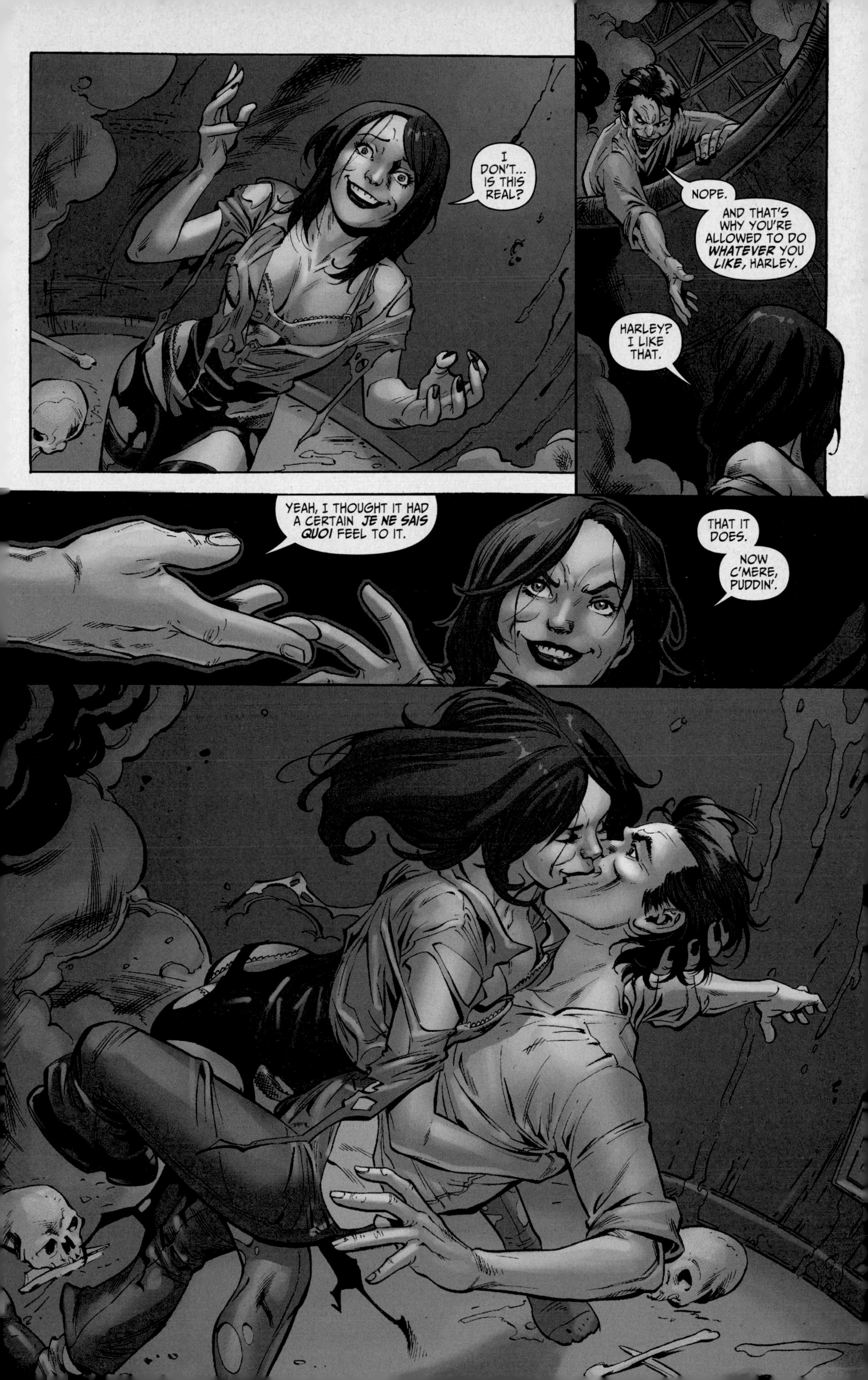
I DON'T... IS THIS REAL?
NOPE.
AND THAT'S WHY YOU'RE ALLOWED TO DO WHATEVER YOU LIKE, HARLEY.
HARLEY? I LIKE THAT.
YEAH, I THOUGHT IT HAD A CERTAIN JE NE SAIS QUOI FEEL TO IT.
THAT IT DOES.
NOW C'MERE, PUDDIN'.

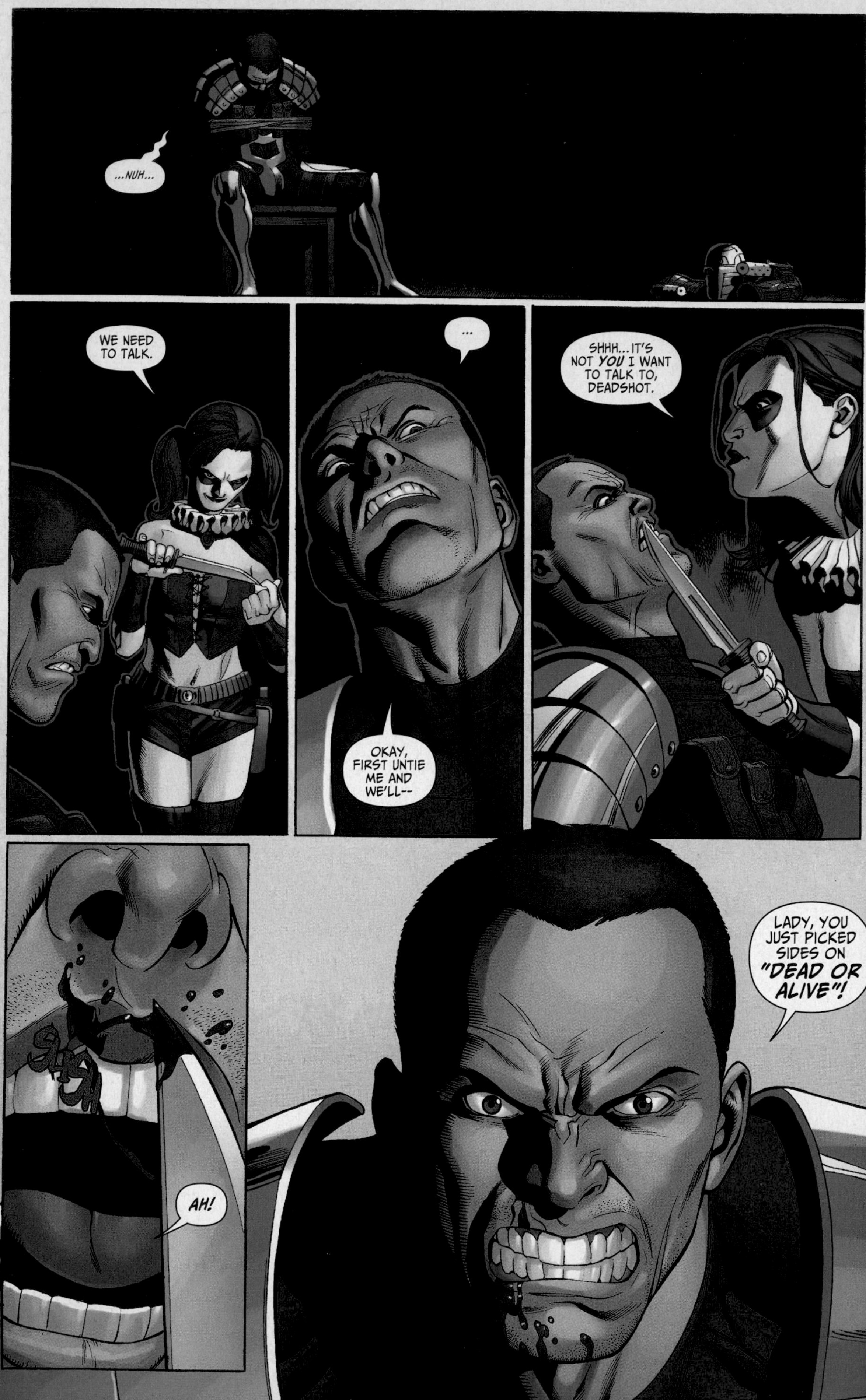
...NUH...
WE NEED TO TALK.
...
OKAY, FIRST UNTIE ME AND WE'LL--
SHHH...IT'S NOT YOU I WANT TO TALK TO, DEADSHOT.
SLISH
AH!
LADY, YOU JUST PICKED SIDES ON "DEAD OR ALIVE"!

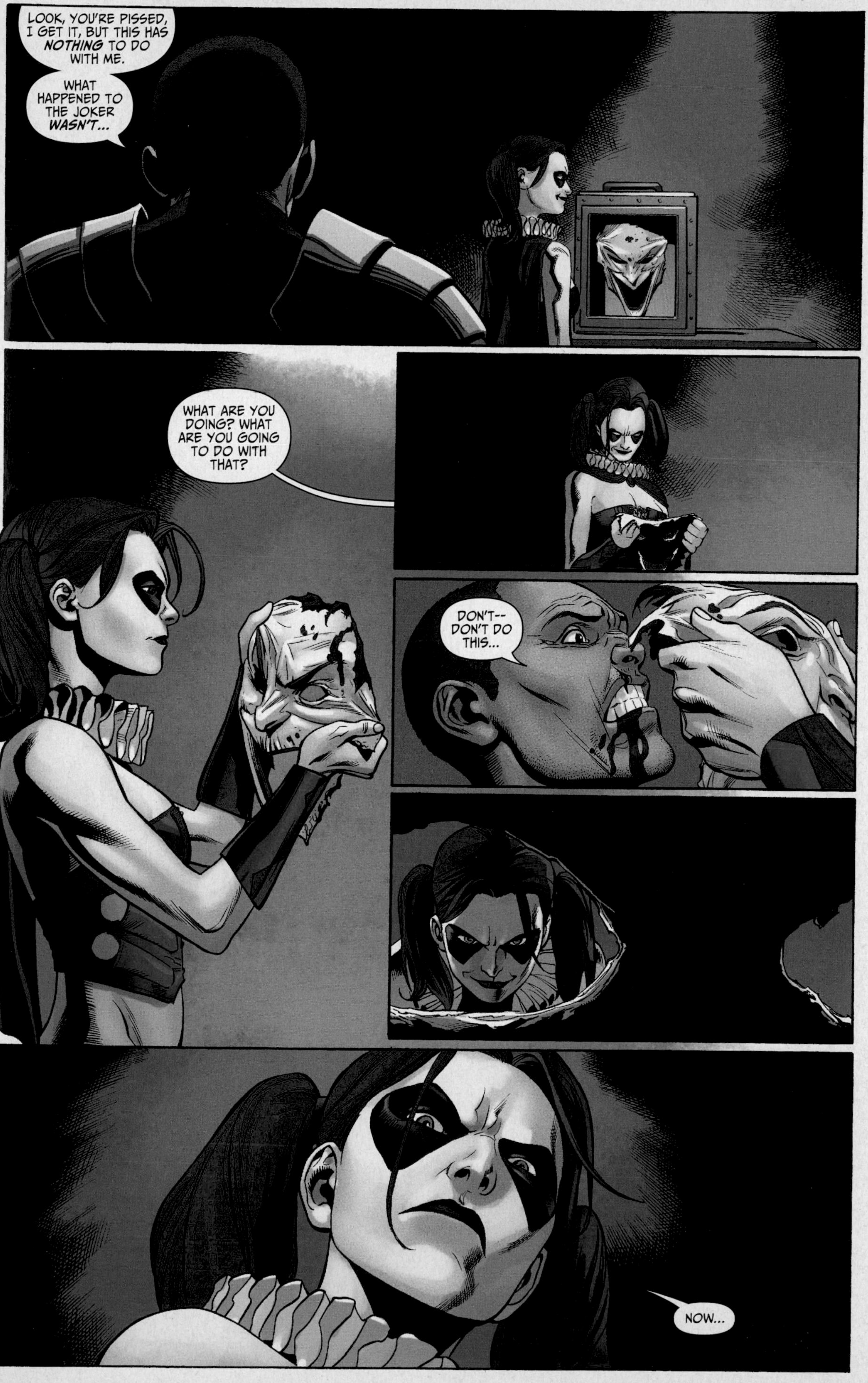
LOOK, YOU'RE PISSED, I GET IT, BUT THIS HAS *NOTHING* TO DO WITH ME.
WHAT HAPPENED TO THE JOKER *WASN'T...*
WHAT ARE YOU DOING? WHAT ARE YOU GOING TO DO WITH THAT?
DON'T-- DON'T DO THIS...
NOW...

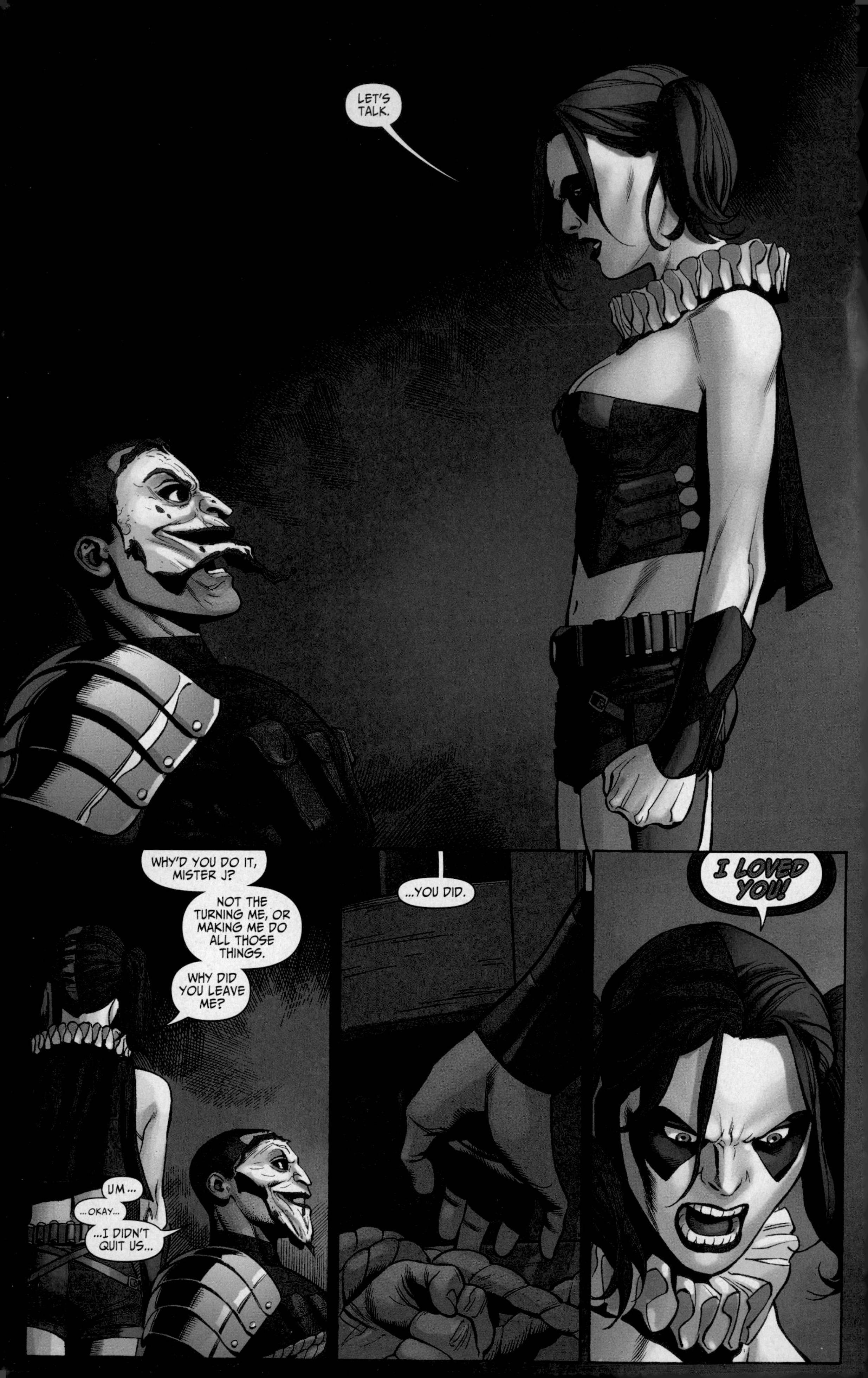
LET'S TALK.
WHY'D YOU DO IT, MISTER J?
NOT THE TURNING ME, OR MAKING ME DO ALL THOSE THINGS.
WHY DID YOU LEAVE ME?
UM...
...OKAY...
...I DIDN'T QUIT US...
...YOU DID.
I LOVED YOU!

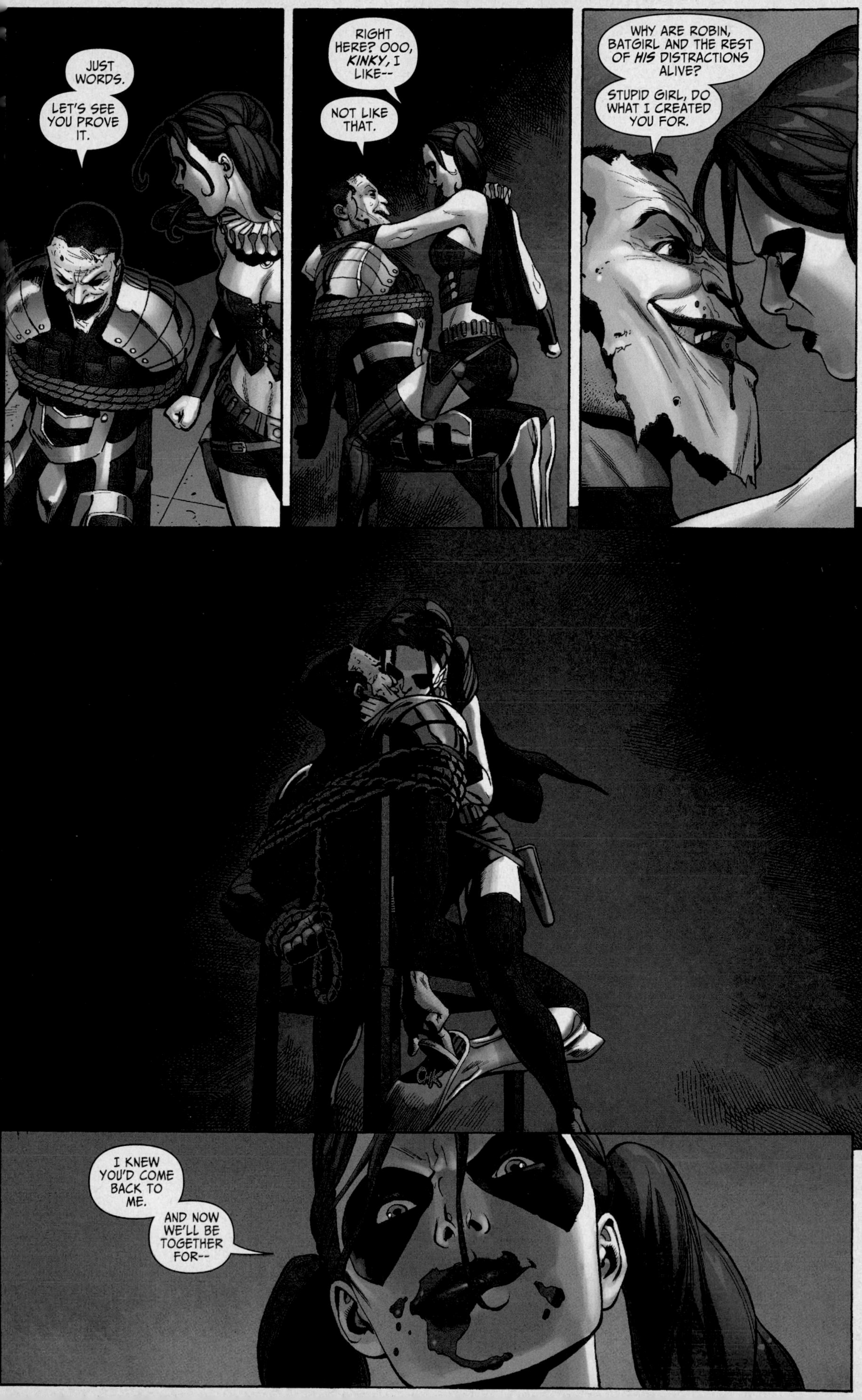
JUST WORDS.
LET'S SEE YOU PROVE IT.
RIGHT HERE? OOO, *KINKY*, I LIKE--
NOT LIKE THAT.
WHY ARE ROBIN, BATGIRL AND THE REST OF *HIS* DISTRACTIONS ALIVE?
STUPID GIRL, DO WHAT I CREATED YOU FOR.
I KNEW YOU'D COME BACK TO ME.
AND NOW WE'LL BE TOGETHER FOR--

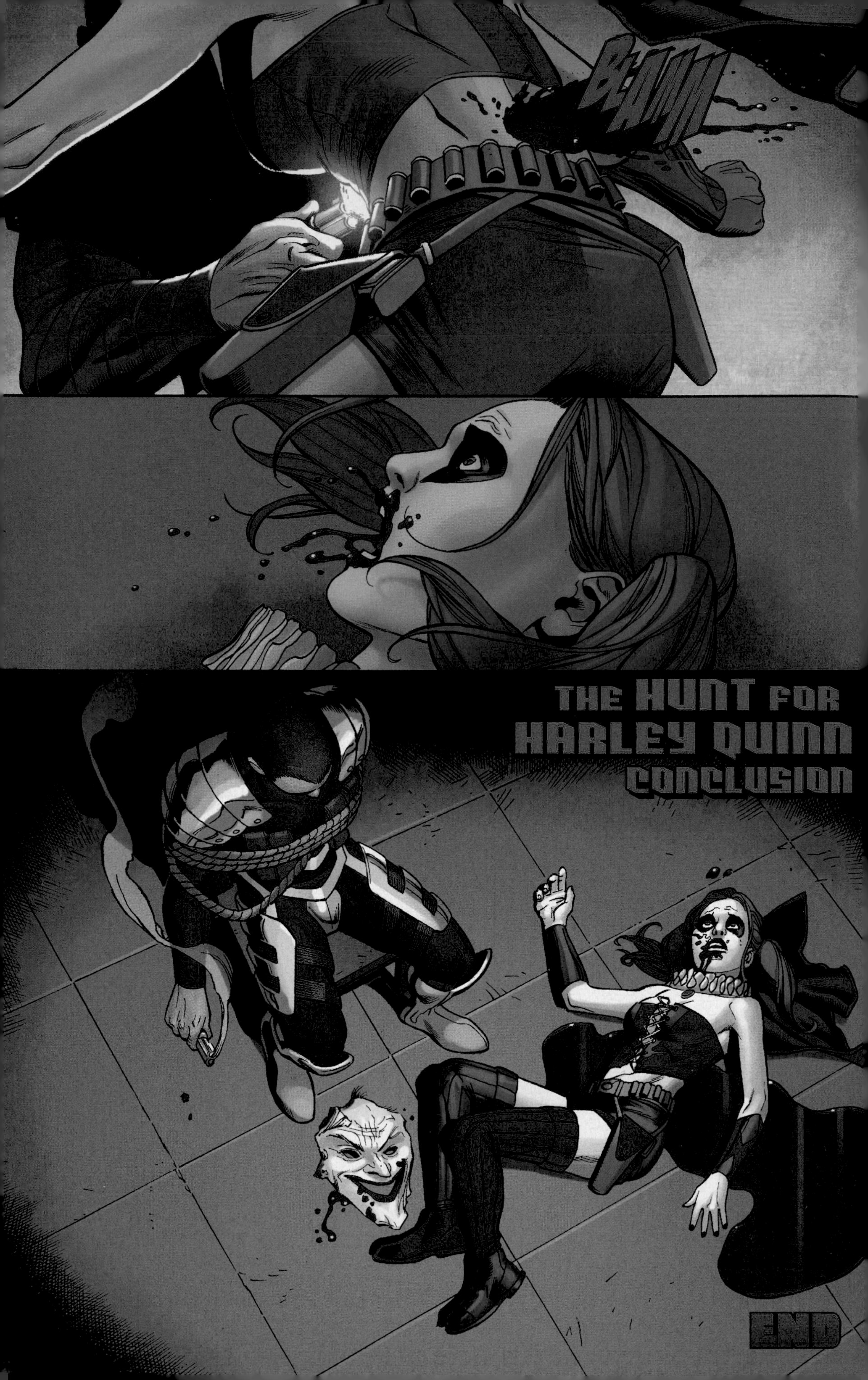
BLAMM
THE HUNT FOR
HARLEY QUINN
CONCLUSION
END

Deadshot sketch by Jim Lee

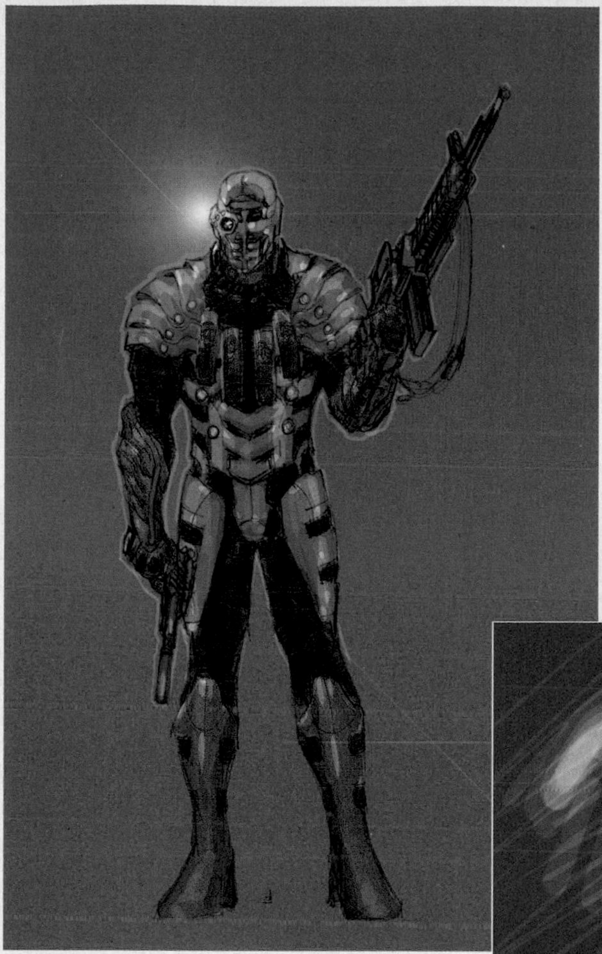

Harley Quinn sketch by Jim Lee

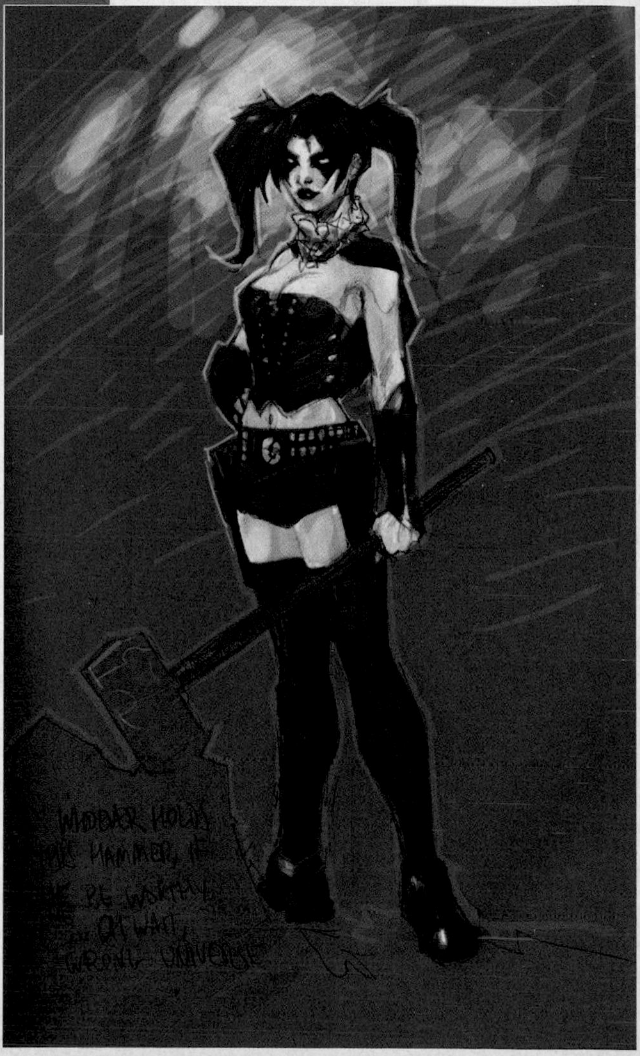

Black Spider sketch by Jim Lee

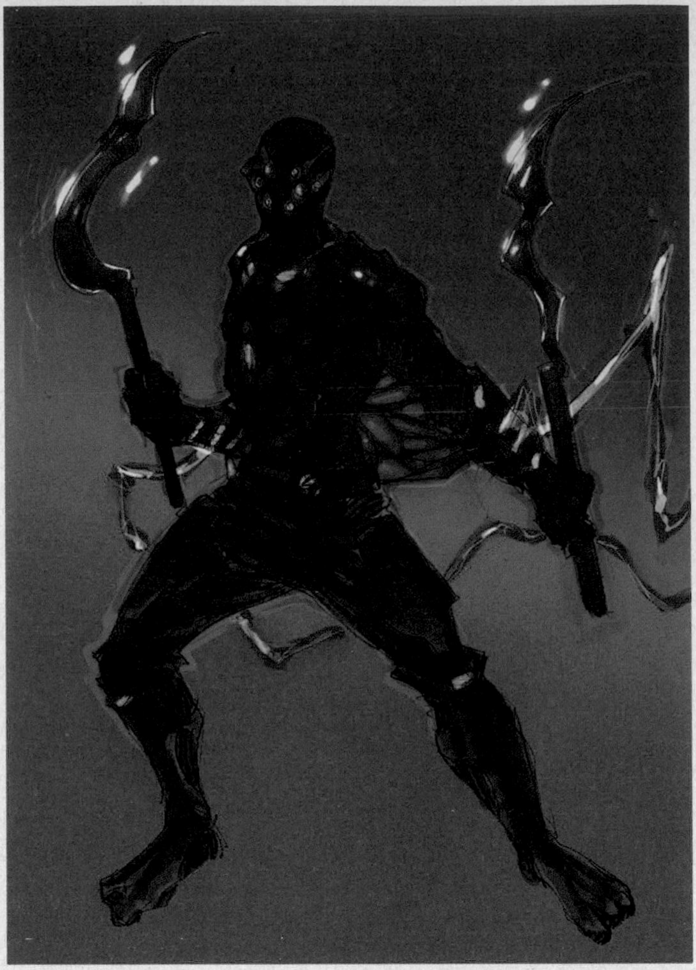

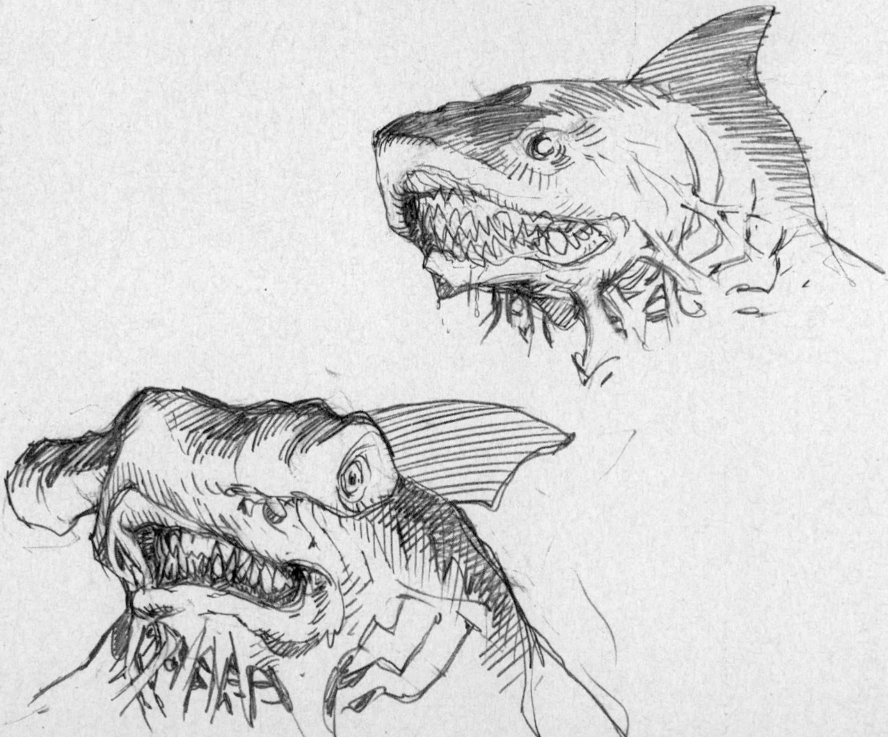

King Shark sketches by Jim Lee